Surviving College:

A "Real World" Experience

Connie Schick

Eileen Astor-Stetson

Brett L. Beck

Bloomsburg University

KENDALL/HUNT PUBLISHING COMPANY
4050 Westmark Drive   Dubuque, Iowa 52002

Table of Contents

Foreword

A student's entry into college is one of those important and, at times, difficult developmental transitions of modern American life. From the moment they appear on campus, students must come to grips with the fact that the first year of college is more than a 13th grade, that their new professors expect more than their former teachers did, and that the habits they bring from high school may not enable success in college. Perhaps even more difficult for new students to reconcile is that while they are enrolled for the academics and the acquisition of new skills (career preparation goals for which someone is spending a great deal of money), they also want desperately to make friends, date, participate in sports, party, and have a good time. Thus planted are the seeds of choice and conflict—and the need for guidance toward their successful resolution.

That's where *Surviving College* comes in. Written in a warm and chatty style, this book provides students with the kinds of friendly and invaluable advice that one normally associates with good mentors. Informed by psychological theory and research (e.g., there are discussions of self-efficacy, self-handicapping, social comparison, intrinsic and extrinsic motivation, stress, depression, and eating disorders), 20 chapters address nitty-gritty practical issues about coping with campus life inside and outside the classroom. Chapter titles include *Survival Test Taking: Dirty Little Secrets Your Professors* Want *You To Know, Coping With Stress: How* Not *To Hide Under Your Bed,* and *Sex: Will There Be A Test on This?* Within each chapter, the reader is treated to an assortment of interesting facts (e.g., I did not know that campus drinking rates are higher in the Northeast than in Western and Southern states, or that the view of college as a venue for partying originates in the days when students came from wealthy families and did not need career training). In addition, all chapters contain writing activities designed to foster self-insight by getting students to stop and reflect on their own abilities, assumptions, motives, and behavioral tendencies. The chapters also provide useful lists of suggested readings and Web sites relevant to the topic.

Adapting to new and unfamiliar life situations is never easy. For first-year college students, many of whom have left home for the first time, there is added pressure to "perform," both academically and socially. For them, *Surviving College* should prove to be just what they need: a survival guide that articulates the challenges, forewarns them of the obstacles, and offers friendly advice on how to adapt, adjust, overcome, and succeed. On campuses large and small, this book should appear alongside textbooks on dorm room shelves and in backpacks. For many, it will serve as an invaluable tool.

Saul Kassin, Ph.D.
Williams College

Chapter 1

Mike and Lauren Matriculate[1]: ## *A Cautionary Tale about "The Real World"*

Let him who would enjoy a good future waste none of his present. — Roger Babson

Let us introduce you to Mike and Lauren, who have just arrived at their new college. Of course, they are apprehensive and a little homesick. Of course, they are lost and a little nostalgic about the "good old days" when they were seniors in high school and experts on navigating its shark-filled waters. But here they are! They have finally begun to live *on their own*—ready to meet new people, have new experiences, and learn new lessons. Here they hope to become prepared for their adult lives. Besides preparing for their careers, they hope to learn how to get along with all types of new people, they look forward to finding some really good friends and perhaps a romantic partner, and—probably most of all—they hope to learn how to get along with themselves. They hope that their old personal criticisms, hesitations, times of boredom, perceived shortcomings, and inability to control themselves will slowly disappear. They want to *really* understand who they are and what they want from life. And they want to see their bad habits turn into the pride of self-control and direction.

In short, they think they have arrived at the door of their adulthood. Ah, but how surprised they are to hear their "elders" tell them that they aren't living in "the real world"! Sophomores tell them to kick back and have a good time—that they can always change their habits "...when you get into the real world." Believing they are reassuring them, parents tell them that their stress isn't real—for them to "...just wait until you experience *real* stress in the real world." And some of their professors keep saying to learn things because "...you will need them in the real world."

What are Mike and Lauren to think after they hear this advice from their "elders"? Does this advice really relax them—or does it just make them indecisive in the face of choices or moral dilemmas? Does the advice make it all too easy for them to goof off, act dangerously, put off selecting a major or career field, or otherwise waste a few years?

And what about you? Have you had your parents, older friends, and even perhaps your professors refer to the future as "the real world" when they talked about your college career? Is this the attitude you lived by while in high school? Were there actions—or things you avoided doing—that you now realize impacted your life in a negative way? Did you ignore good study habits, avoid tough courses, or take risks that could have damaged your health or harmed others? Have you decided that college is your "last chance" to have fun before becoming an adult? Or have you resolved to "change your ways" and become a more serious and responsible person?

[1]Hint #1: Keep a dictionary with you and look up words you aren't sure of!

1

Writing Activity 1.1—Think about how you feel *right now* about being in college. Is it "the real world" or just a rest stop? What do you want to accomplish while you are in college? What would you say is your *main* reason for being in college? Writing your thoughts will help you apply information in this chapter to your life.

Now, look at what you have written and decide whether your thoughts agree with the beliefs of those who tell Mike and Lauren that they aren't in "the real world" or whether you side with them in believing their start in college is indeed an entry into that "real world." Do the goals for your college years center around career preparation? Do they center around "having a good time"? Do they include learning about yourself and working on your social skills? Think about your current attitude about where you are as you read our suggestions because your attitude can either help or damage your progress along your new path.

First, you are no doubt curious about *our* view about the "reality" of your present stage of life. We firmly believe that college—your present existence—*is* "the real world." In fact, we hope to persuade you that *wherever you are at any moment in time is the* **only** *"real world" you can ever experience!* This may sound like one of those Zen statements you have heard or read about, but it actually reflects a large body of research concerning the benefits of living *as though* the present will be an important determinant of your future. Additionally, it is a reflection of how you have been living all the moments leading up to right now. Don't mistake this view for a carefree "live for today" attitude because it is the exact opposite! As you shall see, thinking this *isn't* "the real world" is more likely to lead you to lazy behaviors and an unrealistic belief that what you do here doesn't really count.

The Dangers of Thinking Your Current College Life isn't "The Real World"

Someday we'll look back on this moment and plow into a parked car. — Evan Davis

First, let's look at the pitfalls of accepting your elders' words and deciding college should only be taken seriously when it gives you a chance to prepare for your "real life."

If this isn't "the real world," I don't have to take my role as a college student seriously.

We hope you can see how illogical that statement is right away. Ask yourself—is this how you felt about high school? Are you going to be one of the many students we see each year who say when they receive a bad grade on an exam or paper: "But I never had to study in high school, and I got good grades!" If so, you are still assuming that learning just shouldn't be *that hard*. You may even believe that the professor will "teach" you everything you need to know if you just show up and listen in class (more on this in Chapter 4). And, of course, you have bought into your parents' suggestion that you won't experience genuine stress until you are out there where they are—in "the real world." Indeed, you will tend to take on a victim's role: "Oh, poor me, why are these professors making everything so *hard*!? It's just not *fair*!" This attitude may be even more likely if you *did* study hard in high school and figured that you knew everything there was to know about how to learn. College *really is* much harder than almost all high schools and most courses that you completed while there. You *really are* going to have to develop better self-management skills if you hope to do well here. And this book *really will* help you understand your current skill level and develop an effective learning style for helping you succeed not just in college, but also in the rest of your "real life."

Research on Freshmen Study Habits—UCLA's Higher Education Research Institute study of 282,549 freshmen at 437 colleges and universities (Sax, Lindholm, Astin, Korn, & Mahoney, 2001) found that a record low of 33.4% reported studying 6 or more hours a week when in high school. However, 45.7%, the highest percent ever reported, said they had an "A" average in high school (50.1% of women, 40.4% of men). Freshmen reported immediately learning that their lax habits would not work in college. As one student put it, "I took a lot of (advanced placement) courses in high school, and I thought I was prepared for college. I didn't know how difficult it was going to be. Not only do you have to focus on the tests, but every project is more important than in high school."

Other questions found that drinking and partying by freshmen were at an all time low! Only 46.5% (compared to 73.7% in 1982) reported frequent or occasional beer drinking in the past 12 months, and 52.5% reported drinking wine or liquor in the same time period. In fact, 35.8% said they didn't attend a single party during a typical week.

If this isn't "the real world," most of the information I'm supposed to learn is just "busy work" to be avoided if at all possible.

Unfortunately, you may already feel that way about material you are exposed to in the classroom. By the time they finish high school, many students suspect that information their teachers seem so interested in has little relevance to their own lives. You may think: "Old English literature? American history? Give me a break!" If you had a part-time job in high school, you probably didn't run into employers or co-workers who wanted to talk about such topics, so knowing about them may have seemed irrelevant. However, if you hope to rise in the business or professional world, knowledge of these rather esoteric areas is important. Being knowledgeable can make the difference between being seen as sophisticated or as naïve, even dull. Friendships, love and business relationships, and even opportunities for jobs and promotions are affected by how others view your grasp and perspective on topics such as history, politics, psychology, economics, and the arts. You do not just learn facts and theories in college. Indeed, the skills you develop *as you learn* are the very ones corporations and graduate schools say you will need to succeed in your career. These skills include critical thinking, problem solving, time management, oral and written communication, a good sense of humor, and the ability to work on your own as a self-starter and with a wide variety of people.

If you "skated" through high school, we strongly suggest you choose General Education courses to fill in the gaps in your worldliness. You will be surprised to find that these topics you have denigrated are full of interesting information. Like employers, educators realize that there is more to preparing you for life and for a career than just taking courses in your major. They recognize that college is the place where you hone your skills for carrying on an interesting conversation and where you develop enough avocational interests so that your future will never be filled with the feeling you probably had quite often around the age of 14 or 15: "I'm bored."

Writing Activity 1.2—In high school, which courses did you "skate" through or fail to retain information from? Which areas did you skip completely and now realize contain information you should know? What courses do you need to take in college to make up for not learning this information? List *courses you skipped or didn't apply yourself to in high school* **and** *courses you need to take to fill the holes in your education so far.*

If this isn't "the real world," the only important courses are the ones in my major because they are the ones that prepare me for my real job.

Too often this attitude is formed by the questions your parents or other adults ask about what you are doing in college and what your plans for the future are. In fact, you may have heard them talk so frequently about how important college is for "getting a good job" that you have already decided that they consider the rest of your college courses irrelevant. Consequently, you may decide it is alright to skip classes in non-major courses and cram for exams in them rather than using learning methods that will help you retain the information. The inevitable outcome will be a poor Grade Point Average (GPA). However, if you ask a few seniors who are looking forward to finding a good job or are applying to graduate school, you will hear that your GPA is important to your success. Besides GPA and letters of recommendation, prospective employers and graduate school committees look at which courses you took outside of your major. They will be interested in whether you took only introductory level courses outside your major or attempted more in-depth, higher level courses. The addition of foreign language, ethics, speech, psychology, information processing/computer technology, cross-cultural issues, natural science, and mathematics courses signals your willingness to tackle more difficult topics—an attitude that signals maturity and perseverance to them.

We suggest that instead of merely taking courses that fit your "extracurricular" schedule, that meet later in the morning, or that your friends have signed up for, you find out which ones might be interesting ***and*** beneficial to you. Your college catalogue and Web site list all courses, give very brief descriptions of each one, and alert you to the prerequisites for upper-level courses (a ***prerequisite course*** is one you must complete, sometimes with a particular grade, prior to signing up for certain upper-level courses). Most colleges will not let you take courses for which you lack the prerequisites, so completing these introductory courses during your freshman and sophomore years are essential. We also hope you will talk to upper-level students in majors other than your own about courses they have found particularly interesting and useful in their major. If you live in a dorm, you can begin your search for interesting courses by talking with your Resident Advisor (RA), who is usually an upper-level student. Be clear that you are not asking about *easy* courses, but are interested in learning about topics or specific areas within a major. Another source of information are professors you have for introductory courses. They can tell you about the major in which they teach and about non-major courses they recommend to their advisees. If you are undeclared, it is especially important to begin your search early in your first semester since scheduling for your second semester usually begins in the second or third month of school. Taking a wide variety of courses that sound interesting to you will help you select a major—and possibly a minor and/or concentration you may also wish to pursue.

We have a further suggestion, whether you are a declared or undeclared student: do not take all your General Education courses during your first two years if your college unless they are prerequisites for other courses. There are two advantages for putting off a few upper-level courses. Leaving a few somewhat easier lower-level courses until your junior or senior years will lessen the stress that results from having nothing except hard courses during these semesters. Our advisees lament that they wish they could spend more time on particularly interesting areas within harder courses but that time pressures produced by taking all upper-level courses limit their doing so. Our advisees who do take a few of their lower-level courses later in their college careers have also told us that these courses sometimes surprise and delight them. The perspective they have gained and their more sophisticated study skills allow them to tackle introductory courses with a zeal they would have lacked as freshmen. They use these courses to help them answer questions they have formed as a result of taking courses in other areas, including their major. They realize the interactive and reciprocal nature of knowledge—how information from one major illuminates topics in other areas. Some of them even discover new interests or career fields which allow them to combine two areas of study. One of your authors actually chose a new career field as a result of taking an introductory course as a senior, a path that has never been regretted. Oh, yes, there is one further benefit for taking lower level courses as a junior or senior—you're more likely to make a good grade in them due to your more advanced skill level. Consequently, your GPA will benefit from this strategy!

Writing Activity 1.3—Whether or not you have already declared a major, think about some areas of study about which you are curious and then browse through your college catalogue or Web site. What courses sound interesting? Ask your RA and other upper-class students about interesting courses they have taken. Ask your roommate and friends about courses they have heard are interesting. Which ones do you need as prerequisites for upper-level courses you want to take? Finally, consider courses that you think would help you reach your career and personal goals. Write down these prospective courses and why you want to take them (if you don't write down reasons, you may have to look the course up again when scheduling). Be sure to consult this list when designing your schedule for next semester and next year.

If this isn't "the real world," how I spend my spare time in college will not have an effect on my life after I leave college.

This belief is probably the most dangerous one for both your personal and professional life in the future. Frequent remarks we hear from students are: "When I graduate, I will *start...*" and "When I graduate, I will *stop...*." Since we are educators who study how you learn both good *and* bad habits, these remarks make us shudder. Let us look at some of the negative outcomes you may experience from believing that your actions during your college years won't impact you later.

The party-hardy myth. The belief that college is just a "time out" and will have no effect later on is one of the causes of the well-known "party syndrome." If you ask almost anyone over about age 12, you will hear that college is the time for partying.

This attitude about college being the time to party developed long ago when few people attended college, and almost all of them were rich. Job training was not their goal since most men were going to work for daddy or his friends and most women were learning about the arts, making friends, and hunting rich husbands. The main reasons both men and women attended college were to make connections with other rich people and to develop their social skills. However, after World War II more and more young people began to see college as a way of becoming upwardly mobile. The first wave of "new" students were GI Bill students, most of them older than traditional students and many of them married. These more career-oriented (and poorer) students didn't usually impact the party reputation of colleges since they were less likely to be major participants in extracurricular activities.

In the mid 1960s the atmosphere of most colleges began to change. Beginning at Berkeley and other prestigious colleges, students became more interested first in "student rights" and later in the other "rights" movements of the time. While there was still a hard core party group at all of these schools, there was also a growing number of activists and other "serious" students of both traditional and nontraditional college age.

> *A side note on the middle to late 1960's*: Hippies and student activists were *not* the same people and, in fact, didn't get along very well. Hippies really were there to "party hardy," and they didn't have much time or interest in school *or* in the rights of others. You may have heard their motto: "Tune in, turn on, and drop out" (thanks to Timothy Leary). Activists often had contempt for hippies, whom they considered untrustworthy and not really deserving of a place in the rights movement. Other party hounds were more likely to hang with hippies than with activists, and we are sure you can figure out why!

During the next 10 years the number of college students mushroomed as baby boomers reached college age and a greatly increased number of women and ethnic minority students chose to pursue a post-high school education. As in the late 1940's, the GI Bill again impacted the growth of colleges since many of those returning from Viet Nam either started or resumed their college careers. Many new majors were developed, some of which were job-oriented rather than fitting into the liberal education mode of their grandfather's era. At this time student partying did not differ as much from partying by their non-college peers as had been true before and after this period. You may think of the 1960's as the "psychedelic" era, but it was really the late 1960's and the 1970's.

As the protester and psychedelic eras passed, "the party place" once again became the reputation for colleges. Research during the past 30 years has shown that college students, as a group, drink more than their non-college peers. But it may also surprise you to learn that drinking, especially heavy drinking, among college students is *not* as widespread as you have heard. Additionally, most students who are heavy drinkers during college also drank regularly (even heavily) during high school, and heavy drinkers on campus usually seek out other heavy drinkers to be their friends. So the myth that college *makes* you drink is far from true.

We will discuss drinking and the use of other drugs in more detail later in the book, but we felt it was necessary to introduce the topic here. You won't miss out on a social life by skipping the drinking scene—or at least skipping the drinking when you attend parties! And you will find that studying is more successful and accomplished in *less* time when your brain isn't in an alcoholic fog or distracted by a hangover.

One additional note about a failure to take drinking (or drugging) seriously: The belief that you can magically stop heavy drinking or drugging upon leaving college is ***not*** true for many students (e.g., Sadava & Pak, 1994). Forming the "drink to relax" habit and failure to learn how to socialize without alcohol lay a trap for would-be quitters. Unfortunately, well-learned habits are *very* difficult to break (see Chapter 5 on self-management for more about habit formation and change). Additionally, some heavy drinkers will find that their genetic predisposition toward becoming an alcoholic, paired with their drinking habit, has set a trap they cannot escape alone. These students will eventually have to acknowledge their need for help if they ever hope to break the downward spiral of alcoholism (see Chapter 14 on alcohol use).

Failure to develop self-management habits needed in later life. The other problem with believing there is a disconnect between the college years and later life is that you are constantly strengthening the habitual nature of your behaviors. If you use college as a "time out" from life and just enjoy your freedom from responsibilities, you will fail to develop the skills necessary for personal and professional success in life. Procrastination, poor time management, beliefs that work is unpleasant and to be avoided whenever possible, and failure to take responsibility for learning are behaviors that may have been tolerated in early adolescence. But they are *not* acceptable behaviors in college or in the job place. Such behaviors result in poor grades and inadequate preparation for one's career. Perhaps more importantly, professors are aware of your habits, and both organizational recruiters and graduate schools place heavy emphasis on our recommendations when considering your capacity for success. Research shows that times of change, such as entry into college, are excellent times to work on dropping ineffective habits and adopting new, more efficient ones. For this reason, we have included information concerning how to develop your self-management habits as well as specific tips on how to learn and how to apply these skills in your studies.

The Advantages of Thinking Your Current College Life
is "The Real World"

The doors we open and close each day decide the lives we live. — Flora Whittemore

While much of this book will discuss ways you can benefit from your college years, we also want you to understand the dividends and joys of immersing yourself in all parts of college life while you are here. **College is your *job* for the next few years.** Approaching each day with this realization will encourage you to search out the most efficient and effective methods for doing your job. This belief will also help you choose responsibly when friends pressure you to "blow off" your studies, *and* it will give you a valid explanation to give them when they ask why you don't want to go out with them.

Intrinsic and extrinsic motivation

Test for Self-Awareness—Before reading on, complete and score the Work Preference Inventory on p. A1 in the Appendix (Amabile, Hill, Hennessey, & Tighe, 1994). Knowing how you score will help you better understand and apply the information in this section.

Another important benefit of taking your studies seriously is that you will enjoy them more. You will spend more time looking for something interesting in each lesson rather than adopting an "oh, poor me" attitude. Consequently, you will approach your work with *intrinsic motivation*, rather than *extrinsic motivation.* You are *intrinsically* motivated when you engage in a task because you see it as a challenge, as interesting and enjoyable, or as an opportunity for self-expression (e.g., Covington, 2000). You are interested in performing the task effectively, but you also find that just *doing* the task is reinforcing. Intrinsic motivation comes from within you, whereas *extrinsic* motivation depends upon the reward you hope to receive or the punishment you hope to avoid by completing the task. Intrinsic motivation results in feelings of *self*-control and pride in the ***process*** of learning, regardless of the outcome of your efforts. Because you focus on the process, feedback on your progress is important to you, whether the feedback comes in the form of exam scores or information from texts, professors, and friends. You will be eager to correct your efforts when you receive feedback, instead of lapsing into defensiveness and attempts to blame others for your perceived "failures." Probably because of this strong interest in mastering the task, research shows that when you are intrinsically motivated, you are more likely to use the type of complex, sophisticated learning strategies that maximize good performance and retention of information (Ames & Archer, 1988; Schunk, 1996). And here is a payoff you may not have expected—you'll find that you actually remember something *after* you take the exam!

Sadly, students who are extrinsically motivated and see their learning as externally controlled do only the minimum required for a course. Their sense of adventure and curiosity are stifled by their profit-loss approach. Their attitude is: "Why should I read more, search the Web, or even look up a word I don't understand when I won't get a grade for it?" Research (e.g., Deci, Koestner, & Ryan, 1999) shows that people who are learning to perform a task for *extrinsic* reasons become *less* interested in the task and even choose not to pursue it in their spare time.

This can happen even if they were originally curious or anxious to learn the material or skill! This phenomenon is called the *overjustification effect* and has been found to occur for such varied tasks as sports, school work, and performance of helping behaviors (e.g., doing favors for a friend or family member, doing volunteer work). Extrinsic learners also tend to give up or prematurely ask others for help when a task seems difficult.

> *A note for those of you who will be parents, teachers, coaches, or bosses of any sort.* Beware of constantly rewarding (or criticizing) people learning from you or in your presence. If people come to believe that they are doing it "for my parents," "for Coach," "for my school (or company)," or for the glory they will receive, they will eventually dislike the task and "slack off" unless pushed to perform. You have no doubt seen this happen to a talented friend during middle school or high school. You might have thought your friend was burned out, but a more likely explanation is the *overjustification effect*—that *intrinsic* motivation had turned *extrinsic*. If this has happened to you, we urge you to try the activity again *without worrying about external factors*. With the pressure off, you will probably regain the initial joy you received from the *process* of the activity. In the future, recalling this renewed satisfaction will remind you not to rob those in your care of the ownership of their actions.

Interestingly, for those who remain intrinsically motivated in the face of external pressure or reward, a payoff of some sort (e.g., praise, a good grade, a smile) does *not* reduce their feelings of self-control or their tendency to look further into the topic. Rather than being seen as an external reward, the payoff serves as *positive feedback* confirming that their efforts to learn have been successful (e.g., Eisenberger & Cameron, 1996). *Negative feedback* alerts them to ineffective methods or poor efforts, again serving as a motivator to correct their behaviors rather than a signal to stop trying. In fact, intrinsic motivation facilitates persistence, even on difficult tasks, resulting in experimentation with different techniques prior to asking others for assistance.

Self-efficacy

> **Test for Self-Awareness**—Before reading further, complete and score the Self-Efficacy Scale on p. A3 (Sherer et al., 1982). Knowing how you score will help you better understand and apply the information in this section.

One payoff for mastering a task, especially if you feel at least some intrinsic motivation for it, is that you will develop *self-efficacy* for the task. *Self-efficacy* is the belief that you can perform a task well (Bandura, 1989), a feeling that you are competent in an area. You develop self-efficacy when you see that your actions result in your reaching a desired goal—and you believe that you got there largely *on your own*. As pointed out earlier, pursuing a task for intrinsic reasons encourages you to try harder and longer before asking others for help. Stumbling along on your own may be temporarily frustrating, but it maximizes your chances of "owning" eventual success and producing confidence that you can repeat that success. Belief that you can do a task can also be increased by reading instructions or seeing a person you perceive as similar to yourself complete the task.

Initially, self-efficacy is situational—that is, it is *task-specific*. You may feel comfortable in one class but "over your head" in another. A sport you have played for years may seem easy, while even thinking about giving a speech in front of a crowd or in class may seem scary or impossible. However, self-efficacy will generalize as you try similar activities or learn that certain techniques work *across* tasks. That is why we stress the importance of developing self-management skills. Bandura believes that generalized self-efficacy will lead to success in *any area you consider important*. For instance, developing study habits that let you perform well in your classes produces self-efficacy for learning in general. Consequently, you will be more willing to attempt new tasks as your faith in your own proficiency increases. As you feel competent in more and more areas, you will gain self-confidence. This confidence becomes part of your ***self-concept***, your picture of who you are and what you can do.

Writing Activity 1.4—To better understand how *intrinsic* motivation has affected your efforts to learn in the past, think about activities you have undertaken *because you wanted* to rather than for some external reward or to avoid punishment. Now pick *one* (a sport, video game, other activity or skill) and write about your efforts to become proficient at that task. Has your self-efficacy for the task generalized to other situations? Also write how your behavior on this task differed from behaviors related to an *extrinsically-motivated* task (a chore at home or some other maintenance task) you also performed regularly at the time.

Our Suggestions for Making the Most of
Your Current "Real World"

Don't think we expect you to spend all your time on course work. We certainly don't! We want you to live a balanced life in college. Besides involvement in courses and career planning, we urge you to take part in extracurricular activities, develop friendships and social skills, do volunteer work, and take time to find out who you are and where you want to go in life. If you are a traditional-aged student right out of high school, your relative "freedom" from "adult" duties (e.g., maintaining a home, raising a family) at this point in your life will give you the time to experiment with the person you are becoming, to try out new roles and activities. If you are a "returning" (older) student, you still are at a choice point in your life or you wouldn't be in school. We hope you too will make a point of pursuing the activities just listed. Regardless of your place in life, the development of good self-management skills will enhance your time and opportunities for such adventures, and we hope that this book will increase your options and whet your appetite for the full course of college life.

Suggested Readings, Web Sites, and References

At the end of each chapter, we will suggest readings, web sites, and references to help you learn more about the topics in that chapter. Your college library will have many of these, and if not, they will have a process for getting a copy of an article or borrowing a book from another college. *If you want to find an article in a hurry*, go to your college's library web site and look in the databases available. This address (http://library.bloomu.edu/pages/dbremote.html) takes you directly to our library's web page listing all the databases available through both on- and off-campus access. It also contains instructions on how to access databases and the catalogue of library holdings. You can check your own library's web pages for how to access these resources. Many dorms are wired to allow you to research online from your room 24 hours a day.

There are searchable databases for many interests (e.g., music, sports, current events) and career fields (e.g., business, social work, education, history). You will find uses for many of them during your college career and in the future. Here are a few data bases we found useful while writing this book.

> **EBSCO HOST** (Academic Search Primer) allows access to articles and research in a number of different majors and professions. This resource provides online search of over 4,000 magazines and scholarly journals, with full text of articles available for about three-quarters of them, dating back to 1990. (Some of our references are for articles you can access *directly* through this source.)

> **PsycINFO** has citations and summaries of journal articles, book chapters, books, technical reports, and dissertations in psychology and psychological aspects of other disciplines (e.g., medicine, psychiatry, nursing, sociology, education, pharmacology, physiology, linguistics, anthropology, business, law). Journal coverage includes material from over 1,500 journals. Chapter and book coverage includes worldwide English-language material back through 1987 (updated monthly).

- ➤ **Health Source: Consumer Edition** (under *Medicine/Health*) offers searchable full text for nearly 165 journals, including Consumer Reports on Health. Additionally, you will find abstracts and indexing for nearly 180 general health, nutrition, and professional health care publications.
- ➤ **MEDLINE** (under *Medicine/Health*) provides access to the entire Comprehensive MEDLINE file, including full text for articles in over 75 medical journals dating from 1966.
- ➤ **Periodical Abstracts** (under *General Indexes*) accesses more than 1800 periodicals. About half the citations are full text (back through 1988).
- ➤ **ERIC** (under *Education*) provides abstracts and some full text from over 900 education periodicals and documents (back through 1966).

Suggested Readings

Covington, M. V. (1998). *The will to learn: A guide for motivating young people.* New York: Cambridge University Press.

Deci, E. L., Koestner, R., & Ryan, R. M. (1999). A meta-analytic review of experiments examining the effects of extrinsic rewards on intrinsic motivation. *Psychological Bulletin, 125,* 627-668.

Suggested Web Sites

http://www.bloomu.edu/ The home page for Bloomsburg University, which provides access to the library, academic programs, courses, general administrative topics (e.g., financial aid, General Education requirements), student activities, athletics, and many other topics.

http://www.thesemester.com/ Tips are offered on how to successfully complete the semester.

http://www.collegefreshmen.net/ This site has advice for the challenges facing college freshmen.

http://www.unc.edu/depts/unc_caps/resources.htm The University of North Carolina's Counseling And Psychological Services presents practical information on academic improvement, eating disorders, substance abuse, depression, sleep, grief, stress management, assertiveness, and helping a friend. You can access other sites from this page too.

http://www.psychwatch.com/ This site is one of the best we've found to contain information on all areas of psychology and to give you access to other Web sites of interest. Sign up to receive a free newsletter every Friday that contains links to news releases on current research and books. You can also search the archives for earlier news releases, and there are tutorials on many topics.

Chapter 2

Pitfalls on the Path Through Your College Career

The Seven Deadly Sins:
Procrastination and Self-Handicapping

No one can go back and make a brand new start, my friend,
but anyone can start from here and make a brand new end.
— Anonymous

You have probably heard the term "seven deadly sins" in the past (if you need a quick, but gruesome, review of them, check out the movie *Seven* with Brad Pitt and Morgan Freeman). We have compiled our own list of self-destructive behaviors to warn you of hazards that can lead to failure, regardless of your good intentions. Although we will be discussing their negative effects on college success, these self-defeating habits will also make you less effective in other parts of your life. We start our book with these pitfalls because you need to be aware of them *and* avoid them in order to take an adaptive path through your college career—one that will feel comfortable while also helping you succeed in your academic work, personal life, and extracurricular activities.

In the next three chapters, we will be discussing each of the "seven deadly sins" and showing how each one can negatively impact your life. We will also give you pointers on how to avoid falling into these pits—or how to get out of them if you are already there! The seven pitfalls are *procrastination, self-handicapping, downward social comparison, upward social comparison, perfectionism, setting performance rather than learning goals in your course work,* and *being too serious.*

A general note on the format of the book and how to best benefit from it

As you discovered in Chapter 1, throughout the book we will be pointing you toward scales to complete in the Appendix. Each scale will help you identify your current beliefs and behaviors in relation to the next topic to be discussed. For most scales, you will be told how to interpret your scores and given information on behaviors or personality traits that researchers have found to be related to high or low scores on that scale. We *strongly* urge you to complete the indicated scale *before* reading on in a chapter. Additionally, there will be **Writing Activities**, **Exercises**, and **Quizzes** included with some topics throughout the book. Completion of them will increase your self-awareness, help you understand the material presented, and give you suggestions on how to apply it in your everyday life.

Procrastination

Indecision and delays are the parents of failure.
— George Canning, English statesman

Test for Self-Awareness—Before reading further, complete and score the Procrastination Assessment Scale for Students (PASS) on p. A5 (Solomon & Rothblum, 1984). Knowing how you score, and on which types of academic activities you are most likely to procrastination, will help you understand and apply the information in this section.

No doubt the most widely practiced self-defeating behavior is ***procrastination***, putting off a necessary task for no really good reason. When procrastinating, we usually choose a ***short-term gain***, an immediately pleasant task (e.g., watching TV), instead of tackling a less pleasant task that, when completed, will produce or lead to satisfaction and self-fulfillment (i.e., one that provides us with a ***long-term gain***). Sometimes, in order to make ourselves feel justified in procrastinating, we will substitute some easy or less aversive work task for the one we're putting off. Unfortunately, this substitute task very seldom needs to be done right then—or at all (e.g., putting your CDs in alphabetical order). While at times there are good reasons to delay a chore, those occasions show that we understand the overall task well enough to organize and prioritize our efforts (more on this in Chapter 5 on self-management). All of us procrastinate at times, but if you regularly do so in relation to school work, this is the first problem you must tackle if you hope to become a successful student. *And don't procrastinate about changing this habit!*

Writing Activity 2.1—Think about tasks on which you procrastinate. Do you delay boring, difficult, or other types of tasks—or more than one type? Write about a task you put off when you knew you should have tackled it. Write about the consequences of the delay. Have you stopped procrastinating on this type of task because of these consequences—or are you still a "work in progress"?

No doubt you can think of all sorts of rationalizations for putting off your work. Frequent excuses include "It's boring!" or "It's too hard." You may also assert that you work *better* under pressure and that working to a deadline "energizes" you. You may even believe that doing your work later rather than now will not affect the quality of your work. After all, you can gather more and better information to help you do the task by delaying. And finally, you may be convinced that your current work load or stress level is just too high and that taking on even one more task will push you over the edge. Let's look at each of these excuses and their validity.

"It's boring!" or "It's too hard."

This assertion is a result of what psychologists (e.g., Ellis & Harper, 1978) call "irrational thinking." Two irrational beliefs underlie this attitude: (a) I can achieve maximum happiness through inertia or through passively, uncommittedly enjoying myself (this is known as the "Elysian

Fields syndrome") and (b) it is easier to avoid life's difficulties and responsibilities than to use self-discipline to undertake harder, but ultimately more rewarding, tasks. This latter belief also results in putting off decisions that need to be made—a practice that produces a lot of stress and may even back you onto a path you didn't really want to choose at all. We suggest that you reread the section on *intrinsic motivation* in Chapter 1 (p. 9) and what you wrote in **Activity 1.4** (p. 11) to see that you can work hard and be successful at difficult tasks *if you want to be*. Therefore, this excuse is merely a problem of incorrect labeling. You have *chosen* to think that studying or writing a paper or going to class are tasks you don't like or for which you lack *self-efficacy* (p. 10). Later chapters will introduce self-management and study habits that can help you correctly label course work as more interesting (or at least as essential to do *now*) and give you suggestions for developing skills that will make these tasks more approachable. Besides, you do tasks that aren't fun every day (e.g., commuting, brushing your teeth)—you just don't procrastinate on them because they are either necessary or habitual.

I work better under pressure, and working under a deadline "energizes" me.

You may actually believe that the "motivation" and "energy" you feel when facing a deadline makes you more productive. If so, it's time to realize that they are really just stress reactions, and not very pleasant ones at that! As people who teach about brain physiology, let us assure you that better work is *really not possible* when your stress level is elevated. Your "higher-order" cognitive processes—including efficient learning of difficult material, problem solving, decision making, and creativity—are temporarily short-circuited when you feel threatened by a stressor, such as an impending deadline (e.g., Lay, Edwards, Parker, & Endler, 1989; LeDoux, 1996; also see Chapter 8 on stress). Your brain is mobilized for physical action, and your body is releasing adrenaline and other stress hormones into your blood to energize your body for "fight or flight." While your senses are temporarily sharpened, the result is that you are more easily distracted. Consequently, your capacity to concentrate is actually reduced. Unfortunately, your ability to sleep well is also affected, and your immune system is compromised, putting you at risk for illness. None of these results help you do your work successfully. In fact, the unpleasantness of high stress, illness, and a poor work product will conspire to heighten your dislike for the task, reinforcing your belief that school work is hard and should be avoided. *A warning*: If you know that you are an *adrenaline freak*, one who likes the feeling of being aroused, you are at higher risk for procrastinating just to get the "buzz" from the task and the relief from finishing it. We suggest you finish your work early so you can engage in more fulfilling and pleasurable types of arousal.

Postponing my work until later does not affect the quality of my work.

If you regularly procrastinate on your school work, there is really no way for you to justify this statement. Besides the information just presented on the deleterious effect of high arousal on your work, working at the last minute is ineffective for a number of reasons. A rule in the business world that applies equally to school work (e.g., Buehler, Griffin, & Ross, 1994) is that work takes twice as long as you think it will. As a procrastinator, you have no doubt experienced this pitfall already. Delays inevitably result, including failure to have gathered the correct information and tools prior to beginning your work, lack of supplies (e.g., out of printer paper again!), interruptions (e.g., your noisy roommate), and fatigue from working too long at one time. As the deadline looms, mistakes become more frustrating, making you repeat time-eating procedures or "settle" for poorer quality work. Skipping classes to finish a project or study for an exam is also a risk and will lead to inadequate effort in the courses you slight.

I can gather more and better information to help me do the task if I don't start it now.

This one *sounds* good, but a little self-monitoring will tell you whether it is true or just another rationalization. If you are just putting off an unpleasant task, doing *more* work on it is highly unlikely. If you find that the results mentioned in the last paragraph occur when you finally begin work on the project, you haven't really gotten more information or the supplies you need for the task—*you have just put it off*. And if you really do gather more information so you can do your work more effectively and efficiently, we suggest you correctly re-label your procrastination as **prioritizing** so you won't see these activities as identical. Prioritizing is a good study skill and an effective self-management technique. However, failure to distinguish between these two behaviors will result in *justifying* your self-destructive procrastination rather than seeing it for the problem it really is.

My current work load (or stress level) is just too high, and if I take on one more task, it will push me over the edge.

This rationalization is probably the truth if you regularly procrastinate. Professors tend to schedule papers and exams around the same time during the semester (e.g., midterm, before holidays, the last week or two of the semester), so failure to work *regularly* on assignments will result in a mountain of work coming due at the same time. Cramming for exams almost guarantees that you will have to study the material again for the final because you won't remember any of it (see Chapters 6 and 7 on study skills). Stress and "all-nighters" due to facing a deadline will inevitably lead to sleeplessness, irritability, frustration, illness, and fighting with everyone in sight. The low energy and distractibility you experience in the consequent state will further slow your work pace, darken your mood, increase your pessimism, and result in rotten papers and poor exam preparation. *No, this is not an exaggeration.* Ask upper-class students what one promise they make to themselves at the beginning of every semester, and they will almost invariably give you some version of: "I will work steadily during the semester and not procrastinate because I'm tired of being sick and stressed out…getting poor grades…not being able to party with friends at the end of the semester…sleeping away my vacation."

If you are still skeptical about the dangers of procrastination, read the following **Research** box. (You will find this study and other resources cited at the end of the chapter or in the bibliography if you want more information on changing this insidious habit.)

18

Research on Procrastination—In two studies, Tice and Baumeister (1997) assessed the effect of college students' procrastination on their work and health. On the first day of class they assigned a paper due late in the semester, telling students they could turn in it in early, on time, during an "automatic extension period," or late. Students completed procrastination scales and daily symptom checklists, weekly measures of work load and stress level, and reports of health-care visits. When handing in the paper, each completed a measure of relief. Compared with those who scored low on the procrastination scale, those who scored high handed in their papers later, scored lower on the paper (and on two course exams), reported more symptoms and stress, had more health-care visits, and felt more relief when turning in their paper. *The only period in which procrastinators had fewer symptoms than other students was during the first quarter of the semester*, presumably when they were doing less school work than nonprocrastinators.

A recent semester-long study (Sirois & Pychyl, 2002) found that procrastinating students had poorer health and used ineffective, unhealthy coping techniques. They reported more daily stressful incidents, lower academic satisfaction, lower self-esteem, lower wellness behaviors overall, more health problems (digestive, insomnia, flu, and colds), more likelihood of being a smoker, and more alcohol consumption weekly. They also used poor coping strategies, including denial, ignoring instead of trying to solve the problem, avoiding work, use of alcohol and other drugs to escape their problems, less planning, less social support seeking, and more pessimistic interpretation of events. (See Chapters 8-10 for more on stress, illness, and good coping strategies.)

Ferrari and Beck (1998) also found that college students who put off studying for exams reported more negative feelings and health problems.

OK, so what can I do about this self-defeating habit?

As is evident from the findings in these two research studies, rationalizing that you can work better under stress and believing that procrastination is a benign behavior simply don't hold water. If you are now anxious to attack this habit, here are a few suggestions to get you started.

> *Correctly label your task.* By attacking your tendency to engage in irrational thinking, you can feel better about the task instead of viewing it as awful, boring, or too hard. Remind yourself of difficult tasks you have completed successfully in the past—and of times your procrastination has turned a moderately difficult task into a nightmare. Admit that you don't like doing a paper or studying for an exam, but that you can do it and feel good about the product.

> *Challenge your rationalizations.* Remind yourself that working right before a deadline stresses you out and makes you irritable. Recall the frustrations, delays, and fights with others that have accompanied past procrastination. Admit that you turned in papers and took exams that did not reflect your knowledge or creativity because of your stress level and the limited time available for the task. Think of the times you have been sick, sleepy, or depressed during and following completion of a task you delayed.

➢ *Use environmental control to remove the "reward" of putting off the task.* If you read your e-mail, smoke a cigarette, visit with your roommate, or watch a rerun of *Friends* for the 10th time when you don't want to start a task, stop it! Sit at your desk or go to the library and *get started* on the task (more on minimizing distractions and "chaining" in Chapter 5 on self-management).

➢ *Do something useful.* Making yourself perform a task that is unpleasant, unfamiliar, or difficult will show you that you can do it If memories of earlier incidents are inadequate to spur you to action on the current task, tackle something you have been putting off *just to prove that you can do it.* But be careful that it doesn't become a substitute for the task you need to accomplish! We're sure you have found yourself alphabetizing the cans in your kitchen cabinet, rearranging your closet, or catching up on your letter writing so you feel justified in not doing a genuinely important task, especially school work. The joke in college is that dorm rooms are never so clean as they are during finals week!

➢ *Make your commitment public.* Either write down a schedule for doing a long task and post it over your desk, make a written contract for a shorter task, or tell someone when you will tackle and complete a task. Using a list, calendar, or planner to "publicize" what you plan to get done today or this week makes it harder to admit that you haven't carried out your intentions. Potential drawbacks for this technique are that you will underestimate the time needed to do a task, won't anticipate the interruptions that may occur, will find list-making depressing (the multitude of tasks may look insurmountable), or will feel discouraged at how *little* you get done. Of course, seeing how many tasks you need to do at an *early* point in the semester can motivate you to use better self-management techniques and to get started *now*!

➢ *Be realistic about your attention span.* Nothing is more discouraging than trying to do a big task all at once. The law of diminishing returns guarantees that you will be inefficient in such a situation. You need to be realistic about how long you can concentrate, write, or study before you need to take a break. Because something sweet helps your brain work—really!—you will benefit from an occasional time out to eat an apple. Watch out for depending on cigarettes or caffeine as "pick ups." Both can harm your concentration by increasing your arousal level to the point where you are easily distracted.

➢ *Develop habits and schedules for your work.* Procrastinators tend to be "all or none" workers. To overcome this tendency, schedule recurring tasks (e.g., reading chapters for class, studying for regularly scheduled exams) for the same time periods during each day or week. Once this becomes a habit, you will find that it seems "natural" to do the task at that time and that you will automatically arrange the rest of your time to accommodate each task. Other people will also get used to your schedule and be reluctant to interrupt you, which will eliminate misunderstandings, frustrations, and the need to explain yourself to others.

➢ *Divide large tasks.* Starting early lets you decide what a task requires, gather what you need to do the task, and attack it in pieces. Because you don't always feel creative and your energy level fluctuates from day to day, dividing a task lets you do difficult parts at times you are most capable and ready to concentrate on the task. This works for all types of tasks (e.g., studying for an exam, writing a paper, doing library research, reading a text chapter). You will find that you work more efficiently at certain times of the day and be able to increase your output by scheduling harder course work at such times. Studying when *you* choose to rather than to meet some externally-imposed deadline will help you recognize fluctuations in your energy level and concentration span—and let you take advantage of this insight. You have no doubt heard the expression, "Don't work harder—work smarter." Dividing large tasks is just one of many techniques that will let you work smarter.

➢ *Just get started.* If you don't want to work on a task, set a timer for 10 minutes and promise to work until the buzzer goes off. Then decide if you are willing to do 10 minutes more. This is a good technique for really boring work, but may not work well with difficult tasks since having a timer go off or looking to see how much time is left will distract you. One surprise is that you may find that you merely hate to *start*. Once started, you may be reluctant to stop before finishing and may even find it less boring or difficult than you thought. The smaller amount you still have to do when the buzzer goes off often motivates you to continue to completion. An added advantage is that you will learn how long it takes to do certain types of tasks (e.g., reading a chapter), so you can schedule more accurately in the future.

➢ *Get organized.* Chapter 5 on self-management includes more tips on how to organize your work space to assure you are ready to tackle a task without delay, how to minimize your distractions, and how to post your schedule for the semester.

Writing Activity 2.2—Which of these techniques do you use? Which ones do you plan to adopt? Do you have other methods to get yourself to do tasks you would rather put off?

| |
| |
| |
| |
| |
| |
| |

Self-Handicapping

He that is good for making excuses is seldom good for anything else.
— Benjamin Franklin

Test for Self-Awareness—Before reading further, complete and score the Self-Handicapping Scale on p. A9 (Jones & Rhodewalt, 1982). Your answers and score will help you better understand and apply the information in this section.

Think about the last time you met a friend to play tennis or some other sport—did you make a remark about having a "sore leg" or that the wind was really blowing hard? How about when you talked to a friend before an exam—did you say you hadn't studied much even though you had? Have you ever indulged in a few drinks before approaching someone you really wanted to impress? If you have used excuses similar to these before facing a task, welcome to the club! At times, we all self-handicap to protect our egos. Let's look at how and why we make such excuses.

When you are uncertain of successfully executing a task you performed adequately in the past or one you believe you *should* complete well (e.g., one appropriate for your academic or gender role), there is a tendency to verbally or behaviorally *self-handicap* prior to the task (Arkin & Baumgardner, 1985). The goal is to establish an excuse *just in case* you perform poorly. Self-handicapping usually occurs when you have a need to feel competent and "in control" because the task is tied to your feelings of self-worth.

We all self-handicap. Procrastination is a common example. The self-handicapping type of procrastination allows us to create the excuse that we would have done better if we had just spent more time preparing for an exam or working on a paper. Beck, Koons, and Milgrim (2000) found that college students who scored high on scales measuring academic procrastination and self-handicapping started later and studied less for an exam—and did worse on it than their peers. The damage of self-handicapping was not the same for all students, however. For those with high SAT scores (1045-1290), poor course performance only resulted if they *both* procrastinated on exam preparation *and* skipped classes. In comparison, students with low SAT scores (400-936) did poorly on the exam if they *either* skipped classes *or* procrastinated. Those with medium SAT scores (937-1044) only performed poorly if they skipped classes.

No doubt you can think of times when you told a friend that you didn't study much for an upcoming exam or might not be "on your game" today because your leg hurt. As long as you realize that it is normal to want to disown a potential failure <u>and</u> you don't *create* an actual roadblock (i.e., you just *say* you didn't study, but you really did), you probably won't damage your subsequent performance. ***The danger occurs when a created self-handicap*** prevents ***the occurrence of success***, such as getting drunk the night before an exam or really not studying. Of course, creating an actual self-defeating handicap will let you blame a poor exam score on lack of sleep, a hangover, or not studying rather than on an ***intellectual deficit*** (i.e., "I'm not smart enough for college"). This created excuse will *temporarily* protect your ego (remember, self-handicapping occurs when you *fear* you may not perform well). Unfortunately, such behavior lessens your probability for success in a course. It can even lead to ***ego-damaging*** behaviors, including plagiarism and cheating (Roig & DeTommasso, 1995), when you attempt to catch up.

Writing Activity 2.3—Write about a recent situation in which you self-handicapped. Did you actually lessen your chance for success by doing something to sabotage your performance? Or did you just invent a reason why you might not succeed (e.g., saying you hadn't studied when you really had)? Do you now think you could have done better if you hadn't self-handicapped?

Gender-related differences in self-handicapping

Both men and women self-handicap, but researchers have found that they often prefer different methods. Men are more likely to use an ***acquired (behavioral) self-handicap***, which involves *actually damaging one's performance* by either carrying out a *bad* behavior or not performing a *good* behavior (Arkin & Baumgardner, 1985). Here are some of the self-defeating behaviors that <u>men</u> have been found to adopt more readily than women do. Check to see if you have used any of these behaviors when you weren't sure you could do well on an important task

(Berglas & Jones, 1978; Harris & Snyder, 1986; Rhodewalt & Davison, 1986; Strube, 1986; Tucker, Vuchinich, & Sobel, 1981):

➢ not practicing or studying for a task
➢ withholding effort during a task
➢ avoiding feedback by choosing to do an unrelated task rather than one that would show you how well you would do in an upcoming situation
➢ playing against an inferior opponent so that you didn't have to work hard and wouldn't receive feedback on areas in which you need to improve
➢ selecting a goal so difficult that you have almost no chance to reach it
➢ playing against a much superior opponent
➢ taking on too many tasks at once
➢ studying or performing in an environment that is distracting (e.g., in front of the TV or around people who are noisy, playing when it is windy or the weather is inappropriate)
➢ using debilitating drugs or alcohol prior to attempting a task.

Of course, women also self-handicap, but they usually resort to a *claimed (**self-reported, but not real**) self-handicap* (Higgins, Snyder, & Berglas, 1990). Women will *say* they have a problem that *may or may not* really exist instead of actually acting to damage their performance. Here are some of the behaviors researchers have found <u>women</u> are more likely to use (Baumgardner, 1991; Baumgardner, Lake, & Arkin, 1985; Gibbons & Gaeddert, 1984; Smith, Snyder, & Handelsman, 1982; Smith, Snyder, & Perkins, 1983). Check to see if you have used any of these pseudo-excuses when faced with uncertain success:

➢ saying you have test anxiety
➢ saying you are experiencing the side effects of medication
➢ saying you are experiencing emotional symptoms (e.g., feeling anxious or depressed)
➢ saying you are experiencing physical symptoms (e.g., feeling tired, having a headache)
➢ saying you are in a bad mood
➢ saying you are "just a woman."

Incidentally, this latter excuse isn't as easy to use now as it used to be. But if you were raised in a traditional household or culture, you may have fallen back on it successfully. Did you have "the boys" or maybe some family member regularly tell you that you couldn't do something because you were "just a woman"? If so, you may still use this excuse when you fear you can't do something successfully—or you just don't want to do it (e.g., lift something heavy, kill a bug, build something with household tools). Unfortunately, the same traditional attitude that lets you get away with such statements isn't as kind to men, who are actually expected to magically know how to fix a car or play a sport. But don't feel too sorry for them—they may self-handicap when asked to do something they consider "women's work" (e.g., cook, do the wash, buy their own clothes). The ultimate in such stereotyping of tasks is shown in the following joke: A husband, who manages a large company and makes over $100,000 a year, walks into the kitchen and yells back to his wife in the living room, "Honey, where is the ice cream?" The exasperated wife, realizing he probably wants her to get it for him, says, "It's in the oven." And the husband looks in the oven!

The gender difference in preferred types of self-handicaps appears be related to the tendency for men to think their performance on a task is due to an **unchangeable ability** (e.g., intelligence, athletic skill, strength), whereas women are more likely to believe their performance results from either their **effort** or **luck** (Deaux & Emsmiller, 1974; Rhodewalt, 1994). If men think effort won't help, their self-worth is more at risk if they perform poorly on a task. They have made a **"stable" attribution** for their performance. They believe that trying harder will have little effect on their behavior, that "they are who they are." Instead, women have made an **"unstable" attribution** to a **temporary** deficit (e.g., lack of effort, disinterest, being tired, bad luck), so they believe that today's performance neither predicts their future behavior nor reflects badly on their self-worth.

Women may also be engaging in **impression management** (trying to get others to see them in a positive way). Sometime a woman will practice for a task but then deny that she has done so (e.g., Luginbuhl & Palmer, 1991). Therefore, any subsequent success will be viewed more positively by those who think she is attempting the task *without practicing*—and poor performance will be excused! To test women's tendency to *behaviorally* self-handicap, researchers have asked them to choose between distracting music (or a drug which supposedly would damage their ability to perform) and task-facilitating music (or a performance-enhancing drug). Compared to the choices made by men, women have been far more likely to choose to increase their chances for success (chosen the "facilitating" option) rather than setting up an excuse. In other studies women have practiced more (Hirt, McCrea, & Kimble, 2000) and chosen a situation they were told would increase their performance (Doebler, Schick, Beck, & Astor-Stetson, 2000). In all these situations men were more likely to deliberately sabotage their behavior by choosing the offered self-handicap.

A positive side effect of self-handicapping: awareness that a task is importance to you

Remember that self-handicapping indicates fear of an ego-damaging outcome and uncertainty about your ability to perform "as you should"—it is *not* an effective coping technique by itself. If you catch yourself starting to self-handicap, you can use it as a signal that the task is important to you and that you need to adequately prepare for it. Here are some steps you can take to increase your performance instead of resorting to self-handicapping:
  ➢ ask questions so that you understand the task
  ➢ practice for it
  ➢ allow plenty of time to accomplish the task
  ➢ make sure that the environment in which you work on the task is favorable for doing it well
  ➢ accept feedback so you can adjust your performance on it during the task and in the future
  ➢ acquire skills that will increase your performance (this will also help you gain self-efficacy for the task)
  ➢ remind yourself that denying your fear and uncertainty, avoiding preparation for a task, or not thinking about it will actually *increase* your need to self-handicap.

If you engage in self-handicapping, you need to monitor your actions and thoughts to learn which situations increase your anxiety enough to engage in self-defeating behaviors. Then you can see what coping skills (e.g., asking questions, time management, assertiveness, relaxation) are needed to assure better performance. You will find that increased confidence from being prepared will allow you to face a task in a more relaxed state, which will also enhance your probability of success. As you develop self-efficacy for a task, your need to self-handicap (or procrastinate) will lessen—but you will probably still claim that "sore leg" occasionally!

Suggested Readings

Baumgardner, A. H. (1990). To know oneself is to like oneself: Self-certainty and self-affect. *Journal of Personality and Social Psychology, 58,* 1062-1072.

Beck, B. L., Koons, S. R., & Milgrim, D. L. (2000). Correlates and consequences of behavioral procrastination: The effects of academic procrastination, self-consciousness, self-esteem and self-handicapping. *Journal of Social Behavior and Personality, 15*(5), 3-13.

Ellis, A., & Harper, R. A. (1978). *A new guide to rational living.* N. Hollywood: Wilshire.

Higgins, R. L., Snyder, C. R., & Berglas, S. (1990). *Self-handicapping: The paradox that isn't.* New York: Plenum.

Tice, D. M., & Baumeister, R. F. (1997). Longitudinal study of procrastination, performance, stress, and health: The costs and benefits of dawdling. *Psychological Science, 8,* 454-458.

Suggested Web Sites

http://ub-counseling.buffalo.edu/stressmanagement.shtml This site provides information on a variety of topics for college students (e.g., stress, study skills, procrastination, perfectionism, time management).

http://www.unc.edu/depts/unc_caps/resources.htm The University of North Carolina's Counseling and Psychological Services presents practical information on academic improvement, eating disorders, substance abuse, depression, sleep, grief, stress management, assertiveness, and helping a friend. You can access other sites from this page too.

http://www.queendom.com This site is fun, entertaining, and lets you compare yourself to others. However, do not take all of it seriously!

http://www.psy.ohio-state.edu/social/arkin.htm This site compares the self-handicapper and overachiever, and there are a number of references you can look up to read more about them.

http://www.carleton.ca/~tpychyl/ This site for the Procrastination Research Group at Carleton University in Ottawa, Canada, presents information and research on procrastination from all over the world. You can even take part in their research through this site.

Chapter 3

Pitfalls on the Path Through Your College Career

The Seven Deadly Sins:
Downward and Upward Social Comparison and Perfectionism

We are what we think. All that we are arises with our thoughts.
With our thoughts, we make the world. — Buddha (c. 483 BC)

Now that you have explored your tendencies to procrastinate and self-handicap, let's look at the next three "deadly sins" for college success: ***downward and upward social comparison*** and ***perfectionism***.

Downward and Upward Social Comparison

If you are unsure about *anything* and cannot get objective information about it, you will look to others in the situation to see what to think, how to act, or how to judge your behavior. Festinger (1954) called this ***social comparison***. In fact, ***social reality*** (what others think is occurring) becomes *your* reality. In order to get *useful* information, the others you use as a reference must be *similar to you in that particular situation*. For instance, you might ask classmates if they thought an exam your class just finished was hard or easy.

Based on social comparison theory, Schachter and Singer (1962) developed an explanation of how you decide which emotion you are feeling. According to their theory, you will using the actions or statements of ***those similar to you in the situation*** to interpret ***unexplained physiological arousal***. Additionally, if your culture (e.g., movies, TV) has taught you to expect to experience a specific emotion in the situation, you will interpret *unexplained* arousal you feel at that time to fit your culture's expectation. For instance, you may interpret the excitement of being at a party as "love" if you meet an "appropriate" person, especially if you are inexperienced in intimate relationships (Hatfield & Walster, 1981).

While social comparison is a useful method for helping us understand our current situation, we sometimes incorrectly choose ***dissimilar*** others for comparison purposes. When we do so, we are engaging in ***downward*** or ***upward social comparison*** (Buunk, Collins, Taylor, VanYperen, & Dakof, 1990).

Downward social comparison

This type of comparison occurs when we contrast ourselves with one who is less well-off, less skilled, or less fortunate. We resort to this technique when our self-worth or safety is threatened *if* such a comparison holds a promise of self-enhancement or reassurance. We can also use it to improve our current level of ***subjective well-being*** (how happy we are, how good we feel) (Diener, 1984; Goethals, 1986). The person needs only to be similar enough to make our comparison *seem* realistic (e.g., a fellow student, someone of the same sex or age). Health psychologists (e.g., Wood, Taylor, & Lichtman, 1985) suggest this type of comparison can *sometimes* be a useful coping technique. Patients with a chronic illness which cannot be escaped may experience less distress and handle treatment better when they compare themselves with someone who isn't coping as well. Victims also benefit from using it immediately after a traumatic event (e.g., a car wreck) because it allows them to insulate their feelings until they can accept and deal with reality.

However, downward social comparison can hurt others or our relationship with them when it takes the form of ***derogating*** (belittling, blaming) another person (e.g., "he brought it on himself") or picturing the person as less well off (e.g., thinking about when the person performed poorly). In this case our empathy for and tendency to understand or help others is reduced. Its effect is also evident in a wide range of everyday behaviors, including wanting to be with others when afraid, telling ethnic jokes and other forms of derogatory humor, scapegoating, lacking sympathy for crime victims, and displacing aggression.

Although downward social comparison can help you in a few situation, too often it has a self-destructive outcome. See if you have used any of these negative forms it can take:
  ➢ feeling *inappropriate* relief from anxiety when you should take action to change your behavior ("I can handle my liquor—I won't have a wreck like he did")
  ➢ being lazy due to feeling superior (not working to improve your behavior because you can beat a "beginner")
  ➢ lessening your effort for improvement ("half the class flunked the exam, so my D is OK")
  ➢ denying personal responsibility ("you don't deserve help because you caused your problem; I wouldn't act like that")
  ➢ denying a need to change ("lots of people get good jobs with a lower GPA than mine)
  ➢ ***illusion of invulnerability*** (Weinstein & Klein, 1996; Weinstein, 1984) ("other people get sick from not getting enough sleep, but that won't happen to me")
  ➢ complacency ("no one else has started on the paper yet, and I've at least picked a topic")
  ➢ misjudgment and inflation of one's capabilities ("my roommate must be stupid to have failed an exam—it won't happen to me because I never studied in high school and got good grades")

Threats to one's self-worth may *automatically* result in defensiveness rather than considering the usefulness of this feedback. For instance, a student reminded of repeated absence from class will cite his roommate's tendency to skip more classes. Or a heavy drinker will respond, "You should see how much my friends drink." Therefore, we urge you to *be sure* that when you resort to an excuse, you are *not* missing an opportunity to get valuable feedback. You should also take care that you don't appear to be evading your misdeeds. Inappropriate comparisons and defensiveness can hurt both your future performance *and* your reputation in the eyes of others.

Writing Activity 3.1—Write about a recent situation in which you used *downward social comparison*. Was it an appropriate use of the technique, or were you being defensive or even undermining future performance by ignoring feedback? Now, write what you could have said, to others or yourself, to *avoid* comparing downward and to *own* your behavior?

Upward social comparison

This type of comparison occurs when we liken ourselves to someone who is better off or more fortunate than we are or who has something we think we *should* have because we *mistakenly* consider the person to be a similar other. Like downward social comparison, this process may occasionally have a good outcome for us. We can use it positively for motivation to spur us to improve our performance, to encourage us to persist during a frustrating period, or as a model for showing us how to do something that is new to us.

However, the adverse effects of mistakenly choosing a superior target for comparison can be dangerous to our self-worth and health. The media inundates us with upward comparison targets who perform dangerous stunts and have unhealthy life styles, both of which appear to do them no harm. Rich, powerful, happy, gorgeous people are constantly being shown as the *typical* or *ideal* American. Adolescents consume tremendous amounts of media, often mistaking the people and scenarios in stories and ads as "typical" because of their naïveté about the world. The average American home has television on 51 hours a week (Elliot, 1996), and two-thirds of households have three or more TVs, which probably explains why parents' and their children's reports differ concerning what the children actually watch (Donnerstein, 1998).

We should realize that media people are *not* average and are chosen for their looks (real or airbrushed) to sell products or put the viewer in a good mood. Unfortunately, constant exposure to them has taken its toll. Since the 1950's the *ideal* American woman, as portrayed by media, has shrunk (e.g., Silverstein, Perdue, Peterson, & Kelly, 1986) at the very time that American eating and inactivity patterns have resulted in an increase in the size of teenagers and young adults. The explosion of eating disorders and negative self-concept in this segment of the population is repeatedly tied to the mistaken belief that not being skinny is the source of their misery (e.g., Thompson, 1996).

Additionally, the entire 1960's phenomenon (student activism, disillusionment of American youth, riots, and related violence) has been tied partially to increased media exposure of the *have-nots* to the life style of the privileged *haves*. People are constantly told that they should want—and indeed *deserve*—sometime just because it is available. Once they feel *unjustly* deprived of this item, dissatisfaction and feelings of inequity develop (see Olson, Herman, & Zanna, 1986; Suls & Mullen, 1982). This fabricated desire is called **relative deprivation**. In fact, an emphasis on material success as your major goal can have a negative effect on healthy adjustment. When college students rank ordered their goals in life, those who placed financial success higher than self-acceptance, relations with friends and family, and community service (helping or teaching others) reported poorer adjustment and more behavioral disorders (Kasser & Ryan, 1993, 1996).

Negative outcomes for intentionally or accidentally choosing a superior comparison target in a personally-relevant area are well-documented. One consequence is a false belief that something that is *hard* for you to do is *easy* for others—that things just "fall in their lap." You *ignore* the effort they have put out to reach their goal, what they have given up to reach their goal, or the actually differences between you and the other people that may have helped them reach their goal. See if you have experienced any of these outcomes from comparing yourself to an inappropriate person:
> ➤ frustration, depression, and hopelessness ("I'll never get to be a doctor because I'll never know as much as my biology professor does.")
> ➤ jealousy ("It's not fair that my roommate makes good grades, and I keep getting C's.")
> ➤ anger ("I hate her—she has a good-looking boyfriend, and I just have old Charlie.")
> ➤ cynicism ("He probably got good grades because he cheated.")

- feelings of *anomie* (not belonging, lost in a strange culture) ("My roommate makes friends so easily, but I don't know anyone and nobody seems to care.")
- justifications for revenge ("He thinks he's so great—I'll tell everyone the secret he told me so people won't think he's so great.")
- excuses for self-destructive behaviors (e.g., smoking, drinking, exercise bulimia, eating disorders) ("School is so easy for everyone else—I deserve to drown my sorrows.")
- crime or other immoral behaviors ("Since school is so easy for everyone but me, I guess I'll have to cheat my way through.").

Writing Activity 3.2—Write about a recent situation in which you used ***upward social comparison***. Was it an *appropriate* use of the technique (e.g., using an *expert similar other* as a model when trying something new), or were you comparing yourself to an *inappropriate* person? How did you feel and what did you do as a result of making this comparison?

Perfectionism

I have not failed. I've just found 10,000 ways that won't work. — Thomas Edison

---

Test for Self-Awareness—Before reading further, complete and score the sample items from the Multidimensional Perfection Scale on p. A63 (Hewitt, Flett, Turnbull-Donovan, & Mikail, 1991). This will help you understand and apply the information in this section.

Most students begin college feeling somewhat burdened by the expectations of others and a culturally-reinforced belief that they must do *exceptionally* well in school to be a success in life. This is especially true if their high school performance was above average. Many of these students also suffer from a belief that they must be perfect, at least in important areas in their lives. *Perfectionism* is the belief that we must do something flawlessly, that all endeavors must be successful, and that we must *always* do our "best." Burns (1980) described perfectionism as *compulsive* striving to meet unreasonable, unattainable goals and a belief that self-worth depends entirely on achieving these goals.

This belief is another source of procrastination—we need never admit an imperfection if we carefully arrange *not* to test our real abilities. Instead, we can blame lack of time, too many obligations, and unforeseen roadblocks for our less-than-perfect performance. Putting off a task also allows us to avoid the unpleasant feelings that accompany the impossible struggle to do something 100% right.

Perfectionists overemphasize past mistakes, become angry with themselves, and feel guilty about making a mistake. Perfectionism in college students has been found to result in *low* self-esteem, increased mood disorders, and poor health (e.g., Flett & Hewitt, 1992). In a related finding, perfectionists had lower self-actualization scores, apparently due to low tolerance for failure (Flett, Hewitt, Blankstein, & Mosher, 1991). (*Self-actualization* is fulfilling your potential and is an essential goal, according to humanistic philosophers.)

Perfectionists' traits also put them at risk for interpersonal unhappiness (e.g., Bognatz & Schick, 1996). They report loneliness and problems in personal relationships (e.g., Flett et al., 1991; Hewitt & Genest, 1990). They expect rejection from others due to their imperfections, react defensively when criticized, and easily lapse into sarcasm and pointing out others' faults. Defensiveness alienates others, reinforcing perfectionists' belief that flawless performance is mandatory for acceptance by others. Additionally, they fear that revealing any doubts about their abilities will make them appear foolish or inadequate, and they assume that *any* sign of weakness will result in rejection. Their fears result in forfeiture of the chance for intimate communication with significant people in their lives. Consequently, they fail to receive the unconditional acceptance they crave but believe is contingent upon perfect performance (Burns, 1980).

From our description of the many aspects of perfectionism, you probably realized that it isn't just a matter of "doing well." We assume you have now completed the sample items from the Multidimensional Perfectionism Scale (Hewitt et al., 1991), so here are explanations for what each subscale measures and characteristics of those who score high on each type.

➤ *Self-oriented perfectionism (SOP)* is defined as having *impossibly high* personal goals and standards for performance, along with excessive motivation to meet them (Hewitt & Flett, 1991). In a number of studies, SOP has been linked to self-criticism, emphasis on performance and goal attainment, guilt, disappointment, anger, defensiveness, depression, anxiety, hostility, obsessive-compulsive disorder, phobias, paranoia, self-handicapping, indecisiveness, procrastination, alcoholism, and anorexia. In a study of 18-19 year old students, Bognatz and Schick (1996) found it to be strongly related to feeling insecure about love relationships and to Type A personality, which is also marked by a belief that one's self-worth is based exclusively on performance (Price, 1983). You will note that SOP is *not* related to positive self-worth or successful performance, as many people assume it to be.

➤ *Other-oriented perfectionism (OOP)* involves having *unreasonably* high standards for significant others (e.g., family, friends, lovers). It is related to hostility, blaming others, being "embarrassed" by and ashamed of significant others, *authoritarianism* (believing that relative status determines who is "in charge" and is allowed to boss others), dominance, lack of trust, antisocial behavior, cynicism, loneliness, Type A personality, and family problems. (Chapter 4 discusses Type A and B personalities.) Men tend to score higher than women do on OOP. Men and Type A females were found to be higher on OOP than Type B females (Schick & Bognatz, 1996). In fact, Type A students currently in romantic relationships scored *higher* on OOP than Type A's not in relationships or than either Type B group. Those high in both SOP and OOP find that striving for academic excellence often conflicts with their desire for interpersonal success and that people avoid them because they are so judgmental.

➤ *Socially-prescribed perfectionism (SPP)* is characterized by the belief that significant others hold *unrealistic, unfair* standards for you and that you <u>must</u> strive to meet their standards. *SPP is the type of perfectionism that is most strongly associated to poor adjustment, low self-concept, and psychological distress* (e.g., Fairlie, Flett, & Hewitt, 1993). SPP is related to a compulsive need for approval, fear of negative evaluation, *external locus of control* (feeling that the situation, powerful others, and luck control your life), substituting other people's goals for your own, anger at the unfairness of having to work to please others, borderline personality disorder, and Type A behavior. Behaviors SPP produces include procrastination, shame, anxiety, self-criticism, depression, alcoholism, disordered eating, and avoiding evaluation (e.g., hiding from or freezing in front of others). A feeling of never quite pleasing others can lead to feelings of hopelessness, so it is not surprising that SPP is related to suicide threat and intent (Hewitt, Flett, & Turnbull-Donovan, 1992). SPP destroys *intrinsic motivation* (wanting to perform a task for personal reasons, such as interest or fun). Instead, you feel guilty if you are not constantly working to please others.

After seeing the danger of perfectionistic beliefs, we hope you will abandoned any belief that success requires incessantly striving to be perfect. Actually, seeking perfection results in performing *less* well. Perfectionists experience more anxious arousal, which interferes with concentration. A need to *perform* (rather than *learn*) leads perfectionists to use ineffective study techniques (Chapter 4 discusses performance and learning goals). They also avoid *new* situations because they fear doing poorly and looking bad to others. This narrowing of "allowable" tasks ultimately leads to feelings of boredom—of "being in a rut." Perfectionists end up not reaching their potential, regretting not following their dreams, feeling that work is drudgery, and experiencing guilt because they think they have let themselves and others down.

Irrational beliefs of perfectionists

> *Real knowledge is to know the extent of one's ignorance.* — Confucius

Here are some unrealistic ideas that perfectionists commonly believe. As you read each one, think about areas in your own life that suffer because you cling to these beliefs. Describe your own experience for each irrational belief, so you will have a record of your perfectionistic tendencies. Realizing that you harbor these beliefs is a first step toward redefining your own standards and setting *realistic* goals that can make your college, personal, and professional life more successful *and* satisfactory.

➤ You engage in all-or-none thinking (you are either a success *or* failure, good *or* bad).

_____

➤ You see *reaching* goals as essential for self-worth (I "must"…).

_____

➤ All focus for satisfaction is on the future, ignoring the goals you *have met* by focusing on what you still need to do to be successful in your eyes ("when I graduate…").

_____

➤ You engage in "telescoping" (magnifying the importance of unmet or future goals, worrying that they will not be met, feeling dissatisfied with your present performance or existence).

_____

➤ Because of the last two factors, you *minimize* your accomplishments and *fail to reward* yourself when you meet a goal successfully (rather you tell yourself, "Don't brag" and "Don't rest on your laurels"—or even, "Anyone could have done that"). Incidentally, this latter self-statement is both a reflection of, and a perpetuator of, low self-worth.

_____

➤ Desires become demands ("I would like…" becomes "I must/ought to/should…").

➤ You use *selective attention*, only looking at your flaws and mistakes rather than acknowledging your good points and successes. This focus makes it almost impossible to feel like you have "won," but very easy to believe that you have "lost."

➤ You see average behavior as mediocre and "shameful"—you believe that you have let yourself and others down if your performance is not superior.

➤ You feel unmotivated and unworthy unless others are raving about your "great" behavior, praising you, and complimenting you. You feel conflicted over whether or not to "brag" just in case others are unaware of your performance. You *need* for them to know about your performance so you can win their approval.

➤ Despite needing to tell others of an unseen feat, you fear being labeled a "show-off." Because of this fear—and a tendency to automatically minimize your achievements, as mentioned above—you often ungraciously respond to compliments by pointing out your shortcomings or a flaw in your performance. Doing so is an insult to the person praising you (it denies that others know how to judge behaviors) and will actually result in your getting fewer compliments from this person in the future.

➤ Your anxiety is so high when faced with anything important to you—and what *isn't* important??—that it interferes with your ability to concentrate, learn, and perform. Consequently, tasks become aversive and unpleasant because of the negative feeling you get when thinking about or attempting them. Eventually, a sense of dread and uncertainty becomes "attached" to the task through *classical conditioning* (pairing of an emotion, such as fear or anxiety, with a person, situation, or task that did not previously elicit that emotion from you). Conditioning causes you to think the person, situation, or task *itself* is automatically unpleasant or scary, even if you have never before faced that *specific* person, situation, or task (you "hate" school, "can't do" math, "can't stand" talking in front of a group, "fear" professors).

> Even a task that you once enjoyed and looked forward to (e.g., a sport) becomes more aversive as it gains in importance to you or as your expertise increases. You become more critical of your performance, expect "excellence" every time you attempt the task, and eventually only do it to please others (e.g., parents, coach, the boss)—*intrinsic* motivation (enjoying the task) turns to *extrinsic* motivation.

Escaping the perfectionism trap

> *Success is getting what you want; happiness is wanting what you get.*
> — Dale Carnegie

You may wonder if now is the time to attack and change self-defeating perfectionistic beliefs. After all, you are busy starting your college career! However, late adolescence and early adulthood—in fact, *any time you are making major changes in your life*—is a great time to reassess how you think about setting and working toward your goals. You have probably already decided not to carry some (or most) of your high school habits into college—so, why not get rid of perfectionistic thinking you currently have?

Just reminding yourself that now isn't the *only* time you can set goals or improve yourself will lessen a perfectionistic fear that you might not "get it right" the first time you try. You will have *many* opportunities throughout life to do self-searching and to decide to set new goals and adopt new beliefs. Let's look at some other times when it is easier to reassess and change beliefs and behaviors.

> Times of crisis or change (e.g., personal illness or injury, diagnosis of a chronic problem you must learn to live with, serious illness or death of someone close to you, following dangerous incidents or "near misses," when an event reminds you that you are not "bullet-proof," new jobs, new towns, new schools, new semesters, new people in your life, new intimate relationships, major changes in your family).

> Times when environmental challenges are so great that you must change (e.g., floods, fires, tornadoes, earthquakes, even hot summers or cold winters).

> Times when you are faced with new developmental tasks or taking on a new role (e.g., leaving home for the first time, living with new people or in new settings—especially if you are accustomed to living alone, entering college, taking a part-time job, beginning a career, becoming a boss, falling in love, committing to a serious relationship, getting married, getting divorced, learning to live without someone who has been significant in your life, becoming a parent, hitting a point in your life when you either need or want to slow down, retiring, having to abandon a pastime or move to smaller housing because of your health).

> ➤ Having to "accommodate" yourself to a new situation in which your old habits and behaviors don't work any more (e.g., college courses do not allow you to "slide by" without studying or by cramming for exams like you might have in high school; new relationships require self-disclosure and learning how to compromise and coordinate with another person; having a roommate or housemate forces you to learn to live with and compromise with people who may be very different from your family).

Gaining perspective on important goals in your life

Only those who dare to fail greatly can ever achieve greatly. — Robert F. Kennedy

Remember that perfectionists do not like change or new situations because they would be performing unfamiliar tasks and taking the risk of doing them poorly at first. Your challenge is to endure the changes you have chosen or are forced to make without falling back on old, but unsuitable, habits. ***Knowing what types of situations in your life evoke perfectionistic thoughts and behaviors will alert you to look for and confront these self-defeating beliefs and begin to change them.*** This is a big step in changing perfectionistic thinking and returning control of your choices and reinforcers to *you*.

Writing Activity 3.3—Think about areas or activities in your life that elicit perfectionistic thoughts and behaviors. (You can look back at situations you wrote down while reading about unrealistic beliefs that perfectionists have.) Now, write about an example of *each type* of perfectionism that you are currently experiencing or have experienced in the past. How are you working—or planning to work—on your thoughts and behaviors to regain control in this area? (If an example is one from the past that you have now "conquered," write about how you got rid of your perfectionistic thoughts and behaviors—doing so will give you suggestions for attacking present problems.)

SOP:

OOP:
SPP:

If your self-worth is centered in only one aspect of your life (e.g., school, sports, looks, *or* a love interest) *or* if your significant others only praise your performance in and stress the importance of one role you play, you can become particularly devastated by a perceived "failure" in that area. A quality of older people is that they have learned to play (and leave) many roles during their lives. Therefore, their "worth investment" is not confined to what happens in just one facet of their existence.

Think about people your age who seem unusually mature. If you know them well, you probably realize that they have had to cope with problems or adjust to situations and roles that people your age usually don't face. Development of good coping skills often results from experience with change (see Chapters 9 and 10 on coping with stress). You currently have such an opportunity. How you choose to cope with the new experiences you meet while in college will form habits you will use for years. We hope you won't choose self-destructive coping techniques (e.g., drinking to escape your studies or to "fit in" at parties, depending on others to take care of you and solve all your problems, blaming others when you should be taking responsibility for your own actions). If you take this path, you will have missed a chance to gain the maturity that comes from mastering *controllable* aspects of your life. Emotional coping (e.g., seeking help from a friend, finding humor in your predicament) is an answer in situations that *not* in your control, but adjusting to college and pursuing your education is *not* one of those instances. The following chapters contain numerous suggests for actively engaging in college and in the rest of your life.

Suggested Readings

Buunk, B P., Collins, R. L., Taylor, S. E., VanYperen, N. W., & Dakof, G. A. (1990). The affective consequences of social comparison: Either direction has its ups and downs. *Journal of Personality and Social Psychology, 59,* 1238-1249.

Hewitt, P. L., Flett, G. L. , & Turnbull-Donovan, W. (1992). Perfectionism and suicide potential. *British Journal of Clinical Psychology, 31,* 181-190.

Hewitt, P. L., & Genest, M. (1990). The ideal self: Schematic processing of perfectionistic content in dysphoric university students. *Journal of Personality and Social Psychology, 59,* 802-808.

Kasser, T., & Ryan, R. M. (1993). A dark side of the American dream: Correlates of financial success as a central life aspiration. *Journal of Personality and Social Psychology, 65,* 410-422.

Olson, J. M., Herman, C. P., & Zanna, M. P. (1986). *Relative deprivation and social comparison: The Ontario symposium* (Vol. 4). Hillsdale, NJ: Erlbaum.

Weinstein, N. D., & Klein, W. M. (1996). Unrealistic optimism: Present and future. *Journal of Social and Clinical Psychology, 15,* 1-8.

Suggested Web Sites

http://www.unc.edu/depts/unc_caps/resources.htm The University of North Carolina's Counseling And Psychological Services talks about academics, eating disorders, substance abuse, depression, sleep, grief, stress management, assertiveness, and helping a friend.

http://ub-counseling.buffalo.edu/stressmanagement.shtml This site provides information on a variety of topics for college students (e.g., stress, study skills, procrastination, perfectionism,).

http://www.cybertowers.com/selfhelp/ This Web magazine presents articles on a variety of topics (e.g., parenting, stress, dreaming, eating disorders).

http://www.queendom.com This site is fun, entertaining, and lets you compare yourself to others. However, do not take all of it seriously!

Chapter 4

Pitfalls on the Path Through Your College Career

The Seven Deadly Sins:
Adopting Performance Goals Rather than Learning Goals and Being Too Serious

*Only the curious will learn and only the resolute overcome the obstacles to learning.
The **quest** quotient has always excited me more than the **intelligence** quotient.*
— Eugene S. Wilson, Dean of Admissions, Amherst

Here are the last two of the most "deadly sins" for college life—the pitfalls related to *setting performance goals instead of learning goals in your courses* and *being too grim about college and about life in general*.

The Danger of Setting *Performance* Goals

> **Test for Self-Awareness**—Before reading on, complete and score The Goals Inventory on p. A11 (Roedel, Schraw, & Plake, 1994). Your scores will help you understand and apply the information in this section.

Over the last 30 years evidence has accumulated pointing to the greater effectiveness of approaching a task with a *learning orientation* (i.e., a concern for mastery and personal improvement) rather than a *performance orientation* (i.e., a focus on demonstrating one's ability in relation to others, to meeting some external standard in order to "look good," or to escape punishment). The former is sometimes called a *mastery*, or *task*, orientation, while the latter is also referred to as an *ability*, or *ego*, orientation (e.g., Dweck, 1986; Ames, 1992).

Research comparing the two orientations has helped us understand how behaviors and beliefs affect students from elementary school through college, as well as workers in their job settings. We're sure you have heard repeatedly that children of Eastern Asian ethnicity are "smarter" than American children or that their schools are "better" than US schools. Actually, parents in Asian cultures (e.g., Taiwan, China, Singapore, Korea, Japan) and of Asian-American children emphasize their child's *effort* as making the difference in success and failure in school work and other endeavors. There is no real way to compare innate factors or who has "better" schools. It is really *American* parents and culture which more frequently believe that a child's **ability** (i.e., genetic intelligence) is a more important explanation for performance, achievement motivation, and potential for success. Mueller and Dweck (1998) found that 85% of the parents polled incorrectly thought that praising their child's ability (e.g., "you're so smart!") following good task performance was *necessary* to make the child *feel smart*, which parents believed would increase motivation.

You will remember from the discussion of self-handicapping in Chapter 2 that you can make either a **stable** or an **unstable attribution** for your behavior. If you think your behavior was caused by a *stable, unchangeable characteristic* (e.g., intelligence, being smart), you will also believe that trying harder will have little effect on future attempts at the same or similar task. But if you think an *unstable, temporary state* (e.g., lack of effort, tiredness, being distracted) explains poor behavior, then today's actions neither predict future behavior nor reflect badly on who you are and what you can do. *You don't need to protect your ego because your self-worth is **not** tied to how well you perform at any given moment.*

Researchers have found that people who make *internal, stable* attributions for their behavior tend to set **performance goals** for future tasks, whereas those who make *internal, unstable* attributions for behavior adopt **learning goals** (e.g., Mueller & Dweck, 1998). Let's look at how setting each type of goal affects your behavior in an academic setting.

Consequences for setting <u>performance</u> goals

If people important to you have praised your past academic successes (e.g., exam performance, report card grades, Grade Point Average or GPA) by telling you that you are *smart*, you are more likely to set performance goals for future academic work (Butler, 1987, 1988). Here are some of the **negative effects** that researchers (e.g., Mueller & Dweck, 1998) have found those who set *performance* goals experience:

➢ avoidance of a task that could provide helpful feedback if that task has the risk for mistakes or for showing inadequacy
➢ tendency to chose the "safe" and well-learned path rather than trying something new or interesting
➢ helplessness when frustrated or confronted with negative feedback for performance
➢ tendency to give up if the task isn't *immediately* successful (i.e., if it is frustrating)
➢ tendency to ask for help as soon as the path is unclear or habitual techniques don't work (rather than persisting or trying different techniques to solve the problem)
➢ low feelings of self-worth following "failure" or poor performance (due to behavior being linked to intelligence instead of effort)
➢ tendency to show off, to need to demonstrate their ability to others, especially on easy or well-learned tasks
➢ orientation toward competition with others rather than comparison of their current behavior with their past behavior on that task
➢ need to know how others have done or are doing on the task

41

- tendency to try to escape tasks that might show lack of ability to others
- feeling extreme anxiety when forced to perform threatening tasks (consequently, excess arousal interferes with performance, causing a self-fulfilling prophesy)
- feelings of shame and embarrassment when unsuccessful performance is revealed
- tendency to report better performance than that which actually occurred in order to protect their ego
- reliance on *extrinsic* motivation (e.g., praise, emphasis on outcome) instead of *intrinsic* motivation (e.g., interest, increased knowledge or skill, emphasis on process)
- belief that they can't learn unless they like the topic or the professor teaching the class (both put control of their learning outside themselves—at the mercy of chance)
- use of "surface" learning strategies, such as **rote** (word-for-word) memorization (e.g., Meece, Blumenfeld, & Hoyle, 1988)
- *poorer* performance and a *lower* GPA than those of students who set learning goals, illustrating that performance goals lower achievement (e.g., Albaili, 1998; Greene & Miller, 1996; Schraw, Horn, Thorndike-Christ, & Bruning, 1995)

Writing Activity 4.1—Write about a task for which you set a *performance* goal. How did your *feelings*, *behaviors*, and *outcomes* match those mentioned above that have been found for people who set this type of goal?

42

Consequences for setting <u>learning</u> goals

If people important to you have attributed your past academic successes to your *effort* (e.g., hard work, use of specific strategies), you are more likely to set learning goals for your school work. Here are some of the ***positive effects*** researchers (e.g., Albaili, 1998) have found that people who set *learning* goals experience:

➢ being primarily concerned with acquiring new skills and knowledge, even at the risk of making mistakes along the way

➢ a view that current mistakes are positive because they provide ***feedback***, which allows them to improve their strategies and increase their knowledge (as opposed to craving reinforcement, even when it isn't sincere, because their performance hasn't been very good)

➢ desire to develop competence and understanding—to be able to use skills and information

➢ since poor performance is due to lack of effort or using the wrong technique, self-worth is *not* tied to current performance—therefore, few negative feelings (e.g., shame) occur

➢ willingness to take on difficult and new tasks, to work hard, and to tolerate frustration

➢ emphasis on self-improvement and mastery of the material or technique rather than on competition with others

➢ emphasis on the *process* of learning rather than on the *product* (the outcome)

➢ more use of "self-regulatory" activities, including distributed practice (rather than cramming), planning, goal-setting, organization, and comprehension monitoring (e.g., Miller, Beherens, Greene, & Newman, 1993)

➢ appropriate help-seeking (asking questions to clarify the task, asking for feedback, asking for suggestions concerning new techniques or strategies to try)

➢ more use of cognitive strategies that facilitate understanding of the material and the task (e.g., Nolen, 1988)

➢ more use of "deep-processing" strategies, including monitoring their progress, regulating their attention, and demonstrating ***metacognition*** (understanding of how you think, how the brain organizes memory, and how learning occurs) (e.g., Greene & Miller, 1996; Pintrich & De Groot, 1990)

➢ emphasis on self-improvement and thorough understanding (Kong & Hau, 1996)

➢ *better* grades and *higher* GPA than those made by students who set performance goals (e.g., Albaili, 1998; Greene & Miller, 1996; Schraw et al., 1995)

This final consequence should be a warning to you if you usually concentrate only on your performance, believing that doing so will help you "do well." This type of emphasis narrows your emphasis to concern for *what you have <u>done</u>* rather than *what you are <u>doing</u>*. Performance is a *product*, whereas learning is an on-going *process*. You will have a better chance for excellence in academic endeavors if you shift your concentration away from "a grade" and instead look for interest and challenge in your studies every day.

Writing Activity 4.2—Write about a task for which you set a *learning* goal. How did your feelings, behaviors, and outcomes match those of people who set this type of goal?

You may have noticed how this topic is related to discussions of self-handicapping and perfectionism in earlier chapters. Self-handicappers and perfectionists have much in common with those who set *performance* goals in that their academic strategies and outcomes (poor grades, lower GPAs) are similar. You will remember that people who believe their **ability** may be questioned (who make **stable** attributions for their actions) are more at risk for self-handicapping. This emphasis can actually damage performance if they fail to practice or use ineffective study strategies. Similarly, perfectionists depend more on extrinsic motivation (praise from others), are more competitive, tie their self-worth to performance, and experience excess arousal and worry. All three groups—those who set performance goals, self-handicappers, and perfectionists—differ from students who see their actions as reflecting *evolving* skills and the *process* of learning. These more adaptable students approach tasks with a learning orientation, a desire to learn how to alter their behavior so they can eventually master the task.

The Danger of Being Too Grim

You are here for a spell—get all the good laughs you can. — Will Rogers

You were probably expecting us to tell you that you are a grown-up now and that you have to put away your "childish" ways and be serious about life. However, if you look at how a wide range of personality theorists define "the healthy person," you will find that a regularly appearing characteristic is a good sense of humor and "seeing the whole picture," thus allowing you to maintain a realistic, healthy perspective, regardless of the situation. Being grim is not only unpleasant for you and those around you, it is unhealthy and likely to lead to use of maladaptive methods to escape responsibilities (e.g., drinking yourself into a stupor). So let's look at some of the bad habits you would be better off leaving behind on your journey from acting "adultish" to your goal of actually being mature.

Being humorless

One well-known fact is that you cannot be both relaxed and tense at the same time (see Chapter 8 on stress). Since overarousal (tenseness) reduces your ability to learn and remember information, developing a more relaxed attitude about your studies is an *essential* first step toward efficient learning. Learning how to see the humor in life is one path toward that relaxed state and toward building an attitude of competence, self-efficacy, and confidence in your ability to do well in school and in life. (Chapters 9 and 10 on coping with stress will further discuss humor, as well as other ways to increase your ability to relax.)

We have found an atmospheric difference in freshman and upper-level classes. You would think that harder, upper-level courses would produce more feelings of stress and anxiety than freshman-level courses, but that isn't the usual case. Freshmen more frequently have humor go right over their heads, and they even fail to laugh at obviously funny cartoons and jokes. Some of this is the "zombie" state brought on by lack of sleep and feeling overwhelmed by life. But some is due to failure to realize that they don't have to be so dead serious! Even our senior-level teaching assistants, who are frequently laughing about humor used in our freshman mass-lecture class, remark on how strange it is that freshmen just "don't get it."

We hope that by reading this book and applying the tips concerning academic work, stress coping, and relating to others, you will be able to grow out of the grim stage more quickly than freshmen usually do! A good place to start is to explore your general "grimness level." Being "stuck" in an over-serious mood can keep you from enjoying your college years. Grimness also makes you a poor companion, so your studies aren't all that suffer! Take the following **Quiz**— and be sure that you are truthful with yourself when you answer each of these questions. You will also learn to tell the difference between "taking life with a grain of salt," which indicates a healthy sense of humor, and resorting to destructive humor, which can hurt you and others.

Grimness Quiz

> Is your usual brand of humor to be sarcastic about your own and others' statements and behaviors?

> Do you only seem to enjoy *vicious* types of humor, such as practical jokes, laughing at someone who has made a mistake or is embarrassed, or telling demeaning jokes (e.g., ethnic, sexist, or other prejudicial jokes)?

> Do you disguise aggression toward others as humor (e.g., horse play in which you are too strong or are violent, embarrassing another by telling something "funny" he/she did, reminding the person of something embarrassing he/she did and laughing about it even though the other person is obviously uncomfortable)?

> Do you use self-deprecating humor as just another way of putting yourself down for not living up to unrealistic and "impossible" standards (e.g., giving in to perfectionistic beliefs)?

> Do you make fun of people who tell jokes, make puns, read comics in the paper, or "act silly" because you think they are "babies" and should grow up?

> Do you think that playing games is "childish" and a "waste of time"? (This refers to you attitude toward "fun" or even "silly" games, especially those played with others—*not* to violent video games, which aren't at all funny!)

> Do you think that professors who use humorous examples to help people remember course material should just teach you what you need to know for the exam and stop wasting your time and money on "silly stuff"?

> Do you often fail to understand jokes others tell (even though you may laugh to fit in)?

> Are you the last one to "get" a joke someone tells or to see something as funny when others around you have already erupted in laughter?

> Are you unable to see the humor in serious situations?

> Do you think that being playful, kidding your friends in a *harmless* way, and enjoying yourself are pretty much a waste of time? When you do resort to such behaviors, do you feel guilty because of your "lapse"?

> Do you think that watching a comedy on TV or a funny movie is a waste of time, even though you will watch a serious or violent TV show or movie?

> Can you only laugh if you watch aggressive humor, such as *The Three Stooges*?

> When you *do* see something as funny, do you just smile or barely laugh rather than really laughing uproariously?

> Does your laugh sound forced?

> Do you purposely stop laughing because you think that it is immature to lose control?

> Do you find it hard to remember the last time you laughed so hard with friend(s) that you couldn't catch your breath and/or tears streamed down your face?

> Do you feel superior when you *don't* laugh with others and think they're just "stupid" or "childish" to act that way?

If you answered "yes" to *any* of these items, you need to re-examine your attitudes and behaviors. You need to realize that humor is a healthy part of life as long as it isn't hurtful. You need to change your belief that it is immature. If you become embarrassed or feel silly when you laugh at real, non-hostile humor, it is due to believing that laughter and playfulness are not "proper" for an adult. If you are prone to hostile humor, you need to examine what your payoff is for cutting down others or seeing them suffer—why does it make you feel better? You also need to examine the anger you are harboring concerning yourself, others, or your current situation. Why are bitter laughter and sarcasm necessary, and where did you learn that these are "proper" types of humor? Why are you so tense or preoccupied that you just don't "get" jokes or see humor in situations when your peers do? And why do you then see yourself as superior to them? Once you realize how your attitude toward humor—and life in general—is keeping you so grim, you can actually begin to enjoy the events of your day more.

Writing Activity 4.3—Write about how the above questions have enlightened you about your attitudes about humor. Which questions helped you pinpoint ways you can get more humor into your life?

Type A personality

Whether or not you found yourself harboring perfectionistic beliefs when you read the last chapter, you may have an additional problem holding you back from a balanced philosophy for life. The U.S. has the highest proportion of Type A's in its population of any country, and, not coincidentally, we also lead the world in deaths from coronary heart disease (CHD). The hostility component of Type A personality is known to exacerbate the development of CHD (e.g., H. Friedman, 1992).

Type A college students also suffer more upper-respiratory illnesses, headaches, allergy attacks, and sleep disorders than their Type B peers. While health concern alone is enough to cause us to urge you to avoid a Type A philosophy, we will be addressing *how being a Type A can affect your school work, self-worth, and relationships with others*. Since Type A's are often impatient to start a task, if you didn't complete the Type A scale we just recommended, do so before going on!

Type A personality is characterized by a combination of excessive competitiveness, impatience, hostility toward the world in general, and a dedication to work as one's only *worthwhile* activity (Friedman & Rosenman, 1974; see their chapter on philosophy of life for a good distinction between Type A and Type B personality). Type A's faces and voices also give them away. They explosively emphasize words, speak loudly, speed up the end of sentences, interrupt or finish sentences for others, hurry others' speech by vigorously head shaking and saying "yes, yes" or "uhuh, uhuh," rapidly move their body parts (especially their hands and feet—are you swinging your leg right now?), pound their fists and shake their forefinger to emphasize their speech, tense their facial muscles, have straight and brief smiles, seldom "belly laugh," clench their hands and teeth, sit on the edge of their seats, and sigh a lot when mentioning work-related activities (Rosenman, 1978; Tallmer et al., 1990). Here are some of the attitudes and behaviors commonly found in Type A's of all ages (e.g., Lawler & Armstead, 1991; Thoresen & Pattillo, 1988):

> ➢ believing self-worth is determined by "productivity"—discounting the importance of being a good friend or family member or just plain being a good person (Price, 1982)
> ➢ feeling guilty when not engaged in "productive" behavior
> ➢ feeling restless and unable to relax, even when relaxation is the correct behavior for the situation (e.g., reluctance to take a vacation or day off unless pushed, needing to use excessive alcohol or other drugs to relax at the end of a day)
> ➢ being impatient with everyone and everything that is too slow for them

- feeling that others don't take life seriously enough or have standards that are high enough, leading to feeling they must do everything themselves or it won't be done "right"
- feeling impatient when watching someone else do a task, especially someone less accomplished—feeling they *must* take over, which makes them a poor partner or leader and defeats the other person's chance to learn through experience
- feeling restless in social situations not related to work (thinking that small talk is boring and that sitting around and talking is "wasting time")
- feeling anger and frustration with waiting for anything or anyone (e.g., waiting in line)
- believing that being early or on time is essential (being unforgiving of their own and other's tardiness, even when there is a good reason)
- being poor time managers, partly due to forgetting that tasks often take twice as long as estimated and that activities other than work are also necessary (e.g., eating, sleeping)
- falling "behind" early in the day due to poor scheduling, which increases frustration and irritability concerning mistakes, interruptions by others, and their own inadequacy
- valuing *quantity over quality* of performance (partly to justify error-filled, half-done work caused by their frequent rushing of tasks and poor time management)
- emphasizing *production* goals over *learning* goals (taking easy courses, focusing on getting a good grade rather than on understanding the material)
- valuing *reaching a goal* over the process or actual product (relief from finishing a task and crossing it off a list blots out the need to correct errors or be more thorough)
- seeing others as obstacles rather than friends, companions, and work mates
- setting unrealistically high goals, ignoring feedback that they have failed to meet the goal, and then setting a *higher* goal the next time (e.g., estimating they will do well on an exam, and when they receive a poor grade, *raising* their previous goal on the next exam—*but not actually working on skills to help them do better*)
- turning any activity into a competition—even competing with themselves (e.g., reading more pages than yesterday, jogging faster or further than yesterday)
- becoming upset when others don't rave over how wonderful they are and see them as "the best worker" (this tendency to think that no one appreciates how much they do is called "well-modulated hostility")
- needing frequent reinforcement (especially being told they are better than others), which emphasizes the importance of *extrinsic* over intrinsic motivation
- tending to see *neutral* feedback from others as *negative* feedback, which reveals the insecurities they harbor
- feeling insecure—fearing that they won't be able to live up to their own and others' standards, that they must do *more* than others to be liked, that they won't "win" (Type A's, especially males, usually grow up in an "evaluative" family atmosphere, having their performance constantly compared with others'. They are over-scheduled in activities, good grades are required for "acceptance," they receive more punishment for unsuccessful performance than Type B's do, the competitive aspects of life are stressed, and they are warned that they won't be successful or "accepted" unless they do *more and more*.)

Writing Activity 4.4—Which of these Type A behaviors are currently affecting you? Write about an incident in which you acted as a Type A and then describe how you could have handled it in a healthier Type B manner.

Notice that nowhere is there a statement that Type A's really are *better* than others at doing tasks. The reason why Type A's may sometimes *appear* better (e.g., have a higher GPA in undergraduate work) is purely that Type A's spend *a lot* more time on school work, ignoring as unimportant other aspects of their lives (e.g., friendships, family obligations, lovers, personal "downtime"). Actually, Type A's are *not* more intelligent than Type B's nor do they have higher achievement goals than Type B's do. As life progresses, Type A's actually feel *less* satisfied both with their work life and their relationships with others—marriage, friendships, and family (e.g., Burke & Weir, 1980; Kelly & Houston, 1985; Strube, Berry, Goza, & Fennimore, 1985).

The Recurrent Coronary Prevention Project, which ran for five years in the early 1980's, showed it was possible for Type A's to change their philosophies and lives—although it did require the help of a counselor, a weekly support group, and a supportive partner and co-worker. Kaplan (1992) cited the "list of freedoms" (Friedman & Ulmer, 1984, p. 75) on which this change project was based, suggesting that these are the characteristics and beliefs of Type B's that help explain their better health *and* better humor. Check yourself to see how many you personally include in your life:
  ➢ freedom to overcome your insecurity and regain your self-esteem
  ➢ freedom to give and receive love
  ➢ freedom to mature
  ➢ freedom to restore and enrich your personality
  ➢ freedom to overcome and replace old, hurtful habits with new life-enhancing ones
  ➢ freedom to take pleasure in the experiences of your friends and family members rather than feeling diminished by their successes
  ➢ freedom to recall your past life frequently and with satisfaction
  ➢ freedom to listen
  ➢ freedom to play
  ➢ freedom to enjoy tranquility

We hope that we have convinced you that your life, health, and college experience will be better if you are less grim and reduce your Type A tendencies. Here are some suggestions from Friedman and Rosenman's book (1974) you can follow in your efforts to abandon maladaptive Type A attitudes and replace them with a healthier philosophy.
  ➢ Realize that life is an unfinished task, a *process* rather than a product.
  ➢ Concentrate on what you are doing *right now*—don't "think ahead" or try to do two things at once.
  ➢ Resist the urge to step in and take over when someone is doing something slowly— the person needs to learn to do it him/herself.
  ➢ Learn to prioritize your tasks, doing the important and necessary ones first—and don't rush because errors will just mean you have to work longer on the task.
  ➢ Decide which tasks need to be done well and which just have to be done—and recognize which tasks don't have to be done at all or can be entrusted to others.
  ➢ Remember to schedule breaks, maintenance behaviors, social activities, and travel time into your day—don't just schedule work-related tasks (besides, relaxing or doing "mindless" tasks will actually help you concentrate on harder tasks and do them more efficiently).
  ➢ Learn to really smile, laugh, and enjoy life more—and learn to play without feeling guilty.
  ➢ Smile at people and really listen when they talk (rather than interrupting or redirecting the conversation back to what *you* want to talk about).
  ➢ Thank people when they do something for you and compliment them on their successes—celebrating their wins will help reduce competitiveness and hostility.
  ➢ Abandon the belief that "he who dies with the most toys, wins"—you really can't take it with you!

➢ Be open minded and really listen to new information and others' opinions—remember that your opinions were learned and can be amended.

➢ Put effort into developing some intimate friendships—help people close to you and let them help you; do the same with your family members.

➢ Include people in your life who don't compete with you, who don't judge you by your performance, and who will make you laugh—and then learn from their behaviors!

➢ Before speaking, ask yourself if the person wants or needs to hear it and is this the right time.

➢ Remind yourself that criticism from others may be more about their own Type A behaviors or current frustrations than about you personally—stop and decide if their criticism is deserved; if it is, listen and learn. If it isn't, don't buy into it.

➢ Don't take yourself so seriously—very few things you do each day are going to make an earth-shattering difference in the world or even in your life.

➢ Allow yourself to make mistakes, pay attention to feedback, and accept your current level of expertise on tasks—if you need to change your approach or work harder to develop learning skills, *do so* (don't keep doing over and over things that *don't* work).

➢ Remember that working fast inevitably leads to mistakes, frustration, and low levels of creativity—good time management and realistic scheduling will give you time to complete your work with fewer mistakes.

➢ Remind yourself several times a day that success *isn't* related to *how much* you do or *how fast* you do it—repeat to yourself that *quality* is more important than *quantity*.

➢ Learn how to relax and practice a relaxation technique daily (see Chapter 9 on coping with stress).

➢ Find several cheap, constantly available, enjoyable activities that you can do when you are restless or bored—but don't make one of these things something dangerous or unhealthy, such as drinking alcohol.

➢ Talk back to yourself when you feel guilty for not working all the time—remind yourself that balance in life is important for your mental and physical health *and* for success in school and in life.

In these early chapters we have tried to alert you to some beliefs and behaviors that could make your journey through college (and life) more treacherous. Hopefully, you better understand how to avoid these pitfalls. Now we turn to some practical suggestions for smoothing out the bumps in your path. Come along! They will make your life less stressful—and more fun!

Education is not the filling of a pail, but the lighting of a fire. — William Bragg

*Never forget that life can only be nobly inspired and rightly lived if you take it
bravely and gallantly, as a splendid adventure in which you are setting out
into an unknown country, to meet many a joy, to find many a comrade,
to win and lose many a battle.* — Annie Besant

Suggested Readings

Albaili, M. A. (1998). Goal orientations, cognitive strategies and academic achievement among United Arab Emirates college students. *Educational Psychology, 18,* 195-203. (Available through EBSCO HOST; see the end of Chapter 1 for information on how to access it)

Friedman, M., & Rosenman, R. H. (1974). *Type A behavior and your heart.* New York: Alfred A. Knopf, 1984. (Written for the general public, it is an excellent source for understanding the philosophy of people with a Type A personality and how to change to being more Type B.)

Miller, R. B., Beherens, J. T., Greene, B. A. & Newman, D. (1993). Goals and perceived ability: Impact on student's valuing, self-regulation, and persistence. *Contemporary Educational Psychology, 18,* 2-14. (Available through EBSCO HOST)

Mueller, C. M., & Dweck, C. S. (1998). Praise for intelligence can undermine children's motivation and performance. *Journal of Personality and Social Psychology, 75,* 33-52.

Schraw, G., Horn, C., Thorndike-Christ, T., & Bruning, R. (1995). Academic goal orientation and students classroom achievement. *Contemporary Educational Psychology, 20,* 359-368. (Available through EBSCO HOST)

Suggested Web Sites

http://www.unc.edu/depts/unc_caps/resources.htm The University of North Carolina's Counseling And Psychological Services presents practical information on academic improvement, eating disorders, substance abuse, depression, sleep, grief, stress management, assertiveness, and helping a friend. You can access other sites from this page too.

http://ub-counseling.buffalo.edu/stressmanagement.shtml This site provides information on topics for college students (e.g., stress, study skills, procrastination, perfectionism, time management).

http://www.psych.uiuc.edu/~ediener/index.html This is Dr. Ed Diener's home page. It contains links to information on subjective well-being (happiness).

http://www.queendom.com This site is fun, entertaining, and lets you compare yourself to others. However, do not take all of it seriously!

Chapter 5

Self-Management:
I Know I Should Study, but I Just Can't Seem to Get Started

Without ambition one starts nothing. Without work one finishes nothing.
The prize will not be sent to you. You have to win it.
The man who knows <u>how</u> will always have a job.
The man who also knows <u>why</u> will always be his boss.
— Ralph Waldo Emerson

There are some people who, when faced with an assignment, have no trouble organizing materials, settling down, and getting to work. If this describes you, you are to be congratulated. You have more self-control and discipline than do other people. Most of us have faced situations where we just could not get started on a task we knew we should do. Often other activities were attractive or distracting—and it was easier or more pleasurable to participated in those than to do the task. Most people find they have many more choices in college than they did in high school. You will probably have more choice about what to major in, what classes to take, when to take those classes, etc. However, not all your decisions will involve only academics—a lot will involve choosing between studying and partying. Or between studying and talking with friends. Or between studying and sleeping late. How many more choices like these can you think of?

Writing Activity 5.1—List the things that distract you and interfere with your studying. BE HONEST!

Many people have the best intentions when faced with these choices, but when it comes down to what they actually do, studying loses. They go to the party and not the library; they talk with their friends and then do not have time to study; they sleep late and miss their classes. Of course, socializing—and sleeping!—are good for you. However, if these overshadow academics, you may not only cheat yourself out of your education, but you may jeopardize your academic career. How can you avoid this? From a psychological perspective, how can you manage your behaviors better?

Steps to Improving Your Self-Management

Perhaps the most valuable result of all education is the ability to make yourself
do the thing you have to do, when it ought to be done, whether you like it or not.
— Walter Bagehot

Taking responsibility

The first step in improving self-management is to assume responsibility for your behavior. You have to decide that you have control over what happens to you. I have heard a student complain that he just couldn't study because there were too many parties to tempt him. Well, he could ask everyone he knows to stop having parties—but will that happen? I think not. What he must do is acknowledge that he chooses to go to the parties and can choose to not go. He must take control of his behavior. It may not be easy, but it can be done.

Some people may be thinking that this is an oversimplification, that there are some situations over which you have no control. For example, if people in your dorm make a lot of noise all night long, it will be very difficult to study there. And you probably cannot make them stop the noise. In this case, you still need to focus on what you can do. You can study in the library. You can request a new room. You can study earlier in the day. Sometimes it is difficult to see what choices you have, but you almost always have some alternatives.

Modifying your behavior

Once you have acknowledged your ability to take control, you must decide on your goals. One obvious goal is to learn the material in your classes and earn a good grade. However, if you face a lot of distractions and temptations, this may not be so easy to do. What, then, can you do to maximize the chances that you will meet these goals and not give in to temptation? What techniques can you use to control your behavior?

Writing Activity 5.2—List five major goals that you have for this semester. You may include both academic and social goals. Number them in order of importance to you.

Do you think this order is *best* for your academic career? Why or why not?

There is a large body of research in Behavioral Psychology containing simple techniques that you can use to modify your behavior. Generally, these techniques focus on what you can do to your environment to change your behavior and what you can do directly to your behavior in order to change it.

Manipulating your environment

Chaining. Many people already manipulate their environment in order to control their behavior, even if they do not realize that they are doing so. For example, have you ever put a candy bar or other treat in an inconvenient place so you didn't eat it right away? Of course, you knew where the treat was, but because it was not easy to get to, you were more likely to resist eating it on a whim. By putting the candy in an inconvenient location, you increased the number of steps necessary to perform to eat the candy. In other words, you manipulated your behavior by making the unwanted behavior (eating the treat) more difficult to do.

You can do the opposite, too. If you want to increase a behavior, you can change your environment to decrease the number of steps necessary for performing the behavior. Let's say you have athletic practice at 6:00 a.m., and you really want to be on time. You can set out all the clothes you need for practice the night before. When you get up in the morning, you won't have to look for your shoes, socks, uniform, etc. They will all be out. All you have to do is dress. You have manipulated your desired behavior (getting to practice on time) by making it easier to do.

Psychologists have systematic ways in which to describe why these techniques work. One concept used to describe this is *chaining*. Behaviors that link together are called chains. In general, shorter chains are easier to do than longer chains. By making the chain that leads to getting out on time shorter, you are more likely to get to practice early. By making the chain that leads to eating your treat longer, you are less likely to eat it.

Writing Activity 5.3—Chaining can be applied to many types of behaviors. Here is an example of someone trying to change her behavior. How can she change the length of the chain to help her achieve her goal?

Mary wants to start exercising, but she just can't get started. When she does decide to go to the gym, she can't find her athletic shoes. Then she starts talking to friends. Then, if she does start out for the gym, she walks past the Union and stops in for coffee.

These examples were for fairly simple behaviors. Can you use chaining to help you resist temptations that may interfere with studying, a far more complex situation? Happily, the answer is yes. For example, do you know anyone who intended to study after dinner but ended up spending all night conversing with friends instead? How can this be avoided? How can the unwanted behavior (conversing) be made more difficult to do while the desired behavior (studying) be made easier to do?

One possibility is to take your books with you to dinner. After dinner, do not return to your room. Instead, find a quiet place with few distractions. Such a place may be a study room in the dorm, an empty classroom, a desk in the library. Once you find a good place to study, go there for all your studying. Why will this work? If you bring your books with you to dinner, and if you know where your are going to study, it will be easy to start your studying. The chain that leads to studying has been made shorter. At the same time, since you go to your quiet study place instead of your room, you have made the chain that leads to socializing longer. It will be more difficult to talk with friends since they are not nearby. There is an interesting side effect to going regularly to the same place to study—and only studying there. You will find that it gets increasingly easier to focus on your work in that location. You will also find that people will be less likely to disrupt you there since they know you are really working.

Organization. A second important environmental manipulation is ***organization***. Almost everyone has been in the position where they have decided to do some work only to find that they did not have the material they needed. Their book or notes or assignment sheets had disappeared. This can be a very frustrating experience and a major impediment to studying. However, it can be avoided with proper organization.

A first step in being organized is being familiar with your course outlines. Course outlines describe what chapters are covered on what dates, what assignments are due, and when the exams are scheduled. Once you have all your course outlines, you need to coordinate the assignments for all your classes. You can accomplish this in part by using a calendar to list when all your assignments are due and when exams will be given. By putting all your assignments on one calendar, you will be able to see when multiple assignments are due at the same time.

Once you know what you need to study when, you need to have the proper tools to complete your studying. These clearly include the textbook and class notes. Most people find it best to have separate notebooks for each class. In addition, it may help to keep a folder for assignments and hand-outs in each notebook. Textbooks and notebooks for a given class should be kept together. There are additional tools you will need for each class. For some classes this may be only a pencil and paper. For others you may need computers, dictionaries, calculators, or other tools.

Once you have chosen a place to study, you need to be sure to have all the tools you need with you. If you will be working in your room, you should have your text, notes, pencils, and other supplies arranged neatly on your desk before you start studying. Not only will this make studying less frustrating, but it will also make the chain that leads to studying shorter! If you will not be studying in your room, be sure you have brought all the materials you will need for studying with you. Most backpacks have multiple compartments where everything from textbooks to paper clips can be stored. Decide in advance which compartments will hold your different tools. Check your supplies regularly to ensure you have the tools that you need.

> **Reality check on Organization**—Use a separate sheet of paper for each of your classes. On the top of the sheet, put the name of the class. Write down where you will regularly study for that class. List for that class all the tools you need to effectively study for that class.

Directly Changing Your Behavior

> *There is no such whetstone, to sharpen a good wit*
> *and encourage a will to learning, as is praise.*
> — Roger Ascham

Just as there were established techniques for modifying your environment to control your behavior, there are also techniques that can be more directly applied to your behavior. Some of these techniques include using rewards, shaping, and punishment.

> **Test for Self-Awareness**—Before reading further, complete and score the Frequency of Self-Reinforcement Attitudes scale on p. A15 (Heiby, 1983). Knowing how you score will help you understand and apply the information in this section.

Rewards. Rewards are used to increase behavior. Basically, a *reward* is something that, when it follows a behavior, increases the chances that the behavior will occur again. To use rewards to change your behavior, you must first decide what behavior to increase. You will want to be fairly specific: "try to increase studying" is too general. A better example may be increasing how often you read a boring textbook. Perhaps your goal is to read your General Psychology textbook for an hour every evening or to review your notes after each class. After you have decided on a behavior to increase, you need to decide what to use as a reward. Your reward, of course, must be something desirable, like checking your e-mail or eating a candy bar. It is important to note that what is an effective reward for one person may not function as a reward at all for another person.

There are also different types of rewards. Foods, like candy, coffee, and cereal, can be used as rewards. Activities, like making phone calls or checking your e-mail, can be rewards. Playing games, like computer solitaire, can be rewards. You can also give yourself gifts, like a new belt, to reward your behavior. When you have accomplished small goals, like reviewing your notes, you might want to give yourself small rewards, like a piece of gum, so that you can go back to your studying quickly. When you accomplish larger goals, like reading for an hour, you might want to give yourself a more complex reward, like a coffee break, and then go back to studying.

There is a possible danger when you use rewards: *be sure the reward does not interfere with the behavior you are trying to increase!* For example, if you watch a lot of TV instead of studying, you might not want to reward your studying with TV. Why? Because you might become so engrossed in your TV show that you do not return to your studying. Think about how to pick rewards that are appropriate for the behavior.

Writing Activity 5.4—List three *specific* behaviors you would like to increase.
1.
2.
3.
List the rewards you could use to increase these behaviors. Consider, are the rewards appropriate for the behavior? Do the rewards interfere with performance of the behavior?

When a behavior to increase has been decided upon and a reward has been selected, you are ready to put your plan into action. But what if you cannot do so? What if you cannot force yourself to read General Psychology for an hour every night. What if you find yourself asleep after 10 minutes? Often we have to build up to our desired behavior. To do this, use of a technique called *shaping* can be very effective.

If you are not going to be successful in performing the desired behavior, start with a behavior you can do. For example, if you cannot study for an hour, but can study for 10 minutes, then start out rewarding yourself for studying 10 minutes. After a couple of days of reading for 10 minutes, increase the time you have to read before you get the reward. Do not be too ambitious—it is better to increase by small steps than by large ones. See what works for you. If you try reading 20 minutes and that works well, reward that behavior for several days and then increase to 30 minutes. If 20 minutes is too long, cut back to 15 minutes. Continue to make gradual increases until you have met your goal. When you have reached your goal of reading for an hour, **DO NOT** stop giving yourself rewards. After meeting your goal for a while, you may find that finishing the reading on time is rewarding in itself. You may find that additional rewards are not necessary as often. But continue to give yourself rewards on occasion.

Now try to apply this information on shaping to your own behavior. Are there some behaviors you would like to change, but you need to make the change gradually? Do you want to read more? Lose weight? Exercise more? All of these behaviors can be manipulated with shaping. Decide on a behavior you would like to change and complete this **Activity**.

Writing Activity 5.5—What is your goal behavior (e.g., exercising 30 minutes three times a week)?

What will you use as your reward (see your list of rewards above)?

How much are you performing the behavior *now?* (For example, do you exercise at all? Do you exercise 10 minutes twice a week?)

Given how much you perform the behavior now, what is a reasonable place to start? (For example, if you already exercise for 10 minutes, reward yourself for exercising 12 minutes. If you do not exercise at all, reward yourself for going to the gym and trying out the equipment.)

By what increments do you want to increase your behavior? (Be prepared to change this if it does not work!)

Punishment. In general, using rewards to change behavior is more effective than using punishment. When punishment follows a behavior, it causes the behavior to *decrease*. Sometimes people do not perform behaviors because the behaviors are punishing in themselves. For example, some students report being unable to study because thinking about studying makes them anxious. So, the students avoid studying for a while. When they do think about studying again, they have even more to study and are even more anxious. This creates a vicious cycle. The techniques described above with rewards and shaping can help to break this cycle.

The feelings of pleasure at getting a reward are not compatible with feeling anxious. If a student can accomplish a small objective and get a reward, the student will start to associate pleasurable feeling with studying. Anxiety will decrease. The student will be more likely to study, and the anxiety about studying will not build up. However, if the feelings of anxiety are overwhelming, the student may need professional help. Most colleges have counseling centers where trained professionals are ready to work with students on issues like this. The roles of the college counseling center and dealing with anxiety will be discussed in more detail in future chapters.

Overall, it should be clear from reading this chapter that there is something you can do to take charge of your behaviors. You can manipulate your environment, you can give yourself rewards, and you can shape your actions. Try out some of these techniques. You may be surprised at how well they work! And let us leave you with a final thought:

Have regular hours for work and play; make each day both useful and pleasant, and prove that you understand the worth of time by employing it well. Then youth will be delightful, old age will bring few regrets, and life will become a beautiful success.
— Louisa May Alcott, American novelist

Suggested Readings

If you are interested in learning more about how to control behavior, you can start by reading about behavior modification in a General Psychology textbook. In addition, there are many books on behavior modification available.

Heiby, E. M. (1983). Assessment of frequency of self-reinforcement. *Journal of Personality and Social Psychology, 44,* 1304-1307.

Martin, G., & Pear, J. (1996). *Behavior modification: What it is and how to do it* (5th ed.). Upper Saddle River, NJ: Prentice Hall.

Suggested Web Sites

http://ub-counseling.buffalo.edu/stressmanagement.shtml This site provides information on a variety of topics for college students (e.g., study skills, procrastination, time management).

http://www.unc.edu/depts/unc_caps/resources.htm The University of North Carolina's Counseling And Psychological Services has information on academic improvement and many other topics. You can access other sites from this page too.

http://www.thesemester.com/ Tips on how to successfully complete the semester are offered.

Chapter 6

Survival Note-Taking:
Pencils, Books, and Teachers' Dirty Looks

Will this be on the final?
— scene from every course ever taken throughout academic history

---

Writing Activity 6.1—Think for a moment about the way that you take notes for classes. Write down your top *four* strategies for taking effective notes.

| |
| |
| |
| |
| |

How did you do? Unfortunately, if you're like most students, you simply put "I write down whatever the professor says." This is a recipe for disaster. Without time for preparation and review, note-taking can be an incredibly *inefficient* way of understanding course material. What we present below is a more efficient way to take course notes that will save you time, facilitate your understanding, and hopefully increase your retention of class material so that you will perform better on course exams.

Did we promise you enough? Let's go!

Flashback. How many times have you seen the following situation? A student walks into class late after the professor has already begun lecturing. She noisily places her backpack on the desk and then fumbles for pen and paper. After not finding them, she interrupts one of her classmates to borrow something. She finally settles in to listen to the lecture; however, she has difficulty understanding it since she has begun in the middle. As time goes by, her attention drifts off to everyday activities and problems. When she does realize that something important has been said, she tries to write it down verbatim, and when this proves to be impossible, she gets frustrated and gives up. At the end of class she leaves and never thinks about her notes again until the night before the exam. *Then, when she looks at her notes, they make absolutely no sense and do not help her with exam preparation.* She blames her professor for being unclear in the presentation of material.

Does this sound familiar?
Have you done any—or all—of these things?
What is wrong with this student's note-taking method?

Taking notes is one of the most valuable skills in the academic enterprise. Williams and Eggert (2003) found that accurate note-taking was highly predictive of positive exam performance. You would think that, given its importance, note-taking skills would be well-rehearsed and frequently discussed. However, many students know very little about effective note-taking and assume that it is something that will just happen naturally. *Wrong!* The good news is that note-taking is a skill, and with a little thought and practice you can improve your abilities substantially. We will present the process of effective note-taking in four easy steps: *preparing to take notes, taking notes, reviewing your notes, and evaluating your notes.*

Preparing To Take Notes

In the example given above, the student was wholly unprepared to take notes. How about you? Did you mention anything about *preparation* as one of your top four strategies above? We find that the lack of preparation is a common reason why students take poor notes. Just as you would prepare for having a party or going on a date, you also need to prepare for taking notes in a class. Here are some guidelines on how to become prepared to take notes.

Read the material

Unfortunately, to many of our students the idea of "reading ahead" has almost become a joke. If you are doing great in your courses, you probably don't need to worry about it. However, if you are struggling like many do, reading ahead can be a big help. Read the material before the class in which it will be discussed. Usually, it is obvious what the topic of discussion will be for a class period. If you are unsure of the topic, ask the professor beforehand. Then, read the textbook material corresponding to that topic. Reading ahead costs you no extra time, since you have to read the material anyway. However, by reading it beforehand, you will have a context for taking class notes. This is infinitely more efficient. Material will not seem as new, and you will be able to ask intelligent questions and clarify uncertainties you have from the lecture or reading.

Take down the outline

Many professors provide an outline on the board or an overhead prior to the class lecture. *Be sure to write it down.* Then, as you are taking notes, you can fill in the outline, using the same level of hierarchy and structure as provided. This can be a tremendous help if the professor tends to wander during course lectures. (Yes, it does happen!) Also, if something is missing or unclear, you can ask the professor where it fits on the outline. Similar to reading the material beforehand, using an outline provides you with a context for taking better notes. A final advantage is that the outline alerts you when the professor proceeds from one topic to another, helping you to avoid a minute or two of confusion trying to figure out where the lecture is going.

Review your notes

While you're waiting for class to begin, use your time wisely and review your notes from previous lectures. Doing so not only gives you a context for the day's lecture (which facilitates improved note-taking), it is also an excellent way to study. If you frequently review your notes prior to class, you will find that you already have learned much of the material when it comes time to prepare for an exam.

Take charge of your environment

For the student example given above, the student obviously was not ready to take notes. She not only hurt herself, she disrupted the class for those around her. How about you? Do you set up an ideal environment in which to take notes? If you are unsure, here are some useful tips.

> Get to class early if possible, allowing you time for review and preparation.
> Have your pens and notebook ready.
> Sit in a place that helps you pay attention. For most of us, this is in *the front of the class*. Sitting in the back of the class with the other disruptive, unprepared students can be a major mistake.
> Preparing yourself physically and emotionally can also go a long way in helping you pay attention and take good notes (see Chapters 9 and 10 on stress, sleep, and nutrition and Chapters 15 and 16 on mental health).

Writing Activity 6.2—Honestly discuss how much time you put into the preparation for taking notes. Which techniques are you going to begin using now that you know about them? Are there other strategies you need to consider that are helpful for specific classes? Set some realistic goals for future classes.

Taking Notes

Now that you are finally ready, let's take some notes. We find *two major mistakes* occur at this stage of the process. First, some students *take no notes at all!* Each of us has had the experience of giving a detailed list on the chalkboard or an overhead and, upon turning around, finding that some students are taking no notes. It isn't that they are not listening (although there certainly are always a few of these people). They just choose not to take notes. If we see these students during office hours (often because they did poorly on an exam), we ask why they don't take notes. They state that note-taking interferes with their listening. They believe that if they just listen, they will magically absorb the material and be able to provide it to us at exam time. This is a myth. Research indicates that incredibly few students are able to just absorb and remember the material without taking notes—many can't even recall details of the lecture immediately after class! We have yet to meet the student who can do so.

The other major mistake we see is the student who tries to *write down everything verbatim.* Of course, it's impossible. Inevitably, the student ends up leaving out what escapes the brain prior to being recorded rather than selectively recording the lecture's important points. And there's no time to ask either! The student may even record a lecture and then try to write down everything verbatim. This is an inefficient, time-consuming strategy destined to fail if you have even a few other demands in your life. Yes, we would like you to have a life! Therefore, we propose *a compromise avoiding both mistakes.* Take relevant, efficient notes that are of great benefit in exam preparation. To help you do so, here are a few ideas for taking effective notes.

Be active rather than recording material verbatim

When taking class notes, it is important to process the material actively and not just be a passive word writer. Think about what is the *most* important thing being said—an outline on the board or an overhead often helps you choose this point. Discriminate between important material that you will need to know later and your professor's ramblings that just fill in space. *This is a skill that improves over time, so don't be discouraged if you can't do it now.* Our senior teaching assistants have often remarked how inefficient first-year students are in understanding what is important. What these seniors often don't realize is how well they have developed this skill over their four years of college. It will get better with practice, but you do have to pay attention and work on it. (This is also why reading text material prior to class is so important for providing context for understanding the day's lecture!)

Ask yourself questions

As you are listening and preparing to write, ask yourself questions about the material. For example, what is the point the professor is trying to make? How likely is this to be on the exam? Does the professor value this area? Effective note-taking, and later on effective test-taking, is in some ways an interpersonal skill of getting to know your professor. You need to discover a professor's goals, patterns, intentions, and biases. You can process some of this information early on while taking notes. Later, you can assess how effective your guesses were by thoroughly reviewing your exam (see Chapter 7 on taking exams).

Ask your professor questions

One exceedingly simple strategy for taking more effective notes is to ask questions when the material seems unclear. Simple, yet underused. How about you? Are you willing to ask questions in class if something isn't clear? How about just asking the professor to repeat something or to slow down? This also takes some interpersonal skill and some assertiveness (see Chapter 11). The old adage is usually true: if you don't understand something, it is likely that others don't understand it either. If you have difficulty speaking up in class, we suggest that you sit by a more assertive classmate. When you have a question, get him or her to ask it. Or be expressive, which only works if you sit where a professor sees you well. If you frown, look mixed up, or shake your head, some professors will repeat points or ask if you have a question. It's easier to ask a question if you have actually been asked to do so by a professor.

Figure out the main points in today's lecture

In most lectures of less than an hour, there are a *maximum of four or five central points.* Attempt to identify what these main points are. Then, you can fit the rest of the data and examples as supporting material for these main points. Again, this process will keep you active in your note-taking and help you identify the material that the professor values.

Use abbreviations—and be sure you can remember what they mean!

It is amazing to watch students taking notes in a beautiful, longhand script as though they were writing a note to a close admirer. The process of effective note-taking is often a race against time. Establish a system of abbreviations and symbols to help you in this race. If you don't know a number of common abbreviations, it may be helpful to look in a shorthand textbook. You also might ask classmates and friends some of the abbreviations they find helpful. Some disciplines also have their own set of codes and symbols, and you would do well to learn them. Finally, it can be fun spending some time making up your own verbal shortcuts. Whatever system you choose, be sure to write clearly so that you will be able to understand it when you review. If you miss a class, asking to borrow notes from a student who takes *good* notes will introduce you to new abbreviations. This situation will give you a chance to practice asking questions and learn some new, useful short cuts!

Pace yourself

We mentioned earlier the benefits of using an outline from the board or an overhead. This is useful when pacing yourself during a lecture. When using a hierarchy, you can indent to identify points supporting the main topic. In addition, you can leave a space when you fall behind, but go back and fill it in when the professor pauses or begins some examples. Again, don't overlook the option of asking the professor to slow down. Be sure to fill in the holes in your notes at your earliest opportunity (see section on reviewing notes). Just be aware that professors seldom use an "English" outline, always having a "b" to go with an "a."

Take down examples—and make up your own

We often see students taking notes furiously while the professor is giving terms and definitions. However, once the instructor begins to give an example, students put their pens down and use it as an opportunity to take a brief nap. ***Don't do this!*** First of all, the example may be the very thing that helps you understand the term. In addition, on exams many instructors use application-type questions that require your understanding of the example or ask you to provide a new one. Therefore, we recommend that you write down enough of the example to understand it when you are reviewing your notes. Understanding a professor's example serves as a framework for constructing new examples (see section on exam preparation).

Writing Activity 6.3—Answer all of these questions, and then rate your note-taking ability on a scale from 1 to 100. How well are you able to keep up with the information presented in your classes? How coherent are your scratchings when it comes time to review for an exam? Which of the above strategies do you employ? What are your strengths and weaknesses? Finally, set some realistic goals for improvement *prior to the next class.*

Consider the special case of missing a class

As you can see, the process of taking effective notes is something that is established over time. It is also something very unique to your style of taking notes and understanding of the professor. Therefore, getting notes from other students when you have missed a class can be disastrous. Most students are not good note-takers. Even getting the professor's notes can be less than ideal as they are related to his or her unique understanding of the topic and sometimes only consist of a few words, each of which triggers several minutes of lecture material. If you miss class, you might ask the professor to recommend a good note-taker from whom you can borrow the notes.

A related point is the importance of attending class. Many find the time spent attending class to be *less* than that spent reconstructing a friend's notes. Also, we believe that going to class is a highly efficient use of one's time. You get to hear what the professor emphasizes and learn which information is highly valued. Often, the examples can only be understood in the context of the class. We performed a study (Beck, Koons, & Milgrim, 2000) assessing which variables predicted success in a mass lecture General Psychology course. ***We found the variable that was the <u>best by far</u> at predicting course grades was class attendance.***

Reviewing Your Notes

For most students, class notes remain untouched from the time they are taken until the night before the exam. *Big mistake!* How about you? How often do you look at your notes prior to your last-minute panic? It is imperative that you spend some time reviewing your notes as soon as possible after taking them. Doing so provides another opportunity for learning, serves as a context for future notes, and highlights information that may need to be clarified. Below are some suggestions for reviewing your notes.

Review your notes as soon as possible after the lecture

Take a page from business managers and counselors, who write down the main points of a meeting *right after its occurrence* to remind themselves what was said and what they need to do about it. So take a few minutes after class to review and add to your notes. Here's a scary fact—short-term memory lasts less than 20 *seconds* unless you ***rehearse*** (repeat) it, which helps explain why taking no notes is a fatal error!

Unfortunately, most students wait until the night before the exam to review their notes. Abbreviations, examples, and linkages that made sense during a lecture have long since been forgotten. Information fades from awareness quickly unless you *actively* rehearse it, consolidating it into long-term memory. ***Active rehearsal*** isn't verbatim repetition; it requires you to put notes into your own words, explain them to yourself, and make whole sentences. Therefore, as you will have to look at your notes anyway, save yourself some time and review your notes as soon as possible. Look for holes in your notes while the lecture is still relatively fresh in your mind.

Actively process the material while you are reviewing

We often tell students just to read the material as soon as possible, and there is quite a benefit to doing so. However, if you really want to be efficient with your time, actively process your notes while you are reviewing them. What we mean is that rather than just reading the notes and filling in missing information, look again for main themes and linkages. If necessary, reorganize your notes when you have new insights about what the professor was trying to communicate. Some students like to retype their notes. While we think that a passive retyping of information can be an inefficient use of time, we have seen some recent computer-based voice recognition systems that speed up this process substantially (provided that you speak clearly so you don't have to retype mistakes). Use whatever system that works in keeping you actively engaged with the material.

Clarify unclear information

One of the real benefits of reviewing your notes is to assess whether you understand what has been presented. This, however, is only part of your task. If you are uncertain about anything, it is *your responsibility* to clarify the information. Asking the professor for clarification has a number of benefits. First, it ensures that your notes are clear, providing a structure for studying. Second, it communicates interest to your professor, which may provide a foundation for future learning and recommendations. As we said before, if you didn't understand the material, it is likely that many of your classmates didn't either. Finally, you are spending a lot of money and effort pursuing a quality education. *Be assertive in ensuring that you get just that!*

Evaluating Your Notes

Even if you are on the right track, you'll get run over if you just sit there. — Anonymous

Finally, even with all these steps, you need to assess your level of note-taking ability. The most obvious indicator of this is whether you are performing well on the portion of your exams that come from class lectures. If you are doing *really well*, your note-taking technique is probably sufficient—at least for this class! If your grades are poor, you need to decide where you are going wrong and correct it *now*. Here are ideas for evaluating your notes.

Get feedback from others

Compare your notes with those of peers and/or teaching assistants. See whether you have the same coverage of important information. How clear is your content? How effective and memorable are your abbreviations and symbols? Is your organization sufficient? Do your self-originated examples really fit the material? You may also benefit from showing your notes to your course professor. Just be sure to do so well before an exam so that feedback will be useful.

Take a course

Most universities have courses on study skills and note-taking, in addition to other student support services. The time invested (which may even qualify for credit toward graduation) can pay off dramatically in future performance and time savings. Again, note-taking is a *skill* that can always be improved. Get a jump on the competition by honing this skill!

Consider an additional resource: The Cornell Note-Taking System

A well-known and more formalized system of note-taking was developed by Walter Pauk (2000) over 40 years ago for students at Cornell University. It incorporates many of our suggestions in a more stylized format. Many students have used it successfully. There are hundreds of excellent references to the "Cornell Note-Taking System" on the Internet that explain how you can use it. We also give a citation for his book in the references below.

Looking Back and Getting a Life

Writing Activity 6.4—What do you now realize are your top four note-taking skills? Are they the same as those you listed at the beginning of the chapter?

We hope you have already begun to benefit from the suggestions in this chapter. We also hope that sensitizing you to the complete *process* of note-taking will make you a better student with fewer academic stressors. The idea is to let you do effective and efficient school work that will provide you with *both academic satisfaction and more free time for friends, activities, and yourself.* We challenge you to give it a shot. Once you see the values of enhanced note-taking, please provide us with feedback about what worked for you. You will find a form at the end of the book for giving us feedback on this and other topics discussed throughout the book.

Suggested Readings

Beck, B. L., Koons, S. R., & Milgrim, D. L. (2000). Correlates and consequences of behavioral procrastination: The effects of academic procrastination, self-consciousness, self-esteem and self-handicapping. *Journal of Social Behavior and Personality, 15*(5), 3-13.
Pauk, W. (2000). *How to study in college* (7th ed.). Boston: Houghton Mifflin.

Williams, R. L., & Eggert, A. (2003). Notetaking predictors of test performance. *Teaching of Psychology, 29*, 234-237.

Suggested Web Sites

http://ub-counseling.buffalo.edu/stressmanagement.shtml This site provides information on a variety of topics for college students (e.g., stress, study skills, procrastination, perfectionism, time management).

http://www.unc.edu/depts/unc_caps/resources.htm The University of North Carolina's Counseling And Psychological Services presents practical information on academic improvement, eating disorders, substance abuse, depression, sleep, grief, stress management, assertiveness, and helping a friend. You can access other sites from this page too.

http://www.thesemester.com/ Tips on how to successfully complete the semester are offered.

http://www.collegefreshman.net This site has insightful information about college life and even allows you to talk with other first-year students. It has tips on dealing with college coursework, roommates, and stress/health issues.

Chapter 7

Survival Test Taking:
Dirty Little Secrets Your Professors Want You to Know

All I know is that I know nothing. — Aristotle

As professors, we often have a student come to our office to look over an exam. When the student finishes reviewing the exam, he or she may state, "I think I know the material, but I just don't take tests very well." What would you say? There are numerous questions that come to mind, but here are a few common ones. Why not? What would it take for you to do better? What steps have you tried? Is it just in my class, or are you having trouble in your classes?

Writing Activity 7.1—Imagine that you are looking at in your day/course planner (you do have one of these, don't you?) and see that you have an exam in one of your more difficult course in a week. List *three* strategies you normally do *to prepare for* an exam:

List *three* strategies you employ to improve your performance *during* an exam:

List *three* strategies you employ to improve your performance *after* an exam:

Could you think of anything? Did you have at least three strategies for each point in time? Did you find yourself thinking that your exam preparation strategy really depended on the professor, the type of class, and the type of exam? Were you surprised that we asked about your exam preparation *during* and *after* the exam?

Unfortunately, if you're like many students, your exam preparation strategy goes as follows. First, you put off thinking about the exam for as long as possible. *Chronic procrastination* is cited as a problem by as many as 70% of college students (Ellis & Knause, 1977; Hill, Hill, Chabot, & Barrall, 1978). (We discuss procrastination in Chapter 2, in case you haven't read it yet!) For many students procrastination continues up until the night before the exam. Then, you stay up late—or all night—cramming in as much information about the material as possible, which incidentally isn't very much (see the research on sleep in Chapter 9). This process normally involves a lot of anxiety, as well as a variety of avoidance strategies (e.g., cleaning your room, talking to friends). Anxious and exhausted the next day, you take the exam as quickly as possible and leave the room. Feeling like you choked or did poorly on the exam, you put it out of your mind as quickly as possible. You might even skip the next class, during which the professor reviews the exam. You think, "Nothing new happens today, so why go?"

Look familiar?

The previous scenario is related to the types of questions we get after an exam. You can imagine this student stating that he or she does not take tests well, has test anxiety, and knows more than the test would indicate. The student could be right. (We can also imagine this student blaming us for having constructed a "tricky" exam, but that is another story.) Everything the student did (and didn't do) helped ensure a poor performance on the exam. Effective test taking is *not* simply a matter of knowing "a lot of material," although that certainly is involved. It is the process of **preparing for the exam, taking the exam,** and **evaluating the exam after it is over**. Two students may know exactly the same amount of material; however, one will perform much better on the exam due to better test-taking skills. Indeed, many students complain to us that their friends do better on an exam even though their friends hadn't studied as much. Most likely their friends' scores were due in large part to more effective test-taking skills.

What is their secret?

Now that we have your attention, let's look at each stage of the exam-taking process in greater detail.

Preparing for Exams

*Opportunity is missed by most people because
it is dressed in overalls and looks like work.* — Thomas Edison

Preparing for your course exams actually begins on the *first* day of class. How many students do you know who think this way? Most are busily dropping and adding classes, getting settled, and attending parties. But a few know this time is as important as the night before the exam. It is the logical conclusion of several steps mentioned in other chapters. For example, you must be organized, avoid self-defeating thinking and behaviors, show intellectual curiosity, manage stress, manage yourself (e.g., set rules concerning sex and drugs), take effective notes, and arrange a suitable study environment. If these things have been done, you can prepare confidently, and with the self-efficacy gained from your exam preparation, you can reach your desired result—a good grade. Here are some exam preparation strategies you can adopt *now*.

Know what to expect

This is one of the most important test-taking skills. You should know in advance what is likely to be on the exam. This doesn't *just happen*; it takes active behavior on your part. How can you divine what will be on the exam without being psychic? Well for one, ask the professor. The professor often has nothing to hide in terms of the course exam and likely wants you to perform well on it. He or she may be an excellent source of information about the structure of the exam, the types of questions to be included, and useful preparation strategies. You also might consult other students in the class or students who have taken the class previously. Many professors and students also have a file of previous exams from the course. Don't use these as your only source of learning the material, but rather examine them for clues about test construction, style of questions (e.g., applied vs. definitions), and material that is emphasized. The wise and effective student will be fairly confident about a test format, points allotted for each item, time to allot to each question, and the relative importance of various material.

Understand the professor's tendencies

This step is related to knowing what to expect. In some ways, preparing for an exam is an interpersonal skill that comes from knowing the professor's tendencies and the material that is valued. We've mentioned before that gaining this information is one of the reasons why *attending class is so important*. Here you come to understand what the professor values and emphasizes. Professors, like everyone else, are fairly predictable. If the material has been emphasized in class and was on old exams, the likelihood is high that it will be on your exam. It seems like common sense, but good test-takers are adept at the skill of figuring out a professor.

Study as far in advance as possible

Ah, we hear you wail, "But I do best when the pressure is on." *Wrong!* If there is one truism from psychological research, it is that *frequent, brief studying over a long period of time (i.e., distributed practice) is substantially more effective than studying the same amount of time in one long period (i.e., massed practice).* Also, cramming the night before an exam is hindered by anxiety and fatigue (see Chapters 8 and 9).

Set the environment for studying

We mentioned this before in terms of setting your study environment *in general*. This becomes particularly important when you are preparing for an exam. Your study environment needs to be well-lighted, comfortable, and free from distractions. Many students tell us how much time they spend studying. When we inquire about this, we often find that much of this time is spent watching television, listening to music, talking to friends, falling asleep, and daydreaming. Much of effective studying is figuring out how to avoid these distractions.

Study actively

Think about how you get material from class into your brain. Often, students flip through notes and text, hoping that some magic process of osmosis will occur. We don't discount the importance of spending time with the material. However, the effective test-taker learns that it is easier to remember something when *purposefully interacting with the material.* You can do this in several ways, but the overriding principle is to **constantly test yourself**. If the professor gives an example to illustrate a point, see if you can come up with a new one. Try to predict what the questions will be on the exam *and* how you would answer them. You can use study guides, prior tests, and flash cards to keep yourself actively engaged. We encourage you to quiz yourself in whatever manner you like, especially **speaking the answer out loud** when no one else is there (a great technique, even though you look like a total dork!). Engage as many senses as possible.

Study partners: Pros and cons

Many people like to study with others in the class. This idea of study partners is a good one in that it makes the task more enjoyable and social, and it also reduces the anxiety of having to go through a stressful event alone. Group partners can even help make the studying active. You can generate questions and quiz each other. Sometimes a partner will understand a concept from a different perspective that will enable other partners to comprehend it. *However,* studying with others can also be a source of tremendous distraction and inefficiency. Particularly annoying is the partner who has not sufficiently prepared for the exam and who wastes the group's time by going over simple definitions and concepts. If you are nonassertive, you'll be reluctant to throw the person out of the group (see Chapter 11). Or you may feel sorry for or feel you must "carry" the person (see enabling in Chapter 14). Study groups can also deteriorate quickly into chatting and gossip sessions—you may even decide to chuck it all and go to a party.

Therefore, we give the following *cautions for using study partners.* First, only go to the study group *after* you have reviewed all the basic concepts and ideas. The study group should only be used as a source for new ideas and a different perspective on application of the material. Also, be *very careful* in choosing your study partners. They should be individuals who are as committed to learning the material as you are. This likely will not be the same group of friends with whom you go to a party or the gym. Getting out of a study group is often harder than getting into one, so we cannot caution you enough about your choice of partners.

Take breaks, get plenty of rest, and relax

It is important not to overlook the physical aspects of preparing for an exam. Everyone's attention wanders after sitting for lengthy periods of time—for especially difficult material, it may be after as little as 15 or 20 minutes. So, schedule frequent breaks—and take them! Make sure you eat right, get plenty of liquids, and stretch your body. While you need about 7.5 hours of sleep on a consistent basis, you need to sleep 8 hours the night before an exam (see Chapter 9). Doing so facilitates memory processes. Finally, do things to keep yourself relaxed while studying. Walking around and shaking your hands can restore *relaxed* alertness. Nothing short-circuits committing material to memory like being anxious. Be confident, healthy, and relaxed.

Special cases: Preparing for multiple-choice versus essay exams

The above ideas generally hold true across various types of courses and for differing types of exams. However, there are differences in preparation when an exam will have multiple-choice questions as opposed to essays. Multiple-choice exams usually require preparation that is more superficial, but also more exhaustive. You need to be able to recognize definitions and choose appropriate concept examples provided to you. Questions from a study guide, flash cards, and old exams can be helpful. One caveat is in order. Be sure to study questions that are at the same level of application as the ones you will see on the exam. For example, if exam items will be primarily concept definitions, study the material in this way. However, if questions will require you to apply the material or recognize examples, you should study in this fashion.

An essay exam, while covering the same material, is considerably different and requires some modification in your preparation. Essay exams tend to require more detail but from fewer areas. They also require you to *recall* material as opposed to simply *recognizing* it. In general, recall is more difficult than recognition; however, many students seem to like being able to fully express their understanding of the material. To be prepared, it is important to be able to produce the major points in each topic area. Especially helpful is to outline these major points and practice answering hypothetical questions. You can use **mnemonic strategies** to facilitate memory. For example, students in Psychological Statistics can use "NOIR" ("black" in French) to remember the four levels of data in order (*n*ominal, *o*rdinal, *i*nterval, *r*atio). *Flash cards* will help you learn basic terms and theories; then you can work on recalling major points, comparing and contrasting the terms, and producing examples. (*Flash cards* have a term, theory, or name on one side and the definition or other answer on the other. As is true for recognition tests, you should talk out loud to check yourself. *Practice, practice, practice* in the fashion in which you will be tested.

Writing Activity 7.2—List the strategies we just presented that you currently use. Then, pick a few new ones to use when you prepare for the next exam.
Strategies used now:

| |
| |
| |

Strategies to use when preparing for the next exam:

| |
| |
| |

Strategies for Taking the Exam

How often do you think about your exam technique? Do you have little rituals that you perform prior to the exam? Do you have a lucky pen and/or lucky underwear? While we can't attest to the validity of these objects, which may help relieve your anxiety, we can recommend some strategies to help optimize your performance on each and every exam.

> **Test for Self-Awareness**—Before reading further, complete and score the Achievement Anxiety Test on p. A17 (Alpert & Haber, 1960). Knowing how you score will help you better understand and apply the information in this section.

Before the exam

Get your stuff ready before going to bed. Nothing increases anxiety like having to search for necessary items just prior to an exam. Lay out your notebook, calculator, blue book, etc., the night before the exam.

Get enough sleep. We can't say this often enough: *get 8 hours of sleep before a test.*

Avoid anxiety-provoking issues, including imagining yourself at the test. The hour before the exam is not the time to deal with that big relationship issue or to confront your mother. Be sure to keep your emotional life calm during this time.

Arrive early, but don't socialize. You need to remain calm. Arriving early avoids the anxiety of coming in late and being hurried. However, other students, often unprepared, are walking mountains of anxiety. Don't let them infect you with their hysteria. Stay relaxed and out of their way. When one of the authors was a new teacher, he used to ask if there were any questions immediately prior to handing out the exam. Invariably, some student would ask for an explanation of a detailed question. This would result in a panic among others in the class who either were unfamiliar with the question or lacked confidence in their answer. Either way, it was a devastating emotional beginning to the exam. The professor, now more experienced, refrains from discussing content prior to the exam and simply tries to be calm, upbeat, and supportive. The lesson for you is to stay away from others and keep your own relaxed, confident attitude.

Don't review your notes. This also relates to staying calm. We often see students frantically looking over their notes just prior to an exam. There is nothing new you can assimilate at this time. The only impact we see from note shuffling is increased anxiety and reduced confidence.

Get a good seat and get prepared. If given an option, choose a classroom seat that suits you. You may prefer one away from distractions like other students, loud noises, or windows. Once seated, get out everything you will need for the exam, including multiple pencils or pens, tissues, lozenges, water, and scratch paper, if allowed.

During the exam

The time has finally arrived—the exam is in your hands. Take a deep breath, be sure you have all the pages, and read the instructions. Quickly assess the exam, looking at the layout, points given for each question, and total time allotted (preferably, you know this information in advance). Skim through all the questions, being sure to read any essay questions before you begin. You may find clues to essay answers while completing other exam questions. Write down any key words or mnemonics you want to be sure to remember when you need them.

Proceed wisely and stay calm. Once you have looked over the entire exam, you should go to the more valuable areas (in terms of total points), ***start by answering the easy questions*** there, and then answer easy questions for the rest of the exam. You will find that answering easy items first reduces your anxiety and gives you some confidence for attacking the remainder of the exam. It may also give you hints for other answers. Nothing is more disheartening than watching a student struggle and fail on the first item of the exam. If it doesn't come to you immediately, skip it, save your morale, and come back to it later.

Dig into the hard items, but be sure you know what is being asked. When you have finished all the easy items, you can proceed to more difficult areas of the exam. Be sure to ask your professor about any items that are unclear. This is a "no-lose" strategy because the professor may unwittingly give you some clues to the answer.

Work at your own pace. Don't panic when students get up early and begin to leave. Realize that very few "know it all." Our experience has been that many early finishers, especially if essays are involved, are students who have answered very little of the exam or answered too quickly just because they want to escape the aversive testing environment. There is no prize for finishing early nor will it show up on your transcript.

Remember you aren't alone. Finally, be courteous and polite to others while taking the exam. One of the authors had a student who used to curse at the questions during the exam (literally, she uttered profanity angrily and loudly). This was more than a bit distracting to her neighbors. Another of us had a student put his fist through a wall outside the classroom because he didn't like what one of the theorists believed—he knew the answer, but his stress level was so high that he just "lost it." In the best of all worlds, noisy, restless, or fidgety students would ask to be seated away from others. Just don't let their problems distract you from your task!

Special cases: Taking multiple choice exams

Here are a few tips specifically concerning multiple-choice types of exams. Most professors haven't had classes in test construction, and there are some common habits these professors have. Some of our suggestions obviously apply to these professors. Others apply to all multiple-choice items, regardless of the professor's test-making sophistication.

Eliminate clearly wrong answers. With a four-choice answer, eliminating two clearly wrong answers increases your chances of guessing correctly dramatically. If you don't believe us, watch contestants on "Who Wants to Be a Millionaire?".

Read all the choices. "All of the above" may be a better answer than the particular instance you have chosen, and test banks regularly include items with this answer. In addition, "all of the above" and "none of the above" are the correct answer a disproportionate amount of time, especially if they show up infrequently on an exam.

Look for key words. Most multiple-choice items have a key word or phrase that makes one answer correct and the others wrong. Look for that word or phrase and de-emphasize the other text. Some professors help you by emphasizing these words with italics or underlining.

Look for common disqualifiers. Certain words (e.g., every, all, always, never, must) hold true in few cases. *If you don't know the answer*, eliminate options using these terms.

Pay attention to grammatical construction and spelling. Normally when we write an exam, we pay more attention to the question part of an item *and the correct answer*. And we don't proofread the wrong answers as well. Maybe we're just lazy and other professors aren't, but we think it's a natural human tendency and worth a shot. Sometimes wrong answers don't match the question in grammatical construction—even "a" versus "an" or singular versus plural can give away an incorrect answer. Again, if you are unsure of the answer, incorrect spelling and poor grammatical construction may be an indication of a wrong answer.

Check the longest answer. Often the correct answer is the longest one. This occurs because the professor has to ensure that the option is clearly correct, which may take more words and qualifiers than an incorrect answer.

Check "B" and "C." For whatever reason, options "B" and "C" are the correct answer a disproportionate amount of time. We can guess the reasons for this. Professors believe that the "A" answer is too obvious; they want to give you a tempting answer (i.e., nearly correct) first. Answers "B" and "C" will then likely contain the correct answer and the distracter (sometimes the opposite of the correct answer). Having lost inspiration, professors will just throw something in or park their attempts at humor for answer "D." These rules work best when you have no idea of the answer *and* the professor isn't aware of this tendency.

Answer every question. Look back over the exam, being sure that you didn't leave items blank—unless you will be penalized for guessing *and* you have no idea what's correct. Guessing may get you a point or two, but skipping a question doesn't get you anything!

When finished, review the entire exam. Even if you are a poor changer (i.e., more often change from right to wrong answers), you need to review to ensure that you haven't made any stupid mistakes. The natural tendency is to get out of the room (where all the anxiety is) as quickly as possible. Resist this temptation as, again, there is no award for finishing early. Use all the time you have available.

Special cases: Taking essay exams

An essay exam, or essay items on a mixed exam, necessitates a somewhat different approach. Here are some suggestions to help you master this type of question.

Assess the time available and the value of each question. By doing so, you can allot your time among the items, being sure that you pay more attention to the more valuable ones, even if you aren't as sure about them.

Pay attention to other parts of the exam for cues to the answer. For mixed tests, read essay items first since multiple-choice items may give you clues for answers. If so, jot down reminders beside the essay item.

Read carefully what is being asked. Common essay terms ask you to "describe," "list," "compare and contrast," or "critique." Be sure to do what the item requires. Professors have plenty to read and aren't amused when they have to trudge through the jungle of your answer, no matter how wonderful it is.

Outline your answer. Many students just begin answering an essay question. This can lead to an unfocused answer that may receive less credit than you deserve. Outline your ideas, use your mnemonics, and *then* start writing your answer.

Be organized with your answer. Use headings, spacing, indentations, and underlines to convey your idea. The professor has many papers to grade. An organized and clear answer will usually receive a more favorable evaluation—really!

Write legibly, use proper English, and be neat. You are trying to create an impression through verbal means. You will earn points for doing so in a neat, clear, and easy to read manner. A sloppy, hard-to-read answer is easy to disregard. A professor may miss a poorly-worded but correct answer by reading too quickly (we avoid aversive situations too!).

Get to the point. Some of our students begin their essay answers with "It was a dark and stormy night…." We call this the "shotgun method" of answering questions because they throw out a lot of material, hoping to hit something. Most professors can recognize this strategy and will penalize you for it. Besides, if you are pressed for time, it can penalize you by not leaving enough time to answer all the items. Get to the point, answer the question, and move on!

Try to answer everything. You are guaranteed zero points for a blank answer. Try to put down something. If you don't know the answer, you might give the answer to a question that is similar. If you are running out of time, at least outline what you believe to be the correct answer. Some partial credit here and there can add up to a much better grade.

Read and review your work. Go back and review all answers to see if they make sense. (Look for mistakes we still make in this book even after spell-checkers and several readings of the material!) Again, there's no award for finishing early. Use all the available time.

Writing Activity 7.3—You know the drill. Which test-taking strategies are you currently using? Now, pick a few new ones to use for your next exam.
Ones used now:

| |
| |
| |
| |

Ones to use when taking the next exam:

| |
| |
| |
| |

What To Do for the Future After an Exam

What do you do after the exam? Put it out of your mind as quickly as possible? Take a nap, deal with other crises, or begin to cram for an exam in another course? At what point do you start thinking about how well you prepared for the exam and how effectively you took it? For most students, the answer is *never*.

We find that assessing your test-taking strategies <u>after</u> the exam is the single most overlooked aspect of test taking.

But where do you start if you haven't developed this technique? First, you have to consider your exam preparation. Did you spend enough time studying the text? Were your notes sufficient? Was the exam what you expected and could you predict the questions? Did you talk out loud and practice writing complete answers for essays? If not, why not?

An initial source of information can come from *reviewing the exam*. We are surprised at how many students do not review the exam or even look at their grades. Many skip class on the day of the exam review, and those who did poorly on the exam are most likely to run in to see their grade and leave! *Not going to the review is a* **huge** *mistake.* Reviewing the exams can make you more aware of the adequacy of your exam preparation and test-taking skills. We believe that students avoid the review because they do not want the pain of negative feedback. However, this is a situation in which you have to face your demons in order to prevent them from eating you right out of college.

Here are things to look for which specifically address your test-preparation strategies. Look at the exam and *evaluate your performance honestly*. Consider the following points.

- ➤ Where did you do well and where did you perform poorly?
- ➤ Did you struggle or do well on the material from the class notes?
- ➤ Did you struggle or do well on information from the text?
- ➤ Did you do better on multiple choice questions or on the essay questions?
- ➤ Did you do better on definition questions or application-type questions?
- ➤ Did you use your time wisely?
- ➤ Did you panic and give up?
- ➤ If you changed your answers, did you change them correctly or incorrectly?
- ➤ Did you make any "stupid" mistakes because you were anxious?
- ➤ Were there words or questions on the exam that you didn't understand *and* didn't ask the professor about?

Hopefully, you can answer many of these questions in a positive manner, but if you can't, you have just learned something about how to prepare for your next exam. If you are having trouble evaluating your testing techniques, *get additional feedback* from a teaching assistant or from the course professor. Most students find that their exam grades improve over the span of the semester, at least in part due to their greater knowledge of what is expected. Be sure you use every opportunity to become a wiser test taker.

Here is one last **Activity** to check your post-exam strategies. Be sure you return to this chapter after taking your next exam and check to see how your test-taking strategies have improved and where they still need some work.

Writing Activity 7.4—How much effort do you put in *after* the exam? What are your test-taking strengths *and* weaknesses? In what areas do you need to improve and what can you do beginning now? Evaluate your next exam by the methods we suggest and see how your test-taking skills improve.

A Last Word on Test Taking

Think of the question that we asked at the beginning of this chapter—how do you take exams? We hope that you are now more aware of your strategies than when you began reading the chapter—and that you have found some new ideas to help you prepare for, take, and review an exam. The answer to our question is quite complex and involves what you do from the first day of the course. You should also take into account information from other chapters in this book on managing yourself, your stress, and your life in general. Hopefully, enhancing your test-taking skills will boost you to an optimum level of performance. It is our wish that you never have to tell your professor that your exam grade is not a reflection of what you actually know. Good luck!

Suggested Readings

Ellis, A., & Knause, W. J. (1977). *Overcoming procrastination*. New York: Signet Books.
Pauk, W. (2000). *How to study in college* (7th ed.). Boston: Houghton Mifflin.
Postman, N., & Weingartner, C. (1973). *The school book*. New York: Delacorte.

Suggested Web Sites

http://ub-counseling.buffalo.edu/stressmanagement.shtml This site provides information on a variety of topics for college students (e.g., stress, study skills, procrastination, perfectionism, time management).

http://www.unc.edu/depts/unc_caps/resources.htm The University of North Carolina's Counseling And Psychological Services presents practical information on academic improvement, eating disorders, substance abuse, depression, sleep, grief, stress management, assertiveness, and helping a friend. You can access other sites from this page too.

http://www.thesemester.com/ Tips on how to successfully complete the semester are offered.

http://www.collegefreshman.net This site has insightful information about college life and even allows you to talk with other first-year students. It has tips on dealing with college coursework, roommates, and stress/health issues.

Chapter 8

Stress and How to Live with It

The mind is its own place, and in itself can make a heaven of hell, a hell of heaven.
— John Milton, *Paradise Lost,* Book i. Line 253

AAAUUUGGGHHH! How many times have you wanted to scream at something or someone today? You may be surprised to learn that everyone else has wanted to do the same—or to react to a stressful situation in another way. Unfortunately, our culture doesn't encourage us to admit how stressed out we are. If we could do so, we could benefit in two ways. First of all, we would realize that our feelings and reactions are similar to those felt by others, so we wouldn't beat ourselves up so much for feeling so frustrated. Secondly, we would begin to empathize more with each other about how stressful our lives have become and help each other cope with them. And, yes, professors also suffer from stress every day.

Because of the serious health risks posed by chronic stress, researchers studying stress physiology and the psychology of physical and mental health have learned many techniques to help us cope with our stressful lives. In this chapter you will find information on the effects of stress, and in the next two chapters we will discuss techniques to help you cope more effectively.

Writing Activity 8.1—Before reading on, describe *three* things that are stressing you out *right now*—these may involve school, relationships, or personal growth. Rank order the three in terms of how much each is causing you pain (mental or physical) today, this week, and overall.		
	Today	*This week*	*Overall*
1.			
2.			
3.			

Writing Activity 8.2— Now look at the three stressors that are bothering you and discuss how you *are* coping with *each one* and how you *would like to* cope with *each one*.

_____

_____

_____

_____

_____

_____

_____

_____

_____

_____

_____

The Processes of Stress and How They Affect Us

Reality Check—As you read through the information on the Processes of Stress and The Things That Make You Nuts, try to relate the material to the three stressors you just wrote about. Concentrate on more clearly understanding your current stressors, your level of stress overall, and how it is affecting your life. See if you are more likely to be a *somatic* coper (one who reacts *physically*, with headaches, poor sleep, digestive upset, etc.) or a *psychological* coper (one who becomes anxious, depressed, inappropriately angry, distracted, etc.). Some people are a mixture of the two—which are you?

   Stress is our body's reaction to a stressor. That *stressor* can come from an external or internal source—or from a combination of the two. *External* sources include the argument you had this morning with your roommate, the exam just assigned in your last class, the ticket you found on your car when you left class, and the missed opportunity to eat lunch before you were rushing to another class. For instance, a recent study found that 39% of women and 20% of men entering college admitted feeling frequently overwhelmed with the situation and their work load (Sax, Astin, Korn, & Mahoney, 1999). Some *external* stressors may actually harm your body directly, such as cutting your arm while carving a pumpkin, catching a cold due to a depressed immune system, or being injured in an automobile accident.

Internal sources include thinking about that argument you had this morning and what you should have said, worrying about that upcoming exam and about how you'll pay for the ticket, and even trying to decide what you will do about getting a job for the summer. You will notice that *we, as humans, have the ability to upset ourselves over almost anything at any time depending on how we look at the situation*. Fortunately, as you will see in the next two chapters on coping with stress, we also have the ability *not* to get upset about everything that confronts us—if we are willing to learn good coping techniques.

The physiology of stress

First of all, you need to realize that stress is *real*. You may have heard people say "it's all in your head," but it isn't. In fact, the term *psychosomatic,* which people used to misuse when talking about what they believed was "imaginary" stress, really means how the mind, the brain, and the body interact to make you physically ill. Thus, *psychosomatic* (or *psychophysiological) illnesses* are real damages to the body caused or *exacerbated* (made worse) by chronic stress reactions we experience. Some of the illnesses related to such an interaction include headaches, peptic ulcers, digestive upsets, constipation, diarrhea, heart disease, hypertension, asthma, allergies, backache, TMJ, cancer, and the all-to-common cold. Because chronic stress depresses the body's immune system, almost any type of illness can be exacerbated in a person who either copes poorly or has been driven beyond his or her ability to cope. We teach a large freshman class, and we can almost tell what time of the semester it is by the number of coughs we hear during class.

Every stressor you face doesn't result in your developing an illness or other physical problem. But if you are under a lot of pressure for an extended period of time, even small additional stressors may cause a health breakdown. For centuries medical people have believed that some association existed between a person's daily confrontations, his or her personality, and the quickness with which that person became ill. However, scientific evidence confirming this association did not emerge until the middle 20th century. Hans Selyé (1976) wrote about his *serendipitous* (unexpected, surprising) findings concerning the body's reaction to stress. While developing a new drug, he found that rats' bodies reacted with the same complex of physical changes to injections of different types of chemicals (including saline). When he decided to investigate this strange finding, he discovered these same physical changes when a rat was exposed to chronic shocks, cold, or other physical situations. He named this complex of bodily changes the *general adaptation syndrome (GAS)*.

The general adaptation syndrome (GAS)

Unfortunately for us, the GAS operates in us just as it did in Selyé's rats. And unlike the rat, we have a better and more morbid imagination and a greater tendency to believe that we should be able to control what happens to us in most situations. Let's take a look at what happens in the body when a human confronts a stressful situation (or imagines doing so).

Stage One—the alarm reaction. Although researchers now know that the body's reactions differ slightly when exposed to different types of stressors, Selyé's syndrome remains a good model for what happens when we face a stressful situation. Our immediate reaction to a stressor is a general mobilization of the body to either fight or flee. This ***alarm reaction*** is controlled by activation of the ***sympathetic*** branch of the autonomic nervous system, which is responsible for behavioral readiness. Senses sharpen, heart beat and blood pressure increase, blood moves away from the surface of the skin and from ordinary processes like digestion in order to strengthen the muscles, hormones are released by the adrenal gland to energize the body, and the brain's ability to "think straight" literally takes second place in favor of centering on survival. If the stressor is quickly dealt with, the ***parasympathetic*** branch of the autonomic nervous system, which is in charge of the daily maintenance behaviors of our body, takes over control from the sympathetic branch. We calm down, our digestion and breathing return to normal, and the higher-order cortical processes of problem solving and decision making can operate once more.

This process of switching masters, as it were, may go on in our bodies several times a day as we react to stressors that are sudden or have no immediate solution. Unfortunately, many of these reactions are not really adaptive since we seldom need to fight or flee. Common experiences with these maladaptive alarm reactions include "stage fright" when giving a speech in class, drawing a blank when "test anxiety" kicks in, stammering and being at a loss for words when speaking to a potential romantic interest we hope to impress, and getting a shot of "road rage" when someone slow pulls into our car's path when we're in a hurry.

I have one nerve left, and you're getting on it. — Anonymous

Stage Two—the resistance phase. As a college student, you probably have already experienced the alarm reaction many times. In fact, you may currently be in Selyé's second stage of the GAS, the ***resistance phase***. There are many stressful situations without easy solutions, including that big term paper, the "roommate from Hell," uncontrollable noise in the dorm, and a long daily commute. Freshmen are also trying to master the art of self-management necessary for balancing a busy academic, social, and personal life. "The freshman overload" is a major reason why more illness and exacerbation of chronic conditions (e.g., allergies, migraines) are likely to occur during this year than during the rest of your undergraduate career.

The tricky thing about this second state is that you may not feel like you are stressed. The body is no longer experiencing the alarm reaction, so the symptoms are more subtle. *But they are there.* In this second stage your body is having to run just a little too fast, which tends to "wear down" the body (like revving a car engine while in park). This extra taxing of your body robs it of its reserves, depressing your immune system. You won't have exactly the same symptoms as your roommate, but some reactions are more common than others. Of course, whichever part of your body is weakest due to genetic predisposition, past illness, or damage will be the first to be affected. If you are prone to asthma, allergies, gastrointestinal upset (e.g., diarrhea, constipation), backaches, or headaches, you'll notice they visit more frequently. Colds occur more frequently, and they tend to hang on longer. If you are injured, sprains and broken bones are slower to heal.

Sleep disturbances, indigestion, quickly losing your temper, and difficulty concentrating may also be symptoms you have noticed in yourself and others. Even small problems seem huge, and you lose patience all too easily.

Because the parasympathetic branch can't quite stay in control, it can no longer do the daily maintenance necessary for good health. A poor health cycle accelerates as you sleep and eat poorly and overreact to daily events, setting off the sympathetic branch like a false fire alarm. College health centers do their best to patch up the walking wounded and urge you to get flu shots before the yearly epidemic, but too many students have an *illusion of invulnerability*, an "It won't happen to me" attitude (Weinstein & Klein, 1996). It is during this stage of the GAS that good coping techniques and healthy personality traits can make a difference (see next two chapters on coping with stress and be sure to take the two tests at the end of this chapter). Of course, individual differences in physiology and past health breakdowns, both of which are out of your control, also make a difference in how quickly and in what ways you suffer during this stage.

Stage Three—the exhaustion phase. As you drag home for Thanksgiving, for Spring Break, or at the end of the semester, you may be entering the third stage of the GAS, the *exhaustion phase.* If your coping and preventive health techniques have helped you get through the semester without too much stress and your body's reactions to it, you may actually be able to enjoy a well-earned break from classes. Even then, you will find that many of your friends have not survived as well. This final stage, in which the body's defenses against illness and organ breakdown are exhausted, results in outbreaks of chronic or major illnesses and can even result in death. While your young body is unlikely to succumb to such a dire result, you will no doubt notice the need to recuperate, the ease of getting sick, and the tendency to just want to "veg out" even when you have the chance to go to an exciting, fun-filled event. When asked what they did during semester break, all too many of our students reply with one word, "Sleep!"

Things That Drive Us Nuts and Make Us Sick

Test for Self-Awareness—Before reading on, complete and score the Multidimensional Self-Destructiveness Scale on p. A19 (Persing & Schick, 1999). Your scores will help you understand and apply the information in this section.

When you thought of stressors before taking the Multidimensional Self-Destructiveness Scale (Persing & Schick, 1999, 2000), you may have thought that most stress comes from big demands or big changes in your life—events like floods, moving to a new state, or starting college. While big changes do make major demands on your body and require a lot of adjustment, surprisingly it's the "little" things—including your own beliefs and behaviors—that best predict your daily mood and whether or not you will develop a cold this week. Let's look at the different categories stress experts use to study how stress and our ways of coping with it affect our lives.

Disasters and catastrophes

No matter where you live, Mother Nature can shake up your life—sometimes, literally. Chances are good that you or someone you know well have gone through a hurricane, tornado, earthquake, flood, or other major disaster. When such an event hits a community, a general pattern ensues among its victims. At first people are in a state of shock and numbness; for instance, a person may be seen sweeping the front porch of a totally demolished house. During this short period, large organizations, such as the Red Cross, are needed to take care of and literally direct the movements of victims. In the first few days following the event, people are easily led, the helping of friends and strangers is a common sight, and little dissension is found among survivors. Survivors are easily organized to clean up debris and are willing to work long hours to bring organization and predictability to their lives, which have been turned upside down.

Unfortunately, within a few days of a disaster, people lose their numbness. They begin to realize what they and their community have lost and how difficult returning to normal will be. At this point, it is important for governmental and private organizations to bring aid required for long-term repair and recovery. Many victims lapse into depression as they realize how extensive the devastation is, and they mourn the loss of loved ones, businesses, and community. They may even wonder whether they will ever feel safe or happy again. Psychophysiological illnesses, family disputes and abuses, and alcohol-related problems are elevated among survivors during the 6 months or year following a major disaster. For instance, those living within 5 miles of Three Mile Island following a nuclear accident there in the late 1970's suffered more from such problems than those living even 10 miles away (Baum & Fleming, 1993).

Major life changes

All of us must go through major life changes. We start or finish school, move to new places, lose friends and family members, and suffer through automobile accidents and major illnesses affecting us directly or indirectly. Back during the 1960's and 1970's, researchers believed that major life changes were closely related to development of illness within 6 or so months (e.g., Dohrenwend et al., 1982). However, people react to such events differently, due to their personalities and perceptions of the event, their coping abilities, and how stressed they are prior to the event. For instance, one person may look forward to taking a new job and moving to a new state, whereas another may view it as a threat and may mourn losing closeness with friends and family. Subsequent research showed that although adjusting to change is a stressful process, if we feel we have some control in the situation, and especially if we are relatively healthy and have good social support at the time, we can face problems with little long-term damage to our bodies or lives. (Methods for coping with stress will be discussed in the next two chapters.)

Microstressors

The stressors we experience daily—and often get little sympathy for facing—are called *microstressors*, or hassles. Lack of sympathy and help results from our viewing these little problems as "no big deal" and our failure to realize how much they affect us. *Personal beliefs and behaviors* especially draw little sympathy from others because they believe we can "just stop being like that." And, of course, people thinking or acting as we do often can't comfort us because they are in denial about their having a problem or about their ability to change.

The most even-tempered person is eventually "driven up the wall" by irritations that are too numerous or that last too long. All of us have experienced that "last straw" feeling when we know that we have to get some relief, abandon a situation or task, or find a friendly ear in which to pour our troubles. Health psychologists now spend more time counseling people about how to cope with *chronic* (long-lasting) nuisances rather than with those big, but much less frequent, life changes. Little stressors build up and exhaust our tolerance. We need to learn to read ourselves (and others) well enough so we can stop and use coping techniques *before* we get the headache, have the sleepless night, or start the big argument that is really more about being frustrated with our day than about being angry with our friend or family member.

"OK," you say, "I realize that life is the pits sometimes, but what does that have to do with getting sick?" As it turns out, quite a lot! Remember that stress overloads the body's systems due to the parasympathetic branch's inability to carry out routine maintenance activities. And our immune system also becomes chronically depressed. Studies during the past few years have shown that the consequence of living with small, chronic stressors (e.g., commuting, too little personal time, living with uncontrollable noise or bad neighbors, being unhappy with our job or major relationships, putting up with someone who constantly pushes our buttons) is the occurrence of psychophysiological illnesses, including the common cold. Here is a study on factors related to the development of cold *symptoms* (e.g., coughs, sinus problems, headaches, muscle aches).

Research on Getting a Cold—*Would you risk getting a cold for $800?*

Cohen and his colleagues (1998) paid 276 adults (18 to 55 years old) to take nasal drops containing a cold virus, stay isolated to see if symptoms would develop, and complete questionnaires and medical tests to determine why only some of them actually "got sick." Although 84% became "infected" with the cold virus, only 40% of the total sample developed the symptoms we usually associate with having a cold.

Those with a **chronic** (long-term) stressor were 2 to 3 times more likely to develop symptoms, regardless of age, gender, ethnicity, education, or body mass. There was a linear increase in developing symptoms based on how long a person had been experiencing a stressor (from "no stressor" through a span of 1 month, 6 months, 1 year, or 2 years). An **acute** (short-term) stressor during the past year wasn't associated with occurrence of symptoms. Those with a work-related (un- or under-employment) or chronic interpersonal stressor were more likely to develop symptoms than those with no chronic stressor.

Other findings were that smokers, those who exercised 2 or fewer times a week, poor sleepers, those drinking 1 or fewer drinks per day, and those who ingested 85 mg or less of vitamin C a day were all more likely to have cold symptoms. Less social network diversity (having 1 to 2 roles vs. those with 6 or more roles) was also associated with feeling sick. However, neither health-related habits nor social network diversity detracted from the power of a **chronic** (lasting more than 1 month) stressor to produce cold symptoms.

Feeling out of control

Unpredictable or uncontrollable conditions are especially stressful. Recall the earlier discussion of the benefits of *self-efficacy* (see Chapter 1), the belief that you can perform a task well and that you are competent in an area (Bandura, 1989). The opposite of self-efficacy is the feeling of **learned helplessness**—that nothing you do will change a situation for the better, that your actions just don't matter (Seligman, 1991). A chronic stressor will eventually make you feel hopeless about changing the situation. You are especially likely to be affected if you believe that the situation will continue *with no end in sight*—that you have no power either to change it for the better or escape the situation. Increasing your *feeling of control* is one of the most important cognitive moves you can make to decrease the impact of stress in your life. For instance, living near an elevated railroad is actually more bearable if the trains run on a regular schedule than if they come by at unpredictable times. You will also benefit from feeling that at least you can control how you think and act in a situation you can't change or control.

New situations and new people can be especially scary—but exciting—simply because they are unpredictable. If you can learn to approach a new situation feeling *excited but flexible* (instead of fearing you'll do the wrong thing), you already have a coping technique that can be transferred from old to new situations. It is also useful to remember that the person you are meeting probably feels as you do—after all, you are new to him or her too! Staying relatively calm, using a little self-disclosure so the other person will get to know who you are, and asking questions to make the other person less "strange" to you will help both of you to have a positive first meeting. In fact, just being in a calm, positive mood during an initial meeting increases your liking for the person through the process of classical conditioning. One reason why we like people whom we feel are similar to us is that we think their behavior will be easier to predict. Consequently, we feel less chance of being embarrassed by "doing the wrong thing," and we can also feel freer to be ourselves in the situation.

Feeling overwhelmed by life

Sometimes it just seems that life asks too much of us. Too many demands and too many surprises just exhaust our ability to cope. Freshman year is like this, especially if your health habits are not the best. When your day is too busy, you probably feel tempted to either escape the scene—stop studying and just watch TV, drink, or sleep to blot out the day. While occasional escape is a good idea, using it as your usual coping technique merely results in demands building up until they loom like a mountain. Even freshmen who don't "escape" are tempted to ignore their usual healthy behaviors because they don't seem like a priority at the time. The first to go are the very habits that keep you healthy and help you cope with stress—sleep, exercise, visiting friends, making time to be alone and gather you wits, and eating nutritious food. Because you are young, you can live an unhealthy life style *for a while* with no obvious problem—*but it will catch up with you.* The best way to cope with feeling overwhelmed is the maintenance of good health behaviors, development of efficient academic self-management skills (e.g., time management, good study skills, attending classes, setting up a routine for studying), and developing the courage to say "no" when you have to study (even though your friends nag you to "come play" and your brain plays "oh, poor me" melodies in your head).

One reason that upperclassmen get sick less often and less seriously than freshmen is that they have developed more effective coping skills for dealing with today's incredibly crowded college life. Right now you may think that day will never come for you, but eventually you will look back and wonder why your first year seemed so stressful! When you do, be kind to a freshman. Since building a good social support network is one of the best coping techniques, letting a freshman know you understand his or her panic and that you are there with a kind word and to answer questions can make a big difference. Hopefully, someone has done the same for you by now!

Writing Activity 8.3—Now that you have read about how stress can affect you and filled out the Multidimensional Self-Destructiveness Scale, here's your chance to think again about what stressors are affecting your life *right now*. Has what you read in this chapter caused you to change the ranking of the three stressors you listed in **Writing Activity 8.1**—or are there stressors you didn't list but now realize are affecting you? Write about what is bothering you *most* at this point in the semester and how well you are currently coping with the problem (hopefully, the next two chapters will give you ideas for more effective coping!). Remember that *chronic* stressors, especially those involving interpersonal situations, are most dangerous to your health.

OK, So What Can You Do About All This Stress You're Experiencing??

Life is a horizontal fall. — Jean Cocteau

Right now you're probably thinking, "Well, *that* was depressing!" Yes, it is—but you don't have to end the semester as one of the walking dead and sleep away your vacation! There are many coping techniques to help you get through the first two stages of the GAS without a health breakdown—and to help you avoid getting to the third stage. If you want more stress management ideas not discussed in the next two chapters on coping, there are Web sites with suggestions (see below) and self-help books in book stores and libraries. In Chapter 9 we will describe some quick and easy methods you can start using *right now*. And they *will* help you keep your immune system healthy and your mind less troubled.

But first—there are two attitudes that you may or may not currently have. We suggest that you complete these scales to assess your current level of each attitude before reading the next two chapters on coping with stress. The first of these attitudes, hardiness, is a learned habit, so you can begin working on its three aspects—control, commitment, and challenge—right now. The second attitude, optimism (versus pessimism), is partially **innate** (inherited, genetically-related) and partly learned, so you can become more optimistic even if you don't have the attitude right now. *Both attitudes are related to better adjustment and to good health and longevity.*

> **Two Tests for Self-Awareness**—Before reading the chapters on coping with stress, complete and score both of these scales: the Hardiness Scale on p. A23 (Kobasa, Maddi, & Kahn, 1982) and the Life Orientation Test on p. A25 (Scheier & Carver, 1993).

Suggested Readings

Cohen, S., Frank, E., Doyle, W. J., Skoner, D. P., Rabin, B. S., & Gwaltney, J. M. (1998). Types of stressors that increase susceptibility to the common cold in healthy adults. *Health Psychology, 17,* 214-223.

Seligman, M. E. P. (1991). *Learned optimism.* New York: Knopf.

Selyé, H. (1976). *The stress of life.* New York: McGraw-Hill.

Weinstein, N. D., & Klein, W. M. (1996). Unrealistic optimism: Present and future. *Journal of Social and Clinical Psychology, 15,* 1-8.

Suggested Web Sites

http://tc.unl.edu/stress/ This site provides information on stress management and stress reduction.

http://www.psychwatch.com/ This site is one of the best sources of information on all areas of psychology and has links to other Web sites of interest. You can sign up to receive a free newsletter every Friday that contains links to that week's news releases on research. You can search the archives for earlier news releases, and there are tutorials on many topics.

http://www.clas.ufl.edu/users/gthursby/stress/manage.htm This University of Florida site gives you information on stress and stress management and has links to other sites concerning stress.

http://www.unc.edu/depts/unc_caps/resources.htm The University of North Carolina's Counseling And Psychological Services presents practical information on academic improvement, eating disorders, substance abuse, depression, sleep, grief, stress management, assertiveness, and helping a friend. You can access other sites from this page too.

http://ub-counseling.buffalo.edu/stressmanagement.shtml This site provides information on a variety of topics for college students (e.g., stress, study skills, procrastination, perfectionism, time management).

http://www.teachhealth.com/ This site is focused on providing college and high school students with lots of interesting information on stress. It also includes links to sites on both mental health and physical health.

http://www.cybertowers.com/selfhelp/ This Web magazine presents articles on a variety of topics (e.g., parenting, stress, dreaming, eating disorders).

http://www.collegefreshmen.net/ This site presents advice for the challenges faced by college freshmen.

http://www.thesemester.com/ Tips on how to successfully complete the semester are offered.

http://jama.ama-assn.org/collections/ This is the site for the Journal of the American Medical Association and also allows access to other medical journals and sites.

Chapter 9

Coping with Stress:
How Not *to Hide Under Your Bed*

Part I: "Maintenance" Behaviors

The vigorous, the healthy, and the happy survive and multiply. — Charles Darwin

---

Test for Self-Awareness—Before reading on, complete and score the Health Self-Test on p. A27 (National Health Information Clearinghouse) to aid you in applying the material.

Strong evidence has gathered over the years that you really can't work or learn efficiently when you are ill or your body isn't well-maintained. Here are a few examples. Several studies have found that school children who eat breakfast are more alert, learning and retaining class information better (this supports the federally-supported school lunch programs found in many schools). Evidence has piled up that teens need much more sleep than they regularly get—8 to 10 hours for 17-20 year olds, all in one stretch. Just recently high schools have begun starting their day an hour later in hopes that their students will get more sleep. Researchers have also found that for groups at all ages tested, those who exercise at any level on a regular basis learn and retain information better than sedentary peers. Exercise helps the brain more efficiently use glucose and oxygen, which aids learning. Let's look at further information and suggestions for maintaining your health and increasing your learning effectiveness.

Exercise

No doubt you already know that exercise is good for your physical health, but you may not have thought about its ability to help you manage stress. Because exercise makes your body and immune system work more efficiently, helps you sleep better, and even assists the functioning of your attention and memory, exercise is definitely an excellent preventive measure to include in your life.

You may think you don't have time to exercise, but you will find that exercise actually lets you *save* time. Think about a few realities in your life: how you put off work when you are too tired to think, how often your mind wanders when you haven't had enough sleep or you feel tense, how little work you get done when you have a cold or other aversive health condition (e.g., headache, allergies, diarrhea). Regular exercise will lessen or alleviate *all* of these problems and make your body heal more quickly. Exercise also causes a release of **endorphins** in your brain; endorphins increase your resistance to pain and make you feel happier and more euphoric.

For good aerobic benefits, which will make your body and brain work most efficiently, you need to engage in vigorous exercise *at least* 30 minutes *at least* 3 or 4 times a week. This really isn't much time investment for the benefits you will get from the endeavor! However, you don't even have to exercise that much or as often to get the benefits of endorphins, relaxation, and alertness—all of which help you study, learn material, and commit it to long-term memory. Sleep experts have found that a brisk walk can take the place of napping, if you are feeling lethargic, *and* will actually help you to sleep better at night. (Of course, that doesn't mean it can take the place of sleeping at least 8 hours at night.) We definitely urge you to walk more and, anytime your schedule allows you to, "go outside and play!"

Sleep

Test for Self-Awareness—Before reading on, complete and score How Sleep Deprived Are You? on p. A31 (Coren, 1996), which will help you understand and apply this section.

We're well aware that when you get really busy, sleep is the first thing to go. There just aren't enough hours for classes, studying, partying, visiting with friends, and all the other interesting activities available. However, an essential self-management skill for doing well in college is to get *at least 8 hours of good, regular sleep every night*. Many college students binge and purge when it comes to sleep—getting too few hours during the week and trying to catch up on the weekend. Unfortunately, the body doesn't work that way. You can cut back a little on sleep one night and make it up the next, *if this is a rare occurrence and you are in excellent health*. Be realistic, are you?

OK, let's look at the facts about sleep. The US is the most sleep-deprived country on earth, with an average of a little less than 7 hours a night—and college freshmen are one of the most deprived groups. Being out of the parental grasp is just too much for some students, and staying up late is a way of proving to yourself that you're "in control"—finally! During the first two weeks of a freshmen class, we constantly hear students bragging about how little (if any) sleep they got the night before. Interestingly, by the beginning of the third week the bragging ceases, and students are whining about lack of sleep, no energy to study (or party!), irritability, and an inability to concentrate. We call this the "zombie period." It also marks the beginning of the "catching a cold" season for students!

Some students find sleeping difficult because of noise around their living quarters or a fear of missing out on something exciting. Others are just trying to keep up with course work—especially as they get further behind due to poor time management and inefficient study skills. Late-teen physiology even conspires to defeat going to bed early. Although 19-year-olds (whose bodies will continue to grow for at least 2 more years) still need between 9 and 10 hours of sleep, their brains just doesn't let them get sleepy as early as they used to (e.g., Carskadon, cited in the *UC Berkeley Wellness Letter*, 1995). And then there is that 8:00 class with the professor who always takes roll.

There may be one last problem affecting your ability to sleep well—alcohol. Alcohol consumption peaks during college and, for many, during freshmen year. Consequently, many freshmen go to bed with a good dose of alcohol in their system. Unfortunately, alcohol delays the time it takes for the brain to begin having *restorative* sleep, and the only remedy for this is to sleep *more* than the usual amount of sleep needed (often 10 or more hours). As stress increases during the semester, don't rely on caffeine to energize you and alcohol to relax you. You may *feel* awake, but your brain will function as though it were sleep deprived! And *do not* take sleeping pills or other narcotics. They are addictive and are only effective for a couple of weeks.

So, how *do* you get enough sleep? There is no secret to getting adequate amounts of good sleep, just like there isn't about exercising. The catch is *doing it*! Keep in mind that you need to get at least 8 hours of sleep (see research box), and you need to do so every night. Here are some tactics you can use to increase your chances of sleeping soundly and long enough.

➤ Go to bed and get up at the same time *every day*—if you can only do one of these, *getting up at the same time* is more important.
➤ Develop a 20- to 30-minute pre-sleep routine to get ready for bed; do the same routine every night, and your body will be ready to sleep when you get in bed.
➤ Don't do anything stimulating close to bed time—no fights or heated discussions, no thinking about something that will stir up your emotions, and definitely no worrying.
➤ Get together everything you will need for the next day before you start your pre-sleep routine—get your books together, decide what you'll wear, etc. This habit will guarantee you one less thing to worry about once you get in bed.
➤ Take a *warm* bath or shower, if that relaxes you, but avoid really hot water within an hour of going to bed. If your body is overheated, your brain won't be able to start the sleep cycle.
➤ Sleep in a "cold" room year round—between 45 and 55 degrees is best.
➤ If you are a chronically poor sleeper, don't watch TV, read, or study in your bed—make sleeping the activity for bed, and your body will become classically conditioned to go to sleep when you go to bed.
➤ Don't drink alcohol or caffeine close to bedtime, and don't drink an excess of either anytime during the day. Some people can't handle caffeine after 5:00 or 6:00 in the evening. Although caffeine or alcohol may not keep you awake when you try to go to sleep, they will shorten the time you sleep by causing you to wake up after a few hours—and this isn't just because they are diuretics!
➤ If you must eat or drink late in the evening, make it something relaxing—remember the milk and cookies routine when you were a child? And be sure you don't overdo *any* eating or drinking prior to bed or your sleep will be disturbed. That 1:00 a.m. pepperoni pizza that seemed like a great idea will come back to haunt you by 4:00.
➤ If you are bothered by noise, buy the highest level of noise-defeating foam earplugs you can find. A box will last a long time, and they are also useful when you are trying to concentrate on your studies. Yes, you will still hear your alarm go off, if you aren't too sleep-deprived.
➤ About that alarm—when you get enough sleep and have a regular time to go to bed and wake up, you'll find that you will usually wake up slightly before the alarm goes off. But keep setting it because you may worry about not waking up otherwise.

Research on Sleep and Learning—According to several recent studies, new information and new skills are not "learned" until after you sleep on it. Research in the *Journal of Cognitive Neuroscience* by Stickgold (cited in Blakeslee, 2000) found that more than 6—and preferably 8—hours of sleep were needed following a learning session in order for the brain to encode the new information into memory circuits. In fact, students who were tested later the same day or slept 6 or fewer hours before being tested the next day showed *no* sign of learning. And the sleep needed to be "good" sleep, in which the first 2 hours were spent in deep sleep and the last 2 in rapid eye movement (REM) sleep. (Good quality sleep requires the sleeper to go to bed unaffected by alcohol or other drugs.)

A second finding supports the value of ***distributed practice*** (spacing out your studying over several days) over ***massed practice*** (cramming). Students in the study who slept well prior to their first "test" performed *even better* on the task when re-tested 2 days to a week later. In fact, several factors that the "general public" believes are important for learning and memory were unrelated to ability to recall "test" material—SAT scores, trying hard to remember when being tested, and the prestige and reputation of the high school had *no* effect on differences in performance. *Only sleep made a difference!*

Eating Well

Never eat more than you can lift. — Miss Piggy

This book isn't about nutrition, but good nutrition will help you cope with stress and keep your body healthy. Keep a food diary for a few days so you'll be aware of how poor your eating habits have become. If you are a typical college student, you skip breakfast to sleep, eat out of machines between classes, and favor pizza and junk food over what is available on your meal ticket. Even if you live at home, you no doubt miss meals and try to increase your energy level and alertness with junk. *Stop doing this!* Your body has to have good food and lots of water to withstand the stressful life you are living! Here are some basic musts for good nutrition.

➤ Keep water available *wherever you are*, and drink at least eight glasses a day.

➤ Don't skip breakfast or settle for an energy bar, canned breakfast, or a bagel.

➤ If you have a refrigerator in your room, keep milk, fresh fruit, fruit juice (*not* fruit punch), and a fiber-rich cereal available for a quick meal or snack. If sugar is the first ingredient in your cereal, look for another one, preferably a whole-wheat and high-fiber type. Stone-ground wheat bread (be sure it says whole wheat, *not* enriched wheat flour, as the first ingredient) and peanut butter are other staples you can keep.

➤ Take fruit with you and eat it when you crave "machine food."

➤ If possible, get a microwave and learn to cook something more than popcorn in it. Oatmeal is quick and easy, but avoid instant because of its high sodium content.

➤ Read labels, including those on "machine food." To eat healthier, minimize sodium content, maximize fiber, and minimize saturated fat, hydrogenated fat, and transfat which raise **LDL** (low density lipoprotein, "bad" cholesterol). Remember that the body uses *all* types of sugar in *exactly* the same way, regardless of whether the label lists honey, corn syrup, fructose, sucrose, or some other "fancy" type.

Because you are living a stressful life and often don't eat as you should, we recommend a few supplemental vitamins and minerals. When buying, remember that generics and name brands are almost always identical. To protect your body and immune system, you need a **multivitamin-multimineral pill** (look for 100% rather than mega-doses), **vitamins C** (250 to 500 I.U.), **vitamin E** (containing dl- *and* d-Alpha Tocopherol, 200 to 400 I.U.), **folic acid**, and **calcium with vitamin D** (1,000 mg calcium, preferably calcium citrate, and 200 I. U. vitamin D, especially during the winter and if you get little direct sunlight). ***Note:*** *Supplements* are just that—they do *not* replace a healthful diet.

Your adrenal glands (which produce hormones that energize your body) use vitamin C during episodes of physical stress. Illness and injury also deplete vitamin C. Vitamin E, especially if taken about 20 minutes before eating a high-fat meal, helps keep the level of LDL from building up in your blood, which in turn lessens the risk of hardening of the arteries (***atherosclerosis***). Your body also uses more protein and complex carbohydrates when you are stressed. Good sources of protein include peas, beans, fish, poultry, and lean meats. Complex carbohydrates are found in fruits, vegetables, breads, cereals, and pasta. Protein helps improve concentration and alertness, and glucose (such as that derived from eating fruit) helps the brain work well during learning. Carbohydrates increase serotonin levels in the brain, which helps you feel relaxed and sleep better. Try to choose items for meals that will enhance your ability to study (e.g., protein for breakfast and lunch, an apple while studying, and complex carbohydrates of your choice prior to relaxing and getting ready for sleep).

Writing Activity 9.1—How successful are you *right now* at getting enough exercise and sleep and eating in a healthy way? What do you plan to do to increase your health in each area?   ***Exercise:***
Sleep:
Nutrition:

Relaxation Techniques That Help You Cope

Some type of relaxation is the best method for lowering your arousal level (Benson, 1992). There are many relaxation techniques available, and none are "better" than others. You need to explore several methods and find out which ones work well for you. We assume you already have some method of relaxation, even if it's just watch TV, cruising the Web, or visiting with friends. Here we'll introduce a few more types, but if you want an in-depth description of all the types available, take a look at the Web sites listed at the end of this chapter or visit your campus library or the self-help section of a book store. And let us warn you about substituting relaxation for studying—don't! Researchers have found that studying *and* relaxation work best if you experience test anxiety, but that *studying is better than relaxation if you do only one*!

Breathing

Some methods require practice to learn to do them correctly and to condition your body to relax quickly. But once mastered, they are the most efficient methods since you only need to perform them about 20 minutes a day. One thing common to these techniques is regular, deep breathing. In fact, the easiest type of concentration relaxation is just to lie with your eyes closed and concentrate on your breathing. In order to keep your mind from wandering, several concentration techniques are available. The best way to do these techniques is to lie on the bed or floor. To reduce distractions, be sure you aren't wearing any tight or binding clothing, such as a belt or bra, and be sure you are warm enough. Here are some easy techniques.

> ➢ Visualize your breath going in and out of your nose, seeing it go deeply into your lungs and then re-emerging through your nose. This should be done very effortlessly —the breath should flow in and flow out without your being conscious of controlling either process. You can visualize it as water or a cloud if you need a "solid" visual image to think of as separate from your body.

> ➢ Concentrate on counting your breaths, but you have to be sure this doesn't speed up your breathing. If it does, substitute the words "in" and "out" for numbers.

> ➢ Concentrate on the area of your diaphragm just above your stomach, which should rise and fall as you draw the breath into your lungs and then push it out. Your upper chest and stomach shouldn't move much, if at all, in this technique. If you can't tell if your diaphragm is moving correctly at first, you can place your hand just above your navel until you perfect the technique.

> ➢ Take deep breaths, hold each one for a count of 10, and release it completely. (We commonly use only a third to a half of our lung space when breathing.) This method is both relaxing and energizing, so you might find it useful when you are trying to "jump start" your body in the morning or when preparing to study. However, if you tend to fall asleep easily or are feeling really tired, do this method standing up!

As you become accustomed to using any of these techniques, you will recognize when your body starts to relax. Some people also notice getting warmer as this occurs. When arousal turns on the *sympathetic* branch of the autonomic nervous system, blood moves away from the surface of the body and the extremities (see Chapter 8 discussion of the *alarm reaction* of the

GAS). As the *parasympathetic* branch of the autonomic nervous system takes over when you begin relaxing, blood flows back to the surface and extremities, making the body feel warmer.

Once you feel relaxed, you can begin conditioning your body for "instant" relaxation (which will come in handy when you take an exam, give a speech, or need to resist making a retaliatory remark that could start a fight). As you take and hold a deep breath, silently say the word "calm." After a week or two of practice, you will find that just saying "calm" in your head will get your body to switch on the parasympathetic branch and help you relax. Because the word works through *classical conditioning* (pairing your relaxed state with the word "calm"), you will need to keep doing your deep breathing and pairing of the word a few times a week to maintain the conditioning so you can evoke instant relaxation in threatening situations.

There are two slightly more complicated techniques that require practice, but are excellent for relaxing and for conditioning yourself for instant relaxation: progressive relaxation and meditation. You need to be sure you are reasonably healthy before undertaking most techniques beyond deep breathing. We are assuming you have checked with your doctor if you have a chronic medical condition. Most schools require a check-up prior to beginning school, but if yours doesn't, we urge you to get a thorough check-up now and before attempting strenuous exercise or a relaxation technique.

Progressive relaxation

All progressive relaxation techniques involve some method of tightening and loosening your muscles in a specific order going up or down the body. The idea is to teach yourself what both tightened and loosened muscles feel like, since we seldom pay attention to either process. Once you get into a relaxed state, you can condition the word "calm" just as described above.

Here is an overview of this method, but the best way to use this technique is to *get a relaxation tape* in which the speaker leads you through the whole technique at a regulated rate. The speaker usually tells you exactly how to go about tightening each part of the body, which is essential for doing it correctly and getting maximum tightness. The tape is important because saying the steps in your head will distract you from paying attention to the tightening and loosening of your muscles and often speeds up the process, which is counterproductive.

‣ Lie flat on the floor or a firm bed, remove your shoes, wear loose clothing, be sure you're warm enough, and close your eyes. Rest your arms and legs flat on the surface. Don't cross your feet. Don't use a pillow.

‣ Beginning on your *dominant* side (the hand you use to write), tighten your fist and forearm for about 10 seconds, concentrating on what tightness feels like.

‣ Release the tension all at once, attending to how the looseness feels for about 30 seconds.

‣ Repeat the tightening and loosening for the same muscles, again concentrating on both for the indicated seconds.

101

➤ This same process is repeated going from part to part in this order: upper arm, other arm (lower, then upper), forehead, mid-face, lower face, neck area, chest area, stomach area, hip area (which may be included with stomach area), one leg (upper, then lower), and the other leg (upper, then lower).

➤ At this point you are told to concentrate (or guided through concentrating) on each part again, searching to see if any tightness still exists. If so, you are to tighten and loosen that part using the same method.

➤ Once you check all parts and find that they are relaxed, you are to concentrate on your breathing. As you take 30 deep breaths while remaining relaxed, you say the word "calm" while releasing each one. (This part of the technique is just like the breathing exercise already discussed, and you must practice it a few times a week to keep the conditioning in effect.)

Meditation

Quite frankly, learning *how* to meditate will take about 5 minutes—but you probably won't do it correctly and effectively until you have really worked at it for 6 or more months. Some people never "get it" or find that they get too restless trying it. Progressive relaxation is better for them because they feel like they are "doing something." Even those who are successful find that constant vigilance is required to keep doing it right—at least for the first few years. Meditation is a lot like learning a sport, so you can't expect to be an expert right away or learn it from reading about it in a book—your have to practice, practice, practice!

Here are a few pointers, and if you are willing to work at it, meditation is an excellent and efficient relaxation method. Doing it 20 minutes a day really pays off in increased ability to relax, to take life less grimly, to feel more "centered" and in control of yourself (even in a stressful situation), and to stay in good health! We know that's a lot of promises, but research bears it out.

➤ Be sure you won't be disturbed by *anything* (e.g., phone, people). If you can't escape external noise, use ear plugs, soft instrumental or New Age music, or a tape of non-arousing sounds (e.g., rain, waterfall, forest, seashore sounds). Positioning a clock where you can see it easily will quiet the anxiety of spending too much time.

➤ Sit in an upright position with your spine straight and shoulders back to aid correct breathing. The floor, a firm bed, or a pillow for a seat will keep you from feeling uncomfortable and losing concentration. Cross your legs and rest your hands on your thighs—there are "fancier" positions, but this one is comfortable for most people. A firm, straight back chair is OK, but keep both feet flat on the floor. Don't lie down on the floor or a bed because your need a certain amount of quiet attention and will be too likely to fall asleep.

➤ Close your eyes.

➤ Spend a few minutes relaxing your muscles wherever they feel tight (see above for tips on how to explore muscle groups and relax them).

➤ Get your breathing regulated and slowed.

➤ Put your worries and "urgent" issues away for awhile. One technique is to "write" them on a black board in your head and then see yourself slowly erasing them.

➤ ***This is the hardest step and is where misunderstanding of the meditation process often scares people off.*** You *don't* have to empty your mind—*if fact, you can't do so.* Something will go through your consciousness because that is how the brain works! *The solution is to let your thoughts run on their own*, without becoming interested or involved with them, without directing them, and without getting emotionally aroused by them. Watch your thought pictures and hear words stream by like you were watching something on TV, *but* be sure you don't start thinking *about* them—avoid thinking "that's interesting," which pulls you away from concentration into an analyzer or director role. If you move away from the correct role of just watching, you'll hear yourself saying, "Hey, I'm doing it!", which is a dead give away that you aren't! Your goal is to stay *right here, right now* and be an uninvolved, nonjudgmental participant in your mental life.

➤ Two popular types of meditation are designed specifically to help you avoid following your thoughts right out of the meditative state. One is to say a ***mantra*** (a word that echoes in your head, like "Oooommmmm" or "Ahhhmmmmmennnn," or one with a good feeling for you—just resist one that makes your mind wander from the present). The other method is to concentrate on something—a blue vase is a traditional item. You can "watch" something solid, like a vase or candle flame, or you can attend to your breath, much like the breathing exercises above, *but* you can't get involved with it or guide it! You can also passively listen to the music or sounds, if you are using them to block out distractions. Just float with the sounds, not directing your thoughts. (So, if you find that you can't passively watch your thoughts, try one of these alternatives before deciding that meditation isn't for you.)

➤ There is also a type of "opening up" meditation, which is impossible for beginners because of the opportunities for distraction. However, master meditators can be in an almost constant state of tranquil existence, practicing both the traditional and opening up meditation techniques; this is what experts mean when they say someone is "centered" even when faced with stressful situations. Just like watching your thoughts go by with your eyes closed, this type of meditation involves watching the world go by with eyes open. Since anything we see tends to draw us outside ourselves and distract us from relaxation, this technique is *not* suggested until you really master not getting involved with your thoughts! Even then, it's best to use this method in a quiet location, such as a garden or the woods.

➤ Once you finish meditating, it is important not to jump right up and return to the world. Sit quietly, stretch your neck, arms, and back muscles slowly, let thoughts return without becoming too interested in them. Practice contacting even emotional thoughts as a quiet observer during this period, and it will be easier to do so when they broadside you during the day.

The ability *not* to overreact and panic, *not* to let your emotions drive you nuts, is a primary benefit you will derive from regular meditation. Eventually you will be able to watch your thoughts, worries, and crises without letting them turn on the alarm reaction. Since your higher-order problem-solving abilities are only available when you avoid turning on this fight-or-flight mode, you will eventually be able to decide when you do and don't need to get involved with problems and worries. You will realize that emotions don't just *happen* to you. You will become aware of how often—and inappropriately—you upset yourself by thinking of things from the past or the future that you simply *cannot* do anything about, now or ever. You will learn to put those thoughts out of your mind *without guilt or anxiety*. You will begin to spend more mental energy on matters you *can* do something about and to feel more relaxed and confident as you plan or engage with them. Think of getting rid of useless worries as crossing items off of your "to do" list—it's one less thing you have to spend time and effort on!

Suggested Readings

Benson, H. (1992). *The relaxation response.* New York: Avon.

Blakeslee, S. (2000). "Sleep on it" may be a lesson worth heeding. *Milwaukee Journal Sentinel*, May 1. (in http://www.psychwatch.com/ archives)

UC Berkeley Wellness Letter. (1995, August). *The sleepy teen years*, p. 7.

Suggested Web Sites

http://www.psychwatch.com/ This site addresses all areas of psychology and gives you access to other Web sites of interest. The archives have news releases. There are tutorials on many topics.

http://www.healthscout.com/ This site has tips on diet and fitness.

http://www.unc.edu/depts/unc_caps/resources.htm The U. of North Carolina's Counseling And Psychological Services has tips on stress management.

http://www.clas.ufl.edu/users/gthursby/stress/manage.htm The U. of Florida site gives you information on stress and stress management and links you to other sites dealing with stress.

http://tc.unl.edu/stress/ This site provides information on stress management and stress reduction.

http://www.teachhealth.com/ This site has stress information for college and high school students.

http://www.sleepnet.com This site links to information on sleep.

http://www.neuronic.com This site provides information on sleep and sleep disorders.

http://www.sleepfoundation.org The National Sleep Foundation provides educational information on sleep and sleep disorders along with links to related sites.

Chapter 10

Coping with Stress:
How Not *to Hide Under Your Bed*

Part II: Emotional, Cognitive, and Behavioral Techniques

*Life is not the way it's **supposed to be**. It's the way it **is**.*
The way you cope with it is what makes the difference. — Virginia Satir

The trick to effective coping is to face the reality of the situation and of your current skills and strength for dealing with it. Sometimes you simply cannot change a situation—or cannot do so at the time because of other demands, current health, or skill level. The horror of those times can best be minimized by using some type of *emotional* coping, such as humor, social support, or self-expression. We will consider these useful coping techniques first. Next, we will discuss the value of cognitive restructuring, which can help you cope whether you do or don't try to change a situation. Finally, we will present two active, *problem-focused* methods of coping: problem solving and asking questions. You will also find specific methods of deal with academic, personal, and interpersonal situations in other chapters.

> **Test for Self-Awareness**—Before reading on, complete and score the Multidimensional Coping Scale on p. A33 (Carver, Scheier, & Weintraub, 1989), which will show you the different types of coping you currently use and help you apply the material in this chapter.

Using Humor

A good laugh overcomes more difficulties and dissipates more dark clouds
than any other one thing. — Laura Ingalls Wilder

As discussed in Chapter 4, being grim can harm your school work, interpersonal life, and health. On the other hand, seeing the humor in your daily life helps you cope with stress and improves your mood (e.g., Labott & Martin, 1987). As long as it does not take a destructive form and is used in an appropriate situation, humor relieves tension and is a sign of emotional maturity (Robinson, 1983). The next time you feel overwhelmed by life, try to step back from your situation and imagine that you are seeing it in a humorous movie. How would it be enacted? What can you do to turn it into a more bearable situation? And if you can't find humor in the immediate situation, try this approach when you have gotten through it. Your usual habit may be to dwell on how awful the situation was, how badly someone treated you, or how terrible it is that you have to live such a stressful life. We urge you instead to look for the humor in the situation. We're not suggesting that humor will *solve* your problems or keep you from experiencing stress, but we are saying that you don't have to suffer after an event by continuing to re-live the situation and the stress you have experienced. A more positive mood is also more likely to help you see how you can better handle similar situations or people in the future. An added benefit is that choosing humor has consistently been shown to be physically healthier for you.

Many theorists have studied the physical effects that humor has on your ability to cope with stress. Remember from Chapter 8 that the sympathetic and parasympathetic branches of the autonomic nervous system can't both control your body at the same time. The former prepares you for fight or flight, while the latter calms your body and takes care of maintenance behaviors, such as digestion. When you are chronically stressed, the excess arousal you carry around because you aren't fighting or fleeing instead fuels everything you do or think about—and, *without conscious intervention,* it does so in a *negative* way. You can't think straight, you get frustrated easily, little things annoy you, and any emotion you are experiencing becomes stronger. But you can make a *conscious* choice to control your reactions—the energy can fuel humor just as it does a negative mood. ***You have the ability to look at a situation with anger <u>or</u> humor.*** Additionally, humor releases energy, making you feel better and switching on the parasympathetic branch to relax you. We are sure you have experienced this feeling of relief after a really good laugh. So, next time you feel the pressure building up, find something to laugh about.

Writing Activity 10.1—Write about a time when you and others were in a stressful situation and one of you pointed out something funny about it, cracked a joke, or did something unusual that caused everyone to laugh. How did the humor change the situation or how you looked at it, making the situation more bearable?

Social Support

Friendship improves happiness and abates misery
by doubling our joys and dividing our grief. — Joseph Addison

Humans are social animals: we enjoy aloneness, but we definitely don't like loneliness. Finding people who have attitudes, values, and interests similar to yours should be one of your first missions in college. Many colleges have freshmen come to campus for several days in the summer or before classes start specifically so they can get used to their surroundings and have time to become acquainted with other students. Hopefully, you made good use of those days to meet and get to know people by sharing self-disclosing conversations rather than blotting out the experience by attending impersonal parties, drinking, or staying in your room alone. If your social support network is becoming well-developed, you have no doubt already found how useful it is for helping you handle stress. Having someone to listen to you gripe, to go exercise or visit the library with, and to just hang with is an excellent buffer from boredom and homesickness. We hope you are getting both **emotional social support**, having people listen to and comfort you, and **instrumental social support**, having people materially help you in some way (e.g. answer questions, give you a ride, loan you something). Both types help you keep down your stress level and keep up your immune system to minimize your risk for chronic colds (for a review see Uchino, Cacioppo, & Kiecolt-Glaser, 1996).

Unfortunately, social connections are not always positive or helpful. When you try to change bad habits, such as smoking or not sleeping or studying enough, those same great friends with whom you hang and go to parties can be a big obstacle. If they have the same bad habit, you may find they try to sabotage your attempts to change. They fear you won't continue as their friend if you change, they are forced to examine their own lives when they aren't ready to do so, and they still need you as their social support person! We suggest that when you plan to change any of your habits, you sit down with your friends and explain what and why you are changing, that you are not going to abandon them, and that you actually will need their support and goodwill to succeed in your change program. Gaining their support and allaying their fears will actually strengthen your chance of success—no one is as quick to point out your "back sliding" into your old bad habit as are your friends!

Expressing Yourself

You will not grow if you sit in a beautiful flower garden, but you will grow if you are sick,
if you are in pain, if you experience losses, and if you do not put your head in the sand.
Take the pain as a gift to you with a very, very specific purpose. — Elizabeth Kubler Ross

A consistent finding in the health psychology literature is that *suppressing* your negative feelings is unhealthy (e.g., Gross & Levenson, 1997), while learning to *express* them in a healthy manner can actually increase you health and improve your immune system functioning (e.g., Petrie, Booth, & Pennebaker, 1998; also see the Research box below). Acting like everything is fine when you are actually angrily or sadly brooding affects you in several ways.

> ➤ Physiologically, your body is *more* aroused by suppressing your emotions. Remember that stress produces both immediate and chronic health problems.

> ➤ Trying to hold in your emotions takes a lot of cognitive and emotional effort, which distracts your attention from your other tasks, such as trying to concentrate on your studies or take an exam.

> ➤ Holding in your feelings robs you of the chance for social support from your friends and family.

Application of Research—Must you talk to others to get relief from traumatic events and daily hassles? Apparently not. Writing can be a "stand-in" if close friends are unavailable or you feel uncomfortable telling them about an incident. A review of studies (Smyth, 1998) found that writing about trauma, hassles, or worries helps you sort out your thoughts, gain insight, and remove much of the "baggage" known to accompany emotionally-negative situations. In a typical study (e.g., Pennebaker, 1993; Pennebaker & Francis, 1996) one group of students wrote an essay expressing their feelings about a traumatic experience (e.g., "Write about your deepest thoughts and feelings about a trauma [or current problem]"), while another group of students wrote about non-emotional topics (e.g., "Write about your plans for the day").

The trauma-related writing task led to significantly improved health outcomes in college students, most of whom were freshmen or transfer students. (These groups are most likely to experience stress due to adjusting to college life and to having fewer intimate friends with whom they can talk.) Improvement was correlated with experiencing a *brief period* of increased distress while or immediately after writing, due to thinking about the negative situation. Keeping a journal or just writing weekly were found to have better results than just writing once. Improvement occurred over whatever time period was used in the study, whether 4 weeks or longer. Four types of health measures consistently showed improvement: reported physical health, psychological well-being (happiness, positive mood), physiological functioning, and general functioning. Apparently traumatic memories and problems are stored differently from less negative events. They end up as intrusive, distressing symptoms, hyper-arousal, and thoughts to be avoided or denied (e.g., van der Kolk, 1994). Writing seems to lessen the negative emotionality attached to an incident or problem and allow the writer to gain perspective.

Right now you may feel unable to confide in those around you, either due to the topic of your problem or because you do not as yet feel close enough for self-disclosure. But you can literally "take a page" from Pennebaker's book—write about your problems. His research showed that even students who didn't think anyone would see their thoughts benefited from writing. Because men often find it harder to disclose a trauma or express emotions than women do (e.g., Ptacek, Smith, & Zanas, 1992; Taylor et al., 2000), they appear to get even more benefit from this technique.

When you decide that your emotions need to be expressed out loud to a friendly ear or to the target of your problem (e.g., an errant roommate, friend, or romantic interest), you will have more success if you don't blow up, lash out, or collapse in a sea of tears. Both *holding in* and *over-expressing* negative feelings are related to poorer health (from nervous headaches to development of heart disease or cancer), poorer interpersonal relations, and reduced ability to learn and perform. You may have heard from many pop psychology sources that **catharsis** (letting out your anger in a "safe" or socially-acceptable way) is good for you. *Don't believe it for a minute!* Actually, research shows that catharsis—whether in the form of **displacement** (e.g., beating a pillow, yelling at someone who isn't the source of your problem) or a supposedly "safe" outlet (e.g., playing a contact sport roughly, playing a violent video game)—doesn't accomplish your goal of reducing your anger or getting past the problem.

You no doubt are thinking, "So? What *can* I do?" There are two paths you can take, and you need to learn to chose the one that will alleviate the problem better in each new situation. If there is something you can do to correct or solve the problem, that is the best thing to do. If you can't do anything about the situation, now or ever, you can turn to humor, seek social support, or write about your problems—or you can attack your current attitudes and feelings using cognitive restructuring, which we will discuss next.

Cognitive Restructuring

We are, perhaps uniquely among the earth's creatures, the worrying animal.
We worry away our lives, fearing the future, discontent with the present,
unable to take in the idea of dying. — Lewis Thomas

As you well know, there are some problems that you just can't do anything about. You can't make everyone love you, and you can't always succeed at a task. The saying that "you can do anything if you just try hard enough" simply isn't true. Accepting defeat, knowing when to stop trying, and getting on with your life are marks of maturity, and learning how to do so will actually lead to fewer negative emotions and fewer feelings of helplessness and hopelessness. *Cognitive restructuring* (changing how you think about yourself and the situation you are in) is a technique that can help you adjust to disappointments and stop beating yourself up when you don't succeed. ***Keep in mind that the majority of your stress comes from the way you perceive the world, not from the way the world really is.*** Here are some examples of ways in which changing your beliefs can help you cope with stressful situations.

- ➢ Use feedback from others or from your own task performance to recognize and accept both your good points and your limits. Being realistic about your abilities will help you set achievable goals, reduce competitiveness with others, recognize when you should work with others or ask for help, and accept situations you can't change.
- ➢ Don't beat yourself up when you don't perform "perfectly" or meet goals "on time." Being realistic about what a task requires and how long it will take will help you eliminate procrastination caused by thinking you have plenty of time when you don't.
- ➢ Don't catastrophize. Ask yourself how important the target of your wailing really is for your life goals. Is your current situation or "shortcoming" really so awful?

- Don't hold on to outmoded beliefs or views of yourself. Catch yourself when you say "I have never been able to..."—change your belief to "I haven't learned how to *yet*."
- Learn to make *positive* and upbeat statements. Don't criticize yourself or others; instead, assess how you can improve and ask yourself if you (or the other person) need some help.
- See yourself as a "work in progress." Realize that decisions can almost always be changed if conditions or your interests change.
- Learn to praise yourself and others. Personal praise is really the best reward, so don't think that you are vain for enjoying your good works!
- Learn to tolerate and forgive others—and yourself (intolerance breeds anger, frustration, and hostility). Learn to put yourself in others' shoes, so you'll better understand their motives and feelings.
- Remember that your emotions mostly arise or get out of control due to your thoughts about the situation (excluding tiger attacks, being in an earthquake, or similar situations).
- Don't be so wed to opinions that you constantly fight for them. Remember that opinions are *not* facts and no one has a corner on the truth or "the way it *should* be."
- Be realistic about whether the situation is *your* problem or someone else's. If it is yours, learn to approach it calmly. But if it's someone else's, the most you can do is offer help (if that's appropriate or possible) or lend a friendly ear.
- Learn to "size up" tasks realistically. If the task is big, think about it as a series of tasks (which it is!), prioritize, devise a realistic plan, and work *steadily* to get it done.
- Stop worrying about things you can't do anything about *right now*.
- Avoid **hindsight bias** (thinking that you remember signs indicating something would happen or that you "should have seen it coming"). Many events aren't predictable, and beating yourself up for not seeing them coming is a waste of effort. A better choice is to look back at the situation and learn from it.
- Learn to recognize when your thoughts are unrealistic and condemning. Such thoughts often include words like *should, ought, must, always, never, have to, deserve,* and *owe*.

Problem Solving

Fearful as reality is, it is less fearful than evasions of reality....
Look steadfastly into the slit, pinpointed malignant eyes of reality
as an old-hand trainer dominates his wild beasts.
— Caitlin Thomas, *Not Quite Posthumous Letter to My Daughter*

To solve a problem, you must decide first if you have the skills and information necessary to do so. Here is a beneficial technique that can help you think about and solve all sorts of problems. After using this technique to understand the problem, you still have to carry it out and see if it works. Other chapters can help you proceed. You can figure out why you are "stuck in neutral" (e.g., procrastination, lack of self-efficacy) and how to attack academic, personal, or interpersonal problems (e.g., exam uncertainty, excessive drinking, a roommate from hell).

Thomas D'Zurella and Marvin Goldfried (1971) defined a problem as "failure to find an effective response." If you think you are in a "problematic situation," but you immediately know how to "solve" it *and* you have the resources, time, and motivation to do so without interference from others or the environment, *there really is no problem*. But your situation can become a problem at any step in the problem-solving process: being unable to define the problem, to figure out what to do about it, to carry out the solution, or to have the solution work. Here is a problem-solving procedure you can apply to figure out and hopefully to reach your goal. You will also benefit from occasionally answering the following questions about your problem: Is the problem still the same? Have I discovered a more desirable goal? Have new restrictions or freedoms involving people or the environment become evident to me? Have new alternatives opened up or old ones disappeared? Am I still the "same" person I was when I undertook earlier steps, or do I need to answer them again using newly-realized personal knowledge?

1. *Decide if there is a problem.*
   ➤ Do you feel uncomfortable about a situation, even though you can't figure out what's wrong yet?
   ➤ Do you really need or want a change—or is someone else or the culture making you think a problem exists where you see none?
   ➤ Is an unrealistic belief about yourself (e.g., perfectionism) the real problem?
   ➤ Is someone else the real problem so that you need to change your relationship with the person, including putting distance between you and the person?
   ➤ Is the real problem a conflict between the situation and another existing or desired situation?
   ➤ Is the situation just a symptom of the real problem (e.g., nonassertiveness)?

2. *Define the problem, including where you are, where you want to be, and what is keeping you from getting there.*
   ➤ When, where, with whom, and how often does the situation occur?
   ➤ What do you want the situation or yourself to become or change to?
   ➤ What lack of resources or skills, beliefs about yourself, or elements of the situation are making you unwilling or unable to move to your desired solution?

3. *Generate alternatives to reach your goal or problem resolution.*
   ➤ One effective technique is to talk to people who know you or to a professor or counselor who knows something about the type of problem you face.
   ➤ You might try *brainstorming* (Osborn, 1963). Just be aware that doing so with a group is *not* as effective as having several people brainstorm alone, writing or typing their ideas and then presenting them to elicit ideas from others (Brown & Paulus, 1996; Paulus & Paulus, 1997). Once together, criticism or evaluation is not allowed, wild ideas are encouraged, and combining and improving are sought. A computer-linked method has also worked well (e.g., Paulus, Larey, Putman, & Leggett, 1996; Roy, Gauvin, & Limayem, 1996; Valacich, Dennis, & Connolly, 1994).
   ➤ If you don't need an immediate solution, *sleep on the problem at this point*. Give your nonconscious brain a chance to mull over the problem. Be like Thomas Edison and take a nap when your creative juices aren't flowing! Go back in a day or two and see if there are more (or more elegant) alternatives that have "appeared" in your head.

4. *Consider your alternatives.*
   - ➤ Think realistically about what could happen if you followed each alternative and see if it "feels" right *and* will lead to your goal. You might even find a path that would lead to a better goal than you had originally envisioned.
   - ➤ You must be truthful about how willing you are to follow each option rather than whether it is just appropriate or a "good" idea. An alternative may be possible or may please others, but does it really fit who you are or hope to become?
   - ➤ Talk to those who know you well so they can help you reject alternatives that are how you usually act but may just perpetuate the problem. Avoid people too ego-involved in the problem—or in you—because they will tend to choose what solves their problem rather than yours. Also realize who is a *gatekeeper* for you (one whose ideas or expectations carry *too much* weight, whom you might not question). Recall that extrinsic motivation (acting so others will reward you) is self-defeating.

5. *Develop a realistic "short list" of alternatives.*
   - ➤ Consider what it will take to carry out each potential alternative and what the short and long-term outcomes of each one will be.
   - ➤ Acknowledge your value system and whether you can live with each choice.
   - ➤ Think how each alternative will affect *others*. Will it create interpersonal problems or alienate people important to you? Can you live with shocking friends or employers? Are you willing to be cut off from opportunities you might want in the future?
   - ➤ Is this a "one-shot deal," or are you planning to use this alternative continuously or with similar problems? For instance, dropping a course because you are stressed or sick is different from dropping out of school or adopting quitting as a usual solution.
   - ➤ Do you have the energy, time, and resources to carry out an alternative?
   - ➤ What will you have to give up or *not* choose to do if you use this alternative? Every choice means losing the chance to make another choice, at least right now.
   - ➤ A choice is seldom *final,* but do consider how *permanent* it is. Some require more commitment than others (e.g., it's easier to get a pot plant than have a baby). You may err to either extreme when considering changing. You may underestimate its permanence and serious impact on your life *or* you may see it as "life or death" or feel that you must make the "perfect" decision. The former will cause you to make decisions too late or without thought; the latter will keep you from changing *at all*.

6. *Develop a plan for carrying out your chosen alternative.*
   - ➤ List the steps to be taken, your time frame, and the costs involved. This gives guidelines for action, lets you plan the sequence of executing your plan, alerts you to material and mental resources you will need, and helps you be realistic.
   - ➤ Behavioral contracting can be used at this stage to "keep you honest" and boost your motivation. Use a verbal or written agreement, but avoid contracting with someone who is too lenient or too rigid—choose someone who understands that "slips" are not failures, will remind you when you backslide, and won't sabotage your plan.
   - ➤ *Realistically* re-evaluating the options you chose *and* rejected is essential. The situation may have changed or you have found a new alternative or goal by now. Be sure you aren't engaging in wishful thinking or being affected by irrational "should's."

> ➤ Decide if you are willing to live with the consequences of your actions or reaching the goal? Keep in mind that changing your mind, now or later, is *not* a character flaw!

> ➤ *You may realize that while you want to pursue this path to a desired goal, this just isn't the time to make that move!* If you aren't ready emotionally or materially, admit that you don't have to act right now. The plan can still be used later, and taking time can give you a chance to amass more experience and resources to assure success.

7. ***Carry out your plan, being sure to evaluate your progress and your situation after you have met your goal.***

> ➤ Did the solution give you the outcome you were hoping for? Many people think that some change (e.g., losing weight, starting a serious relationship) will bring them love, happiness, or success. But a *material* change seldom solves an emotional or cognitive problem, which may be based on negative self-labels and irrational beliefs.

> ➤ If you still haven't solved your problem satisfactorily, be aware that you may not admit it, especially if reaching the goal took a lot of effort or sacrifice. This is the time to admit that you can make another choice if you don't like this one.

> ➤ This step is more easily accomplished if you *honestly* consider these questions: Were you realistic about how it would feel, what it would accomplish for you, and how others would react or what they would expect? Do you plan to continue solving the problem like this or would another alternative-or goal-be better? Has it changed your life as you wanted it to or does it have the potential to eventually do so? (Realize that some changes are painful for quite a while [e.g., not smoking or drinking, ending a destructive or dead-end relationship].)

> ➤ How are your significant others taking the change? Be aware of whether their reactions are due to discomfort with *any* change or with this *specific* one. Let them know if there will be consequences they haven't anticipated, if you have decided you haven't solved the problem, or if you have decided you don't have a problem after all. Remember the value of having a social support group.

Asking Questions

Asking questions is behavior. If you don't do it, you don't learn it.
— N. Postman & C. Weingartner

Another way to end frustrations about how to do a task is to ask for help! That may seem obvious, but some students feel that asking for help reflects badly on them. Whether you ask friends in your classes, a professor, or another professional, you need to learn that asking doesn't make you look "stupid" or show that you can't work on your own. Actually, the exact opposite is true! Many educational experts (e.g., Postman & Weingartner, 1973) believe that learning *how to ask questions* is a mature, life-long learning skill and that you will benefit from developing the skill. Anyhow, if you already knew everything and had all the skills you will need for a successful life, you wouldn't need to be in college at all! Take advantage of the "free" experts all around you—ask for help whenever you need it (for more on this topic, see Chapter 11 on assertiveness).

Writing Activity 10.2—Flexibility is an important element in coping with stress. Think about the techniques you currently use when you become anxious, overwhelmed, and stressed out. List *three* different techniques and decide whether each one is useful or not.

Look over the different methods discussed in this and the last chapter, and choose *two* you don't currently use to help control or minimize your stress. Write about how each of these methods can help you cope better with stressful situations you are currently facing.

Now that you have learned some new ways to cope with stress, let's look at some of the "challenges" you probably have already heard about and perhaps are currently facing. These include dealing with both personal and interpersonal problems and being happier with yourself.

I wanted a perfect ending. Now, I've learned, the hard way, that some poems
don't rhyme, and some stories don't have a clear beginning, middle, and end.
Life is about not knowing, having to change, taking the moment, and
making the best of it, without knowing what's going to happen next.
Delicious ambiguity. — Gilda Radner, on her cancer and approaching death

Suggested Readings

D'Zurella, T. J., & Goldfried, M. R. (1971). Problem solving and behavior modification. *Journal of Abnormal Psychology, 78,* 107-126.

Ellis, A., & Harper, R. A. (1978). *A new guide to rational living.* N. Hollywood: Wilshire.

Labott, S. M., & Martin, R. B. (1987). The stress-moderating effects of weeping and humor. *Journal of Human Stress, 13,* 159-164.

Pennebaker, J. (1993). Putting stress into words: Health, linguistic, and therapeutic implications. *Behavioral Research Therapy, 31,* 539—548. (Available through EBSCO HOST)

Pennebaker, J. & Francis, M. (1996). Cognitive, emotional, and language processes in disclosure. *Cognition and Emotion, 10,* 601—626. (Available through EBSCO HOST)

Robinson, V. M. (1983). Humor and health. In P. E. Mcghee & J. H. Goldstein (Eds.), *Handbook of humor research.* New York: Springer-Verlag.

Taylor, S. E., Klein, L. C., Lewis, B. R., Gruenewald, T. L., Gurung, T. L., & Updegraff, J. A. (2000). Biobehavioral responses to stress in females: Tend-and-befriend, not fight-or-flight. *Psychological Review, 107,* 411-429.

Uchino, B. N., Cacioppo, J. T., & Kiecolt-Glaser, J. K. (1996). The relationship between social support and physiological processes: A review with emphasis on underlying mechanisms and implications for health. *Psychological Bulletin, 119,* 488-531.

Weinstein, N. D., & Klein, W. M. (1996). Unrealistic optimism: Present and future. *Journal of Social and Clinical Psychology, 15,* 1-8.

Suggested Web Sites

http://www.psychwatch.com/ This site addresses all areas of psychology and gives you access to other Web sites of interest. The archives have news releases. There are tutorials on many topics.

http://www.unc.edu/depts/unc_caps/resources.htm The U. of North Carolina's Counseling And Psychological Services has tips on stress management and other topics.

http://www.clas.ufl.edu/users/gthursby/stress/manage.htm The U. of Florida site gives you information on stress and stress management and links you to other sites dealing with stress.

http://tc.unl.edu/stress/ This site provides information on stress management and stress reduction.

http://www.teachhealth.com/ This site has information for college and high school students. The information is available in English or en Espanol.

http://ub-counseling.buffalo.edu/stressmanagement.shtml This site provides information on stress and a variety of other topics for college students.

Chapter 11

Assertiveness:
How to Stand Up for Yourself Without Knocking Someone Down

I just can't ask my Statistics Prof. for help. He's too scary.
— College freshman

My roommate threw out my couch.
I'd like to strangle her, but I don't think it's a good idea.
— College senior

College students must interact with many different kinds of people in many different situations. It makes sense, then, that college life will be easier and smoother if the student interacts effectively with others. For example, students must learn to live with a roommate—or two. They must interact with many kinds of authority figures: professors, secretaries, administrators, etc. And, of course, the student will probably want to make new friends. One key to effectively interacting with people is *assertiveness*—knowing how to stand up for oneself without knocking down others. Students must learn how to make their own needs and desires known in a polite, clear, non-aggressive manner.

> **Test for Self-Awareness**—Before reading further, complete and score the Assertion Inventory on p. A39 (Gambrill & Richey, 1975; 1976). Knowing your level of assertiveness in different areas will help you apply the material in this chapter.

How assertive do you feel you are? Can you make your needs clear? Can you do so in a way that is not offensive or aggressive? When are you comfortable acting assertively and when are you not comfortable? When do you think you will actually act in an assertive manner and when are you probably unlikely to act?

In this chapter how to be assertive will be described for a variety of different situations. How to live peacefully with a roommate will be presented. There will be a discussion of how to approach professors, including things students might do and things they should probably avoid doing! Finally, special situations will be discussed: what the registrar's office does and when you need to know this; how you learn to find your way around the library; and when you might want to talk to a dean (and, what is a dean, anyway?).

Roommates — the Good, the Bad, and the Impossible

I like long walks, especially when they are taken by people who annoy me.
— Fred Allen

Most college freshmen share a room with another student. Sometimes, they room with a friend. Often, freshmen room with strangers. Regardless, their lives will be easier if the roommates learn to live with each other in harmony.

What, then, can facilitate the development of a harmonious relationship? Courtesy, communication, and compromise are key ingredients in any relationship. Each roommate needs to make clear what he or she expects. The roommates must also pay attention to each other's expectations. They must then agree to some ground rules. This often means that all parties have to accept some compromises.

There are some common problems students face when living with roommates. For example, one person may like to stay up late while the other goes to bed early. One person may be very neat while the other is, well, not as neat. One roommate may like to have sexual partners stay in the room while the other is not comfortable with this. What are effective strategies to approach these kinds of situations?

First, decide if a situation bothers you enough for it to be worth addressing. If your roommate did some small thing one time, like forgetting to shut off the alarm clock one Saturday, do you really want to pursue this? Remember, you do need to make some compromises. People who complain about everything will eventually not be taken seriously.

So, let's pretend you like to go to sleep early. In contrast, your roommate comes into the room very late, turns on the light, and wakes you. How might you deal with this? You probably should not say, "You are so rude. You come home late all the time and wake me up." Yes, this response does make the problem behavior clear and your feelings clear. But it is **aggressive**—you are blaming your roommate. Rather, you might say something like, "I like to go to bed early, and when the light is turned on after I'm asleep, it wakes me up, and I can't fall back to sleep." You are most likely to be taken seriously and not ignored if you express your needs in a calm, reasonable manner. Speaking reasonably does not *guarantee* you will get your way; your roommate may see things very differently than you do or your roommate may not be reasonable. But assertiveness is most likely to be effective.

Some people reading the above example are probably thinking the solution was pretty obvious. Other people might be thinking that the example is too "sweet"; they would just tell their roommate what an obnoxious creep (you may substitute other adjectives) the roommate is and to stop coming in late. And other people might be thinking that they could never confront their roommate. However, neither calling names nor saying nothing is as effective as a rational discussion. Responding aggressively, like name calling, tends to lead to more name calling. It also creates more resentment. It does not lead to communication and compromise. Similarly, saying nothing is ineffective—saying nothing leads to no change. It leads to more frustration and hurt feelings.

Writing Activity 11.1—Read the "Assertive Rights" on p. A43 (Smith, as cited in Alexander, 2000). Think what each right means to you. Now, write about *four* that are especially important to you. How do you make sure you are given these rights? How do you respect these rights for other people?

Everyone can probably improve how they express themselves in an assertive manner. People who tend to be somewhat aggressive may ask themselves what they want to get out of a discussion with their roommate. If they do not want an argument, and they probably do not, then how should they change their approach to still get their needs met without the fight? Simple things like avoiding "you," avoiding blame, and avoiding guilt really work. Practicing how to express the problem with friends before actually confronting the roommate is also effective.

People who believe that they would never say anything to their roommate also need to reevaluate their position. Why would people say nothing about a situation that makes them uncomfortable? They might be afraid that their roommate will not like them or will get angry with them. However, why should they make this assumption? They might be wrong. The roommate might be unaware of the problem and happy to make changes to reduce it. Most people do not wish to be the cause of someone else's unhappiness. In addition, if an individual is unhappy, is it healthy for that person to ignore his or her feelings? NO! Not only is it unhealthy, but it is the person's responsibility to stand up for his or her rights. People's personal happiness and mental health can be influenced by their ability to do so.

Can people learn to stand up for their rights? Of course. But it takes some practice. A person may wish to try it out with friends before actually using it in a real situation. It might help to develop a script of what to say in different kinds of situations.

For each of the following situations, consider what you could say to your roommate. If you are not confident that you can actually say it, you might want to try acting some of these out with a trusted friend. This techniques is called ***role playing***. It is like being the actor in a play, except you are making up your own lines!

Writing Activity 11.2—Scripts for Coping With Your Roommate.

1. Your roommate tells you that your part of the room is really messy and is encroaching on his/her side.

2. Your roommate asks to borrow your math book, but you really need it yourself.

Writing Activity 11.2 (continued)—More Scripts.

3. Your roommate has a paper due for an English class. You have written a similar paper. Your roommate would like to borrow it, explaining that you are not in the same class and have different professors for the course.

4. You need $5.00 until you get paid in two days. You know your roommate has extra money. You would like to ask your roommate for a loan.

5. You like to stay up late while your roommate goes to bed early. Your roommate tells you that he/she has been waking up when you come in and it is disturbing.

Professors — Most Aren't As Scary As You Think

Students spend a lot of time interacting with their professors. From an academic perspective, these will be among the most important interactions the student will have while in college. Therefore, effectively communicating with professors is essential. How to effectively communicate depends, in part, on why the student is meeting with the professor in the first place.

Many students think of their professors only as the people who stand in front of the class, talk, give exams, and decide on grades. If this is how the student sees the professor, then the student's interactions with the professor will concern only class material. That is not bad, but it is very limited. Professors can play a far more active role in the student's academic life.

First, professors expect to advise students. Most of the students reading this will be assigned a faculty advisor. Advisement may address immediate concerns. What are the required classes for a major? What kinds of classes outside the major may be important to prepare the student for future goals? What combinations of classes should or should not be taken together to maximize the chances the student will do well in all classes? Advisement can also involve future concerns. Students may talk to professors about what they want to do after graduation. Do they want to go to graduate school? If so, in what area? Do they want to get a job? If so, what kinds of jobs are available?

Second, professors usually expect to provide students with additional experiences beyond the classroom and advisement. They may expect to involve students in research projects. They may expect to provide students with field placements where the student can gain practical experience. Professors also expect to write students letters of recommendation for jobs or graduate school. Too often, however, students do not make use of the many ways in which the professors are available.

There are a number of reasons why students may not seek out their professors. Sometimes the professors seem unapproachable—they seem mean, sarcastic, or scary. Sometimes the students do not realize that approaching the professor is acceptable. Sometimes the student does not know that research opportunities or community placements are available. Sometimes students do not seek interaction with their professors when they realize they can because the student is not assertive enough to do it. Sometimes students just do not know how to go about getting the attention of the professor for the particular concern the student has.

Are any of these really legitimate reasons for the student not to have contact with the professors? The answer is NO. Just as it is the professor's job to make educational opportunities available to the student, it is the student's job to make use of these opportunities. Students need to learn how to talk to their professors even if the professor seems to be an ogre. Students need to learn about opportunities available in their department and college. Basically, students need to take charge of their education. How then might students approach their professors in different situations?

Talking to professors about course material

The first point you should keep in mind when talking to professors, or anyone else, is to be polite. Telling a professor he or she is mean or incoherent or incompetent is not going to get you very far. Second, think about when you want to talk to the professor. If you have a question about text material that was just assigned or lecture material that is being presented, it is best to ask the question as soon as possible in class. Sometimes students do not like to ask questions in class because they think it makes them look stupid. This is unfortunate because the majority of the time when one student has a question, others do too. Very few questions are actually stupid questions. At other times students do not like to ask questions in class because of the professor's reaction. Although most professors expect questions and work hard at answering them in an appropriate manner, some professors may be rude or sarcastic. This tends to reduce the number of questions asked during class.

If, for whatever reason, you are unwilling to ask the question during class, there are other things you can do. You can ask a more outgoing or thicker-skinned friend to ask the question. You can jot the question down and ask the professor immediately before or after class. In this way you will get your answer quickly, which may help you understand the next set of material. You may also be surprised at the number of times a professor will say, "That's a good question. Why didn't you ask it during class?" You may even be surprised that the professor who seems so rude during class is actually quite pleasant after class.

If you have complex questions, or you do not have time to talk to the professor before or after class, you should see the professor during office hours. All professors are required to have office hours when they are available to discuss material with their students. It is best to go to office hours with your questions prepared. When you go, it is probably a good idea to introduce yourself and say which class you are taking. Your professor might or might not recognize you or know your name. If you go to office hours, the professor will now be more likely to recognize you in the future.

Talking to professors about grading

Students may also want to talk to professors about grades. Most professors present their grading schemes in the beginning of the semester, including things like the number of exams, papers, and other assignments and the point values of each. Some professors are very explicit. Some are less explicit. If you have questions about the grading scheme, they should be asked as soon as possible.

Asking questions about grades you received on an assignment can be a trickier situation. Most professors indicate where they give points or deduct points. If you think this may have been done incorrectly, it is appropriate for you to get more information. Be aware, however, that you may be crossing a mine field. Most professors will not hesitate to explain the correct answer and give their criteria for how points were assigned.

However, most professors will not want to argue about a point here and a point there on an essay exam or paper. If forced to reread an essay or paper, they may decide the grade should be lower rather than higher. On the other hand, if you think your points may have been incorrectly calculated, you should definitely point this out to the professor. Again, do this in a polite manner. It will not help your case if you make accusations of incompetence. Most professors have given much thought to the kinds of assignments they give and the way those assignments are graded. Any complaints need to be well thought out.

Talking to professors about course material when there is no problem

One of the goals of a college education is to teach people to see the relevance of course material outside the classroom. This means having students think about the material in different contexts. If you read an article relevant to class or see a TV show that deals with some course issues, is it appropriate for you to mention this to your professors? The answer is, of course. Your professor might not only be pleased by the fact that you are applying course material, he or she might even be pleased to receive a copy of the article that you read. In addition, discussing the material will result in a pleasant interaction between you and the professor and make you better known.

There are a variety of times that you can approach the professor with information like this; office hours, before class, and after class are all reasonable. One word of caution—do not commandeer a professor's time. Remember that the professor has other students and other classes. However, if you are truly interested you should make that clear. You will appear to be a serious student. You and the professor will have an opportunity to get to know each other better. This can result in better advisement and more opportunity to engage in relevant experiences.

What if it is impossible to have a discussion with a professor?

Have you ever had a teacher who was incomprehensible? Or one who just never seemed to care about the students? Or one who was arrogant and demeaning? If not, you are lucky. Unfortunately, many students eventually run into a professor with one of these traits. If you have had a teacher or professor like any of these, you may have found it very difficult to ask questions or to request help if you needed it. But you were still required to take exams and finish assignments. And you were still given a grade for the course. For better or worse, it is your responsibility to learn the material, regardless of how poorly the professor presents it. What, then, should you do when you are in a situation like this?

First, try discussing the material with the professor outside of class, especially during the professor's office hours or during a time you schedule with the professor. Sometimes, either because of the professor or because of the student, one-on-one meetings are far more effective in transmitting the information than the regular class is.

Be aware, however, that most professors will not act as tutors. They will answer specific questions, but they will not review the whole lecture.

Sometimes students find their professors are unwilling to help them. This is actually *VERY* unusual. If, however, you find professors who rarely meet office hours, or refuse to answer questions, or demean or belittle the students, go to the department chairperson. Do *NOT* do this if you are simply angry at a professor or if the course is demanding. The department chairperson is almost certainly familiar with the faculty member and will already be aware of his or her reputation. Almost all faculty have little patience for students who complain that a class is too hard. It is appropriate for classes to be hard! It is not appropriate for faculty to regularly miss office hours, to refuse to speak to students, or to make fun of students. Going to the department chairperson does not guarantee that any changes will be made. However, if you do not go to the chairperson, there is no reason for change.

What if you meet with your professor, who turns out to be a nice enough person who answers your questions, but you find you are still not adequately learning the material? *Find a tutor.* Most colleges offer tutorial services. Frequently the department will help students find a tutor. Sometimes tutorial services are free. At other times students have to pay for tutors. This is money well spent. Tutors cost less than having to repeat a class. Also tutors sometimes teach students study techniques that can be used in other classes, making future use of a tutor unnecessary. Accept the fact that regardless of how effective or ineffective your professors are, you are still going to receive grades from them. In order to receive an adequate grade, you are going to have to learn the material.

What Professors Might *Not* Tell You — and Who Will

Sometimes students want academic information that their professors will not, cannot, or simply do not provide. For example, most professors will not tell a student which is the easiest or best professor for a course. It is generally not appropriate for a professor to make that kind of judgement. In addition, if a student is having trouble with registering or with parking tickets or with library fines, professors often do not know the best (or kindest) person to talk to about the problem. Where can students get information on these kinds of topics? Other students!

The value of other students

The other students, especially those in your major, are an excellent source of information. Their perspective is going to be somewhat different than the perspective of the professors. They may have more insight into such things as which classes go well together. They may understand the ins and outs of using the computer system for registration. They may know who to cry to about library fines. Other students may not always be correct—you must use caution and common sense when evaluating their information. However, sometimes other students' insights can be very valuable.

Other students are also often a good source of information about opportunities available to undergraduates outside the classroom. For example, if your department offers students the opportunity for research, field placements, community service, or jobs, you can learn about these not only from professors, but also from classmates. Both students and faculty can share with you what they consider especially worthwhile activities. Depending on your goals, research experience, field work in an organization related to your major, and community service can be important kinds of preparation. For students who want to go to graduate school, research experience may be especially important. Talking to students and faculty will clarify the kinds of research being done in your department, who is doing it, and when you should become involved in it. Other kinds of graduate programs and many jobs want students to have some practical experience. Participating in field work or community service can provide that. Again, both faculty and students can be excellent sources of information concerning the kinds of opportunities available.

Participating in activities like research, field study, or community service allows students to improve their chances of getting accepted to graduate school or finding a job. However, these experiences do more. They allow the students to clarify what their interests and skills are. Participating in these experiences will help you identify what kinds of things you find fulfilling and what you find unrewarding. Finally, students are part of the community in which they are attending school. Participation in community service not only helps the student prepare for the future; it is also a way for the student to give something to the town or city where the student is living.

If your department has a student organization, it is probably a very good idea to join it. These organizations almost always include discussion of the kinds of activities available to students. They also often invite faculty to attend some meetings, which provides students with an additional, informal, opportunity to interact with the professors. Students who are uncomfortable approaching faculty in class or office hours may find that meetings of student organizations provide a more comfortable environment for doing so. Go by yourself or take a friend—but definitely join!

Secretaries, librarians, and administrators

Colleges and universities are basically bureaucracies. There are a lot of offices, a lot of secretaries, and a lot of administrators. Students inevitably have to interact with some of these people. In order to be effective interacting with these officials, it is best to be polite and to be assertive.

The first person, and perhaps the only person, you may interact with in some offices is the **secretary**. Secretaries are generally very well informed about the department they are in and the offices with which they interact. In fact, it is often the case that secretaries know more about some aspects of the university than the professors know. For example, secretaries may be more informed about whom students should contact about non-academic problems like financial aid, work study positions, and policies in the registrar's office. Secretaries may also know about topics like faculty schedules, what classes are available and when, and how to use the computer system to schedule classes. Some students seem very hesitant about approaching secretaries for help. However, it is part of the secretaries' job to interact with students; most secretaries are priceless resources.

Another group that can provide students with invaluable information is **librarians**. Almost all students who go to college must use the library at some point to research assignments. Again, many students seem embarrassed to approach librarians for help. Many librarians, however, seem delighted to provide help. They may not only provide students with an orientation of the library, they may also show students how to use the Internet to search particular topic areas and provide students with information on other kinds of reference materials. If you are hesitant to ask the librarian for help by yourself, there is no problem with bringing a friend with you. That way both of you can benefit from the librarian's expertise.

One non-academic office all students must someday use is the **registrar's office**. The registrar's office is in charge of such things as scheduling classes, keeping students' academic records, and evaluating whether students have met the requirements necessary for graduation. If you need a copy of your transcript, you must get this from the registrar. If you change your address, you need to contact the registrar. If you are incorrectly registered for a course, and you cannot correct this on the computer, you will need to go to the registrar's office. Many forms related to class registration are available from the registrar. As usual, when you need to interact with the individuals in this office, be polite and clearly state your problem. It will be easier if you know what to ask for when you get to this office. However, if you do not know what the form you need is called, be prepared to describe it as clearly as possible. Most individuals are happy to help students.

An office that is infrequently visited by students is the **dean's office**. Deans are administrators. They are middle managers in charge of a college. There are different kinds of situations that may involve a visit to the dean's office. Students facing academic dismissal or probation may need to meet with the dean. Students facing disciplinary action may need to meet with the dean. If a student has a complaint about a faculty member, it may be appropriate for the student to meet with the dean.

At other times, it may be necessary for students to go to the dean's office but not see the dean personally. In most colleges there are a number of forms that must be submitted to the dean's office for approval. Permission to participate in research courses, permission to participate in field courses, permission to transfer credits from another college or university might all require forms signed by the dean. In these situations the student will often get information about the forms from a secretary and deliver the forms to a secretary. Being polite to secretaries and getting the necessary information from them is obviously very important. Again, it helps to be prepared before you meet with the secretary. You should be able to say what your goal is. The secretary will then be able to ensure that you complete the correct forms. In these contexts, students often never actually meet the dean.

Sometimes students have problems or need help and do not know which office to contact. That is not a disaster. If you do not know whom to contact for some information, ask a professor. Just be prepared to find out that, for some issues, especially non-academic questions, the professor, too, may not know what office is in charge. If that is the case, ask the secretary of the department in which you are majoring. The secretary will probably either know what office to contact or will know whom to ask.

Successfully Traveling Bureaucratic Pathways

Many students find it takes a while to adjust to college life and college bureaucracies. However, most students do eventually become adept at working with the system. It is important that you learn how to stand up for your rights and have your needs met—while doing so in a polite, friendly manner. College offers much more than classes. Students enjoy the college experience most when they learn how to participate in all that is available.

Suggested Readings and Resources

Alexander, T. (2000). *Adjustment and human relationships.* Upper Saddle River, N. J.: Prentice Hall. (You can find Psychology of Adjustment books in the book store or the library, and you may wish to take the course to polish your interpersonal skills.)

Gambrill, E. D., & Richey, C. A. (1976). *It's up to you: Developing assertive social skills* (pp. 158-159). Millbrae, CA: Les Femmes. (These authors are trailblazers in the area of assertiveness. If you want a self-help book on the topic, we suggest theirs.)

Your college catalogue and student handbook
Your college guide for scheduling
Your college Web site

Suggested Web Sites

http://www.unc.edu/depts/unc_caps/resources.htm The University of North Carolina's Counseling And Psychological Services presents practical information on assertiveness and many other topics. You can access other sites from this page too.

http://ub-counseling.buffalo.edu/stressmanagement.shtml This site provides information on a variety of topics for college students: stress, study skills, procrastination, perfectionism, time management and others.

http://www.shyness.com/ This site presents information on shyness, questionnaires about shyness and links to resources.

Chapter 12

Sex:
Will There Be a Test on This?

My favorite magazine is Cosmo: *100 pages of naked women and a very entertaining quiz.*
—Anonymous male college student

So, have you had sex yet?

Wait, before you answer that, what exactly is meant by "having sex"? Is it kissing, petting, cunnilingus (oral sex performed on a female), fellatio (oral sex performed on a male), anal sex, vaginal intercourse, some of these, all of these...?

When most people talk about having had sex, they tend to be referring to vaginal intercourse. But does it really make sense to limit discussion of sexuality to only one activity? Doesn't sex involve a variety of behaviors in addition to intercourse, from kissing and touching to cunnilingus and fellatio? In addition, does it really make sense to limit sex to a heterosexual activity, vaginal intercourse, implying that homosexual individuals then do not have sex? Before continuing, complete this **Quiz** and check the answers on p. 135.

Sex Quiz
How much do you really know about sex?

T F   1. Cunnilingus and fellatio are practiced by very few people in our culture.
T F   2. Most college students have engaged in vaginal intercourse.
T F   3. Diaphragms are as effective as condoms in protecting against STDs, including HIV.
T F   4. Very few, for example, less than 10%, of 18- and 19-year-olds are virgins.
T F   5. Most college students have engaged in anal intercourse.
T F   6. One cannot get STDs from oral sex.
T F   7. Most students are influenced in some way by their friends' values.
T F   8. Gay men and lesbians may face pressures that straight students do not have to address.
T F   9. Students almost never get useful information about sex from their peers.
T F 10. Any difference in values between you and your friends is bad.

Clearly, a discussion of sex can include a variety of behaviors. But such a discussion is still incomplete. Sex involves far more than behavior. Most people have some emotional involvement with the individuals with whom they have sex. Many issues arise from the complex interactions between individuals engaged in a sexual relationship. Because of the complexity of the topic of sexuality, this chapter is divided into two sections. The first section addresses ways "having sex" may be defined and what issues you might want to think about before engaging in these behaviors. Because peoples' decisions are often strongly influenced by their friends and associates, the second section of this chapter addresses peer pressure and how to balance the behavior and attitudes of your friends with your own values.

What is "Sex"?
And What to Think About When Deciding to "Do It"

Writing Activity 12.1—What is "Having Sex"? Recently there has been some debate about what it means to "have sex." Write down the activities that YOU feel fall under this heading. Write down WHY you feel these activities are examples of "having sex." There is no right answer for this: include only what you feel to be appropriate.

Oral sex

Data indicate that the majority of college students have engaged in either cunnilingus, fellatio, or both (e.g., Friant, Astor-Stetson, & Beck, 1996). Why college students may engage in these behaviors seems pretty obvious—they can be quite pleasurable for oneself and one's partner. In addition, many people think that oral sex does not really count as sex. People may hold this belief first because oral sex does not involve the kind of penetration found in vaginal or anal sex, and second because there is absolutely no risk of pregnancy. Some people debate whether people who have engaged in oral sex are still virgins. The debate seems fairly ridiculous. What is more significant is that individuals decide on the sexual behaviors they deem appropriate for themselves. Once individuals decide what behaviors they will engage in, they should protect themselves and their partners from the negative outcomes that may result from these behaviors—that is, disease and unwanted pregnancy.

It is established that oral sex cannot make one pregnant. However, can one acquire sexually transmissible diseases (STDs) from oral sex? Unfortunately, the answer is clearly "yes." The chances of getting STDs, including HIV, from oral sex are less than the chances of getting STDs from vaginal or anal sex; however, the chances are not zero. Oral sex is a physically intimate activity. It involves sharing body fluids with another individual. It is probably not a very good idea to share body fluids with lots of other people. **Imagine going to a party and allowing 20 people to spit in a cup and then drinking it.** Disgusting, isn't it? Just as the exchange of body fluids can be avoided during intercourse, and the risk of disease decreased, the exchange can also be avoided during oral sex. Men can wear a condom during fellatio. There are also female condoms available that can help prevent exposure to vaginal fluids during cunnilingus. Some people report using plastic wrap instead of female condoms. There are no methods that guarantee you can avoid STDs, but you can reduce your risks.

Vaginal intercourse

This is, of course, the activity most people think of when they are asked "what is sex?". It is also an activity in which the majority of college students have engaged. Data indicate that about 70% of 18-19 year olds have engaged in intercourse (e.g., Singh & Darroch, 1999). However, if you have not had intercourse, you are obviously not in a tiny minority; the other 30% of 18-19 year olds are virgins (Singh & Darroch).

For those of you who do engage in vaginal intercourse, there are still many issues that you should consider in terms of your sexual behavior. For example, are you in a stable relationship? If the answer is "yes," you may wish to continue the sexual component of your relationship as it is. If the answer is "no," you may want to think about some criteria you will use to decide which sexual behaviors you will engage in with new individuals. For example, will you engage in *casual* sex (that is, sex with someone whom you do not know well)? If you answer "yes," what kind of sex would you have casually? Intercourse? Cunnilingus? Fellatio? Do you carry protection (e.g., condoms) with you in the event you have the opportunity for a casual encounter? Or would you not engage in casual sex at all? If you would not, what might be your criteria for when you would again engage in intercourse? It may not be realistic, or even a good idea, to have a rigid list of all the traits a relationship must have before you will engage in specific sexual behaviors. However, it probably is a good idea to have general values that you are comfortable with to guide your behaviors. And it is very foolish to have unprotected sex in any circumstances—unless you are in a relationship, probably marital, in which you wish to get pregnant!

If you are not yet engaging in intercourse, there are several issues that you may want to consider. First, people have not engaged in intercourse for a variety of different reasons. Some people are waiting until they are married to have intercourse. Some people are just waiting for the opportunity to have intercourse. And some people are not waiting for marriage, but neither are they just waiting for the first possible opportunity to have sex. In which category do you fall?

If you are waiting for marriage, you still might want to think about the kinds of activities you wish to engage in and the circumstances in which you will perform them. For example, will you engage in kissing, hugging, petting, oral sex? Will you do some of these casually? Do you need to be in a serious relationship?

If you are a person just waiting for the opportunity to have intercourse, you still might want to think about what would be an appropriate situation for sex and who would be an appropriate partner. You also should think about what you will use for protection from pregnancy and STDs.

If you are neither waiting for marriage nor looking forward to having sex at the first possible moment, the issues you need to consider are very similar to those posed for people who are no longer virgins. What kind of relationship do you want for your first sexual experience? Would a casual encounter be acceptable? Do you want to be in love? Do you want to have sex with someone you are close to, but love is not a prerequisite? Again, having an explicit list of criteria may not be a realistic or healthy approach to this issue. However, having some idea of what your values are may make this situation less stressful and less confusing. And remember—People can get pregnant the first time they have sex. People can get STDs the first time they have sex. *Do not have sex without protection.*

Special issues facing homosexual students

The section on vaginal intercourse above may seem to have little relevance for gay men or lesbians. However, the section on oral sex can apply equally to heterosexuals or homosexuals. A section on anal sex would also apply to both heterosexuals or gay men—so this is not what this section is about. (OK, because you are probably interested, Friant et al. [1996] found neither gay nor straight college freshmen were likely to engage in anal sex.)

The reason this section is included is that gay men and lesbian students tend to be marginalized on college campuses. This means these students are often not totally accepted by the campus culture. Because gay and lesbian students often do not feel accepted, it may be difficult for these students to be open and honest about their sexual preferences; they may be afraid of how people are going to treat them. Given the fact that people have been killed just because of their sexual preferences, these fears are understandable. However, when people are afraid to admit who they are, it may be difficult for them to meet people to date. In addition, when people feel they cannot really discuss who they are, it may be difficult for them to form close friendships, which is true even for those that are not sexual. Also, if it is difficult to be open about being a gay man or a lesbian, then it is going to be difficult to get information or advice about sexual behaviors or relationships.

What is most significant about the sexual relationships that gay men or lesbians have is simply that they are sexual relationships. All the issues, with the exception of pregnancy, that were discussed for people already engaging in vaginal intercourse or people not yet involved in vaginal intercourse still apply. What kind of relationships are you comfortable with? With what kind of person do you want to have a relationship? What kinds of activities do you wish to engage in and under what circumstances? And, of course, do you have protection from STDs? Again, having some idea of your values, including what kind of relationship you want and what kinds of activities you wish to engage in, will make decisions about sexual relationships easier.

Peer Pressure

We are what we pretend to be, so we must be careful what we pretend to be. —Kurt Vonnegut, Jr.

By now, you have probably given some thought to your values and the kinds of sexual behaviors that are consistent with those values. But decisions like when and with whom to have sex are also influenced by other people. Clearly, a person who wishes to have sex with you may try to convince you to agree. Even the behaviors, attitudes and expectations of your friends and acquaintances—people with whom you have no form of sexual relationship—will influence your decisions. Sometimes, when your values and the values of others conflict, you may feel a great deal of pressure to conform to the expectations of the other people. Sometimes, when exposed to the ideas and behaviors of other people, you may willingly change your own opinions. The function of this section is to discuss some ideas about how other people may influence your behavior —and to encourage you to not just blindly go along with the crowd. Rather, consider what are your values, compare them to the values of other people, and make a reasonable decision about what will be good for you. To think about these questions, you may wish to complete this.

Writing Activity 12.2—How are your friends' *values* similar to your own? How are they different? You may wish to list the similarities and differences below.
Similarities:

Differences:

How are your friends' *behaviors* similar to your own? How are they different? You may wish to list the similarities and differences below.
Similarities:

Differences:

Do any of the differences between your friends and you make you uncomfortable?

Do you feel pressured to change because of these differences?

The first half of this chapter emphasized thinking about your values concerning the types of sexual activities in which you wish to engage. Why? So you can develop an idea of what you *do* and *do not* want to do *BEFORE* you are confronted with the varying attitudes of your peers.

This is not meant to imply that your peers will have only a negative influence on you. Sometimes peers can be excellent resources. They can provide you with points of view you may never have considered. For example, many students with gay friends are surprised to find their gay friends have the same kinds of positive and negative characteristics that their straight friends have. Peers can give you information you are unlikely to get from other sources; for example, where reliable condom machines are located. Peers can advise you about potential sex partners and how you might want to act with them. Problems arise when your peers are either acting in a way that makes you uncomfortable or when they are pressuring you to act in an uncomfortable way.

What do you do when your friends act in a way that makes you uncomfortable? Of course, there is no one answer for this. If your friends' behaviors are not harmful to you or themselves, you probably need to do nothing. For example, if a friend has mentioned his intention of being a virgin until he gets married, that is none of your concern. If another friend is having sex with someone she is fond of but not in love with, again, that is probably none of your concern. When does it become your concern? If the behavior is harmful to a friend or to others, that is worthy of concern. If a friend inappropriately imposes his or her beliefs on you, that too is worthy of concern.

If a friend is acting in a dangerous manner, for example getting drunk and picking up strangers for sex, you may want to talk to your friend about it. If the friend is bringing these sex partners back to your room, even if you are not there at the time, you definitely want to talk to your friend. You also might want to call you college counseling center, or another agency, to see what they can suggest.

If friends impose their beliefs on you, you do not have to passively accept that. It does not matter whether those beliefs are more conservative than your own or less conservative than your own. Discuss with your friends the basis for your beliefs. Ask them to respect your choices. If, on the other hand, they can demonstrate that your behaviors may in fact be endangering you, seriously consider what your friends are saying.

Writing Activity 12.3—What are you friends' expectations? How do you think someone might feel in each of the following situations?
1. It is Thursday night. Joe wants to stay home and study. His friends are going to a party with the main goal of picking up women. They tease Joe about what a loser he is as they leave.

---

2. Janet spent two hours with a very interesting guy at a party. He asked her to his room. She was not comfortable with that and so turned him down. He said "OK," left her, and started hitting on someone else.

Neither of the characters in these situations must comply with what their peers expect; Joe does not have to go to the party; Janet does not have to go to the man's room. However, both are being pressured to conform to meet other people's goals. Although the pressure to conform in these examples is obvious, it is not always so clear. When a group of friends tells another friend that they do not mind when that friend chooses studying over partying, it is still clear to the studious friend that the expectation is to party. When a group tells a friend that it's so interesting that she wants to be a virgin until she is married, it is clear to the virgin that her choice is not a popular one. Sometimes, individuals are not even aware that the differences between their values and someone else's values may cause the other person to feel pressured. Are people influenced by this kind of peer pressure? Do the expectations of others have an effect on behavior? The answer is: "OF COURSE!!"

Writing Activity 12.4—Think about some situations in which your expectations and your friends' expectations may differ. How do your friends express their differences with you? How do you express your differences with your friends? Do you think you may have ever pressured someone to conform to your expectations? Can you think of examples in which you did this *intentionally*? Can you think of examples in which you might have *unintentionally* pressured a friend?

Other people's expectations may or may not directly cause people to change their behaviors. However, all of us have probably given in to our peers' expectations at some point. Even when people do not change their behaviors, they still probably give some thought to what their friends expect. This is a context in which it helps to know what your own values are. If you have thought about your own views, you will be better able to recognize when what you want and what your friends want differ. You will be better able to make a choice with which you are comfortable.

To further consider the topics in this chapter, use the Exercise which follows to think or write about how you would act in each of the situations.

In the present chapter statistics on sexual behavior were presented, issues to consider when entering a sexual relationship were discussed, and some ways peers might influence your decisions were detailed. Chapters 13 and 14 on alcohol and other drugs will remind you that you may not always be thinking straight when you meet people with whom you may or may not want to have a sexual relationship!

Here are the answers for the Sex Quiz at the beginning of the chapter:
1. F **2.** T **3.** F **4.** F **5.** F **6.** F **7.** T **8.** T **9.** F **10.** F

Exercise: *Write your responses for each of the five situations that follow.*

(1) **Imagine you are in a relationship with someone you really like. This person is pressuring you to have intercourse. You do not want to do that—at least, not yet. You do want to maintain the relationship, but you are afraid your partner is going to drop you if you do not have sex.**

1. What do you think you would feel in this situation?

2. What would you say to your partner?

3. What do you think you would do?

Now imagine that YOU are pressuring your partner to have intercourse, but he/she is unwilling to do it. You really like this person.

1. What do you think you would feel in this situation?

2. What will you say?

3. What will you do?

(2) A friend of yours regularly goes out, gets drunk, and brings strangers to bed.

1. What do you think you would feel in this situation?

2. What would you say to your friend?

3. What do you think you would do?

(3) You have just found out that a friend of the opposite sex is gay.

1. What do you think you would feel in this situation?

2. What would you say to your friend?

3. What do you think you would do?

(4) You have just found out that a friend, who is of the same sex as you, is gay. This friend has never made sexual overtures to you.

1. What do you think you would feel in this situation?

2. What would you say to your friend?

3. What do you think you would do?

(5) You have a friend who uses people for sex. This friend regularly lies to people—talking about love, commitment, and sharing—just to get them into bed. Once your friend has made a sexual conquest, the lover is tossed away.

1. What do you think you would feel in this situation?

2. What would you say to your friend?

3. What do you think you would do?

Now imagine that your friend encourages you to adopt the same strategy.

1. What do you think you would feel in this situation?

2. What would you say to your friend?

3. What do you think you would do?

Suggested Readings

Friant, P., Astor-Stetson, E., & Beck, B. (1996). *A comparison of the safe sex behaviors of a college community and an adult homosexual community.* Poster session presented at the meeting of the Eastern Psychological Association, Philadelphia, PA.

Singh, S., & Darroch, J. (1999). Trends in sexual activity among adolescent women: 1982-1995. *Family Planning Perspectives, 31,* 212-219.

Suggested Web Sites

http://www.psychwatch.com/ This site is one of the best we've found to contain information on all areas of psychology and to give you access to other Web sites of interest. You can sign up to receive a free newsletter every Friday that contains links to news releases on research and books for that week. You can also search the archives for earlier news releases, and there are tutorials on many topics.

http://health.org (Prevline: prevention online) This site provides many links related to risk prevention. Information is provided on topics as diverse as drug use, teen issues, gay and lesbian issues, parenting, and multiculturalism.

http://healthfinder.gov This page provided by the U.S. Department of Health and Human Services provides excellent links to information on teens, families, and mental and physical health.

http://www.nyacyouth.org The focus of this site is on advocacy for gay, lesbian, bisexual, and transgendered individuals.

http://www.pflag.org Information is presented for gay and lesbian individuals and their families and friends.

Chapter 13

Drugs:
What are the Facts? What are the Risks?

Caution: Cape does not enable user to fly. — Batman costume warning label

A few of the students reading this will never have a drink or take any drug that was not prescribed for them by a doctor. They should read this chapter anyway. Why? Because the vast majority of students will take some kind of consciousness-altering substance (i.e., drugs or alcohol) for non-medical use. Therefore, almost everyone will have the experience of interacting with someone under the influence of drugs or alcohol.

Writing Activity 13.1—*What drugs do people use recreationally?* List all the drugs that the people you know use recreationally, that is for fun, not for medicine. Be honest. DO NOT write down people's names!

One chapter cannot describe in detail all the drugs available for recreational use on college campuses. This chapter will, therefore, address only a few commonly used drugs. It will also focus on more general issues: how to recognize and resist peer pressure and how to stay safe.

The drugs that will be covered here include alcohol, marijuana, stimulants (such as cocaine and amphetamines), and club drugs (such as Ecstasy and Rohypnol). These drugs were included either because they have been found to be very commonly used, as is the case with alcohol and marijuana, or because they are currently of major concern, such as the club drugs.

Before you go on, complete the **Quiz** on the next page about your knowledge of these drugs. Some students are very knowledgeable; others know less than they realize. Where do you fall? After completing the **Quiz**, check the answers on p. 147.

Quiz on Alcohol and Other Drugs
How much do you really know about alcohol and other drugs?

T F 1. Most high school students have not consumed alcohol.

T F 2. Despite what most people say, having food in your stomach does NOT influence the effects of alcohol.

T F 3. Recent surveys indicate very few teenagers (less than 20%) have smoked marijuana.

T F 4. Marijuana has been found to be useful medically.

T F 5. Smoking marijuana can result in an overdose of the drug.

T F 6. Smoking and injecting cocaine are more dangerous than inhaling cocaine.

T F 7. Use of Ritalin is always illegal.

T F 8. Although roofies are unlikely to be fatal when taken alone, they can cause death when mixed with alcohol.

T F 9. Ecstasy is a hallucinogenic.

T F 10. Research indicates that Ecstasy poses no long-term health risks.

Alcohol

Alcohol is by far the drug used most frequently by high school and college students. National surveys (e.g., Centers for Disease Control, 1996) indicate that over 80% of high school students have had at least one drink. The chances are very high, then, that you have had a drink or, at the least, that you know someone who has done so. However, college students frequently do not simply limit themselves to a drink. It has been found that 45% of 21-year-olds binge drink (Substance Abuse and Mental Health Services, 1999). That means these students drink more than five drinks for men or four drinks for women during one occasion. Given how common drinking is among college students, is it really a bad thing? Could so many people engage in a behavior that is harmful?

In order to answer that question, just what alcohol does to the body must first be addressed (McKim, 1997). Basically, when an individual takes a drink, the alcohol goes into the digestive system where it is absorbed into the bloodstream. The amount of alcohol in the bloodstream can be measured; it is assumed that one's blood alcohol level is related to the degree to which one is affected by the alcohol. The higher one's blood alcohol level, the more drunk one is. A number of factors seem to affect blood alcohol levels. Alcohol seems to be absorbed most easily not from the stomach, but from the small intestine. If the alcohol stays in the stomach, it is subjected to chemical reactions that break it down. This means that if an individual has food in his or her stomach, less alcohol will be absorbed into the blood and so the alcohol will be less likely to have an effect on the individual. In addition, food in the stomach will result in the alcohol going to the small intestine more slowly. So, again, blood alcohol levels will be lower, and the effect the alcohol has on the individual will take place over a period of time. This is why people get drunk faster when they drink on an empty stomach. If there is no food in an individual's stomach, the alcohol passes to the small intestine quickly, very little of the alcohol is broken down, and the alcohol has a large effect quickly.

A number of other factors also affect blood alcohol levels and so affect the influence alcohol has on the individual (Kuhn, Swartzwelder, & Wilson, 1998). For example, women seem to metabolize alcohol differently than men do. If a woman and a man of the same size have the same amount to drink, the woman will probably have a higher blood alcohol level than the man will. Weight also influences blood alcohol level. In general, bigger people can absorb more alcohol than can smaller people.

Once the alcohol is absorbed into the bloodstream, it is distributed throughout the body, including the brain (Kuhn, Swartzwelder, & Wilson, 1998). The effects of alcohol on the brain are apparently inhibitory; that is, the alcohol makes the firing of nerve cells less likely. Overall, alcohol can result in either positive or negative outcomes. The negative effects of alcohol impact a number of bodily systems, for example, physical coordination, cognitive skills, and sexual functioning. Alcohol consumption can make one clumsy. It can interfere with memory and problem solving. It can result in decreased sexual desire and decreased sexual performance. More specifically, five drinks in an hour may result in an individual suffering slower reaction times, slower reflexes, impaired fine motor coordination, impaired judgment, slurred speech, and nausea. Sixteen drinks in an hour may put the individual into a coma. Twenty-five drinks in an hour can kill the person.

On the positive side, a couple of drinks can make a person feel happy and relaxed. If you are a middle-aged man, a glass of wine with dinner might be good for your heart.

What can be concluded about college students' drinking? Could all those students engaging in heavy drinking be wrong? The answer is "yes." Far too often students binge drink. Binge drinking can interfere with thinking, with coordination, and with sexual performance. It can even kill. It is not a good thing. Because alcohol is such a frequently used drug by college students, Chapter 14 will discuss the personal and social impact of alcohol in more detail.

Marijuana

Researchers have discovered that chocolate produces
some of the same reactions in the brain as marijuana.
The researchers also discovered other similarities
between the two, but can't remember what they are.
— Matt Lauer, of NBC's "Today" show

Marijuana is by far the most widely used illegal drug. Recent surveys indicate 40% of teenagers have tried marijuana (Partnership for a Drug Free America, 2003). Over 62% of 16- and 17-year-olds know someone who has used marijuana (Substance Abuse and Mental Health Services, 1999). What is known about this very popular drug?

Unlike alcohol, marijuana cannot result in death due to overdose (Kuhn, Swartzwelder, & Wilson, 1998). However, it does have a number of effects on the body. Marijuana is usually, although not always, smoked. The active ingredient in marijuana, THC, is absorbed from the lungs into the bloodstream. From there, it goes, literally, right to your head. If one eats the marijuana instead of smoking it, the effects will be less immediate. First, the THC will not go as quickly to the brain. Second, because of the digestive process, some of the THC will be broken down before it has an effect. A given amount of THC smoked will have a greater, but shorter, effect on an individual than will the same amount of eaten THC.

Once ingested, THC has a number of effects on the brain and other parts of the body (Kuhn, Swartzwelder, & Wilson, 1998). There is evidence indicating that marijuana interferes with memory. It decreases the ability to concentrate. It causes changes in perception. THC may also affect hormone production, which in turn may affect sperm count. THC speeds up the heart rate. And, of course, when smoked, it affects the lungs. Evidence indicates that smoking THC may cause lung cancer.

Are there positive uses for marijuana? The answer is "yes." Marijuana relieves nausea associated with chemotherapy. It decreases pressure in the eyes of people with glaucoma, a disorder of the eye that may result in blindness. Some research has looked at the use of marijuana for treating pain. Although positive uses for marijuana are documented, you must keep two points in mind. First, there are also negative effects of marijuana. And second, in most instances, marijuana use is illegal.

Stimulants

There are many different kinds of stimulants. Stimulants cause increases in energy, alertness, and feelings of well-being. The most widely used stimulants are cocaine, amphetamines, and methamphetamines (Kuhn, Swartzwelder, & Wilson, 1998). Ritalin, which is often used to treat children and adolescents with Attention Deficit Disorder, is also a stimulant (methcathinone). Many researchers believe that recreational use of Ritalin is increasing because of its availability: people prescribed Ritalin may sell pills to their friends; siblings of children prescribed Ritalin may help themselves to a few pills; etc.

Stimulants come in a wide variety of different forms, including leaves, powders, pills, and rocks. Amphetamine and methamphetamine are most often either powders or pills. Cocaine is most often either powdered cocaine or crack cocaine, which is in the form of chunks.

The means of ingesting stimulants has a major impact on how fast the drug gets into the bloodstream. Powdered stimulants are generally, but not always, either inhaled (that is, snorted), injected, or swallowed (i.e., in capsules). Crack cocaine is smoked. Smoking and injecting distribute the drug to the brain more efficiently than do snorting or swallowing. Snorting, in turn, is often more efficient than swallowing since the digestive process will decrease the strength of the drug. Because of the speed with which the drug enters the system, smoked or injected drugs are more likely to result in addiction or overdose.

Once in the body, stimulants have effects on the brain. They apparently affect the chemicals that *neurons* (nerve cells) use to communicate with each other. The changes in the brain result in other changes in the rest of the body. Sleep is suppressed. People report feeling energized and alert. Mood is reported to improve. However, not all of the effects are good.

Heart rate and blood pressure increase. Body movements and talking increase. High doses of amphetamines or cocaine can cause people to develop psychotic symptoms. People suffering from amphetamine psychosis may report delusions. For example, they may believe other people are out to get them. They may have hallucinations, for example, hearing voices that are not there. Some people showing psychotic symptoms as a result of cocaine abuse report the feeling that bugs are crawling under their skin. Stimulants can also be addictive. When one is addicted, once the drug is not taken, one will go into withdrawal. Overdosing on stimulants can result in death.

Club Drugs: Rohypnol and Ecstasy

The two drugs that are covered in this section are not similar pharmacologically. However, they are similar in where many people tend to use them (e.g., bars, clubs, raves).

Rohypnol

Rohypnol (roofies) is known as a "date rape" drug. It is a benzodiazepine, a kind of sedative. Sedatives depress the functioning of the central nervous system. They seem to effect GABA, a chemical in the brain whose function is inhibitory: it signals neurons that they should not fire. The depressive effect of Rohypnol may be enhanced when the drug is mixed with alcohol. For example, Rohypnol will probably not cause death due to overdose when taken alone. However, when taken with alcohol, it can be fatal.

Rohypnol, like the other benzodiazepines, is usually available in pill form. Also like the other benzodiazepines, it causes tiredness and clumsiness, and it interferes with memory. Unlike other benzodiazepines, it dissolves easily in alcohol. It is because of this last effect, combined with the effects on memory, that there have been cases reported in which women have been raped and have had no memory of the event. It seems that Rohypnol was dissolved in the drinks of these women without their knowledge. If these women had consumed large amounts of alcohol before ingesting the Rohypnol, it could have killed them.

Ecstasy

I'd stay away from Ecstasy.
This is a drug so strong it makes white people think they can dance. — Lenny Henry

Ecstasy is also available in the club scene. About 10% of teenagers have tried this drug (Partnership for a Drug Free America, 2003). Ecstasy, known pharmacologically as MDMA, is an amphetamine that was created in the laboratory. It has complex effects on the chemicals in the brain. Many people report great feelings of well-being when taking Ecstasy. Some people believe it is the perfect drug: it makes you feel wonderful and has no major, negative side effects. However, this assumption is not clearly true.

At high doses Ecstasy may cause damage to internal organs such as the heart or kidneys. As is the case with other stimulants, high doses may also result in amphetamine psychosis. Whether Ecstasy can cause permanent brain damage is not resolved. Increasing evidence indicates Ecstasy may, in fact, have long term effects on some chemicals in the brain.

How to Resist Peer Pressure

It is easier to resist at the beginning than at the end. — Leonardo Da Vinci

Let's face it, the majority of college students engage in under-age drinking. Large numbers also smoke marijuana or know someone who does. The first step, then, in determining how to resist peer pressure is to decide just what behaviors are those in which you wish to engage. For example, if you plan to neither drink nor take drugs, that's wonderful. If you plan to drink socially, but not to get drunk….well, that may not be legal, but it may be honest. If you plan to get drunk, you might want to rethink that—you definitely want to take precautions to keep yourself out of danger. Take a moment to think about it now: What are the behaviors that you think are appropriate for *you*?

Having clearly articulated standards for your own behavior will help you adhere to those standards. It will be less easy for someone to convince you to do something questionable when you *know* you do not want to do it. But sometimes peer pressure can be very forceful. What do you do when you are at a party where everyone but you seems to be drinking? What do you do when people are smoking pot and offer you some? What do you do if people seem to exclude you from social activities because you will not "party" by consuming drugs or alcohol?

One way to resist peer pressure is to think of scenes where you may be offered drugs and alcohol and create dialogue for yourself. That is, think of yourself as similar to an actor in a play. What would you say in scenes of given types? If you have friends with values similar to your own, it would help to role play these scenes with those friends. You might even want to practice with family members. Of course, when you go to the party, or club, or rave—where you might find yourself in the situation of turning down drugs or alcohol, the experience will not be identical to the scenes you have constructed. However, at least you will have had *some* practice in handling the situation; you will also have some phrases that may be useful.

Complete the **Exercise** at the end of the chapter. These role-playing situations will help you to articulate your own values about using drugs and alcohol. You can also develop some possible responses to use when faced with situations where drugs are used.

Creating dialogue for yourself is only one step in resisting peer pressure. Another way to resist peer pressure is to avoid situations where you will be pressured. If certain parties are notorious for the drugs and alcohol available, maybe you do not want to attend those events. Unfortunately, this will not always work. You may attend an event where you do not expect to find drugs but they are there. In situations like this, it always helps to have social support. That means, it helps to have other people with you who will back you up.

On college campuses there are many different people with many kinds of values. The chances are you will be able to find people whose standards are similar to your own. One place to find people with similar values is in extracurricular activities. For example, if you are an athlete whose coach has a strictly enforced "no drinking, no drugs" policy, your team members will be facing the same regulations. They will certainly support your decision to abstain from drugs and alcohol at social events. If they do not, you probably do not want to go out with them. Another place where you may meet people with standards similar to your own is in the classes in your major. Often, particular majors attract individuals with similar goals. For example, students majoring in social work are not usually motivated primarily by money. They are interested in helping people. You may find that other values are shared by people in your major.

When you have identified friends who share your beliefs, it is very wise to go to parties with them. You can all support each other in your decisions. It is also more difficult for other people to try to change the minds of a group as opposed to an individual. In fact, once you are in a group, it is not likely that anyone will question your decisions.

You might want to consider a final strategy for avoiding peer pressure. This may not be as effective or well-thought-out as the others, but it can work in some situations. Basically, you can lie. You can be drinking a soda, but tell someone offering you a beer that you are having a mixed drink. When offered marijuana, you can say you have already had enough. It may be better to use the strategies suggested above, but if you find yourself in a situation where those are either unavailable or not working, do what you have to do to maintain your standards.

Keeping Safe

There are a number of ways in which you want to keep safe. These range from not drinking and driving, to not falling victim to Rohypnol, to not getting in trouble with the law.

Let's address the last issue first because, in some ways, it is the easiest. If you do not want to get in legal trouble, do not break the law. Do not use illegal drugs. Do not drink under age. Bear in mind, once you are 18 years old, you are legally an adult, even if you cannot legally drink. It may not seem fair, but that is reality. Furthermore, convictions for drug use, even for use of marijuana, may eliminate your ability to enter certain careers. Is it worth it?

What are other dangers you might face, and how may you keep yourself safe? Physical dangers are an unfortunate reality when it comes to drug and alcohol use. Accidents are the leading cause of death of young adults. And many of those accidents are related to alcohol or drugs. However, you do not have to get into an accident for drugs or alcohol to result in your death. As indicated in the descriptions of the drugs presented above, many of them can be fatal if consumed in high amounts or if used with other substances. Clearly these dangers apply regardless of the age of the individual involved or the legality of the substance being used—people over 21 can die of alcohol poisoning or in alcohol-related accidents. How can this be avoided?

145

Almost everyone has heard about "designated drivers." These are the people who have agreed to not drink or drug at a party so they can safely drive their drunk friends home. This is a very good idea, even if you and your friends are not driving to the party. However, it takes a little planning and a little self-control. People need to decide in advance on the group of people with whom they will attend the party. They then need to agree on who will be the designated driver. Students who effectively use this strategy either have a friend who does not care to drink or they rotate who is the designated drive. If most of the people in the group would like to drink, just think how little peer pressure—and how much social support—the non-drinker in the group will get!!

Writing Activity 13.2—*Designated Drivers*. Make a list of the friends with whom you like to attend parties. Think about which of these friends you would trust to be a designated driver.

Develop a tentative rotation for designated drivers.

Of course, many people reading this chapter may be thinking that since they do not drive to parties, they do not need a designated non-drinker. They are wrong. Other things can happen if no one is sober enough to realize when there is a problem.

If everyone at a party is drunk, how likely are they to notice if someone has alcohol poisoning? Can one drunken student determine that another drunken student has consumed far too much and may be risking death? Can a drunken student adequately evaluate whether the breathing of another student is so labored that maybe it would be a good idea to call an ambulance? If a student passes out due to alcohol consumption, will that person's drunk friends have the presence of mind to turn the student on his or her side and so reduce the risk of their friend *aspirating* (that means choking on your own vomit)? This may sound gross, but it does happen and can kill the person. Some of this could be avoided if there are sober people at the party—the designated non-drinkers. The non-drinkers will still have the cognitive capacity to make decisions about a friend's safety. It is an enormous responsibility, but it is well worth it.

Designated non-drinkers can also help their friends in other ways. Have you ever known anyone who got drunk at a party and ended up having unprotected sex with a stranger? Hopefully, your friends will not find themselves in this situation but many people have done exactly that. A designated non-drinker may help prevent this from happening. An agreement about appropriate sexual behavior should be made between friends before the party. If the non-drinker then sees a friend engaging in questionable activities, such as going to a stranger's room, the non-drinker can intercept the couple. Some people feel such a scenario applies only to women. NOT SO. Many young men have found themselves in similar, highly uncomfortable positions.

Related to this situation, non-drinkers can help their friends avoid being victims of date rape or of being accused of date rape. Drunken people are often unable to protect themselves. Or they make poor decisions about whom to spend time with alone. Or they may make poor decisions about places to go alone. A sober friend may be able to intervene. Similarly, drunken individuals are more likely than sober people to misread signals sent to them by others. One may engage in what was perceived to be consensual sex only to find out later that it was less than that. Again, a sober friend may be able to intervene and prevent an unfortunate sexual encounter from taking place between two drunken students. This is not to say students cannot meet potential dates at a party. However, it is probably best to postpone decisions about intimate activities, like sex, until both parties are sober. If you meet someone who is unwilling to wait to make a decision like this, do you really want to have sex with that person? Do you think you would be very good at answering this question when you are drunk? Might it be nice to have a sober friend watching out for you? One sober person at a party cannot take care of everyone. However, if enough people stay sober, and if enough people assume responsibility for themselves and their friends, some problems can be avoided.

A final suggestion for safety involves Rohypnol and other possible drugs that may be added to drinks. Basically, do not leave your drinks unattended. Do not accept drinks from strangers. If someone pushes a drink into your hand, say "thank you," put the drink down, and do not consume it. If your drink has been unattended, throw it out and get a new drink. Even if the probability of being drugged is low, it is not worth taking a chance.

The reality is that most college students will drink and many will use some kind of illegal drug. Make your own decisions about these issues. Do not allow others to force you conform to their values. And, regardless of the decisions you make, try to keep yourself and your friends safe.

Here are the answers for the Drugs and Alcohol Quiz at the beginning of the chapter: 1. F 2. F 3. F 4. T 5. F 6. T 7. F 8. T 9. F 10. F

Exercise: Role play. What follows are four possible situations in which you may feel pressured to use drugs or alcohol. What would you say or do in each of these situations? Write down some possible conversations that may result in each of these scenes. Consider: What would you say? How do you think the other person would respond? What would you say in return? Etc. Try to be as detailed as possible. After you have written your responses, try to find someone with whom you can act out each of the situations.

Role Play: Scene One

1. You are at a party where there is clearly a lot of drinking. An attractive individual approaches you and asks if you want a drink. You do not want one, but it seems that this is the way the individual is trying to get to meet you—and you do find the person attractive!

Role Play: Scene Two

2. You are at a party and a very drunk individual asks you why you are not drinking.

Role Play: Scene Three

3. You want to have a single drink, but a friend starts teasing you about "Is that all you're having? You're such a wimp…"

Role Play: Scene Four

4. A lot of people you know are using illegal drugs. They start to harass you about "Narking them out."

Suggested Readings

Kuhn, C., Swartzwelder, S., & Wilson, W. (1998). *Buzzed*. New York: Norton.

Suggested Web Sites

http://www.psychwatch.com/ This site is one of the best for information on all areas of psychology and access to other Web sites of interest. You can sign up to receive a free newsletter every Friday that contains links to news releases on research and books for that week. You can also search the archives for earlier news releases, and there are tutorials on many topics.

http://www.cdc.gov/tobacco This site provides information and links specifically on tobacco use.

http://www.samhsa.gov This is the Web site of the Substance Abuse and Mental Health Services Administration. A wide variety of information, from statistics on drug use to treatment facilities, can be found here.

http://www.unc.edu/depts/unc_caps/resources.htm The University of North Carolina's Counseling And Psychological Services presents practical information on a wide variety of topics of interest to students, including substance abuse, assertiveness, and helping a friend. You can access other sites from this page too.

http://www.miami.edu/ctrada/   See this site for the University of Miami Center for Treatment Research on Adolescent Drug Abuse for treatment programs for adolescent substance abuse.

http://health.org Prevline: Prevention Online This site provides many links related to risk prevention, including the topic of drug use.

http://www.cdc.gov This site from the Center for Disease Control and Prevention provides information on a wide variety of public health issues, including substance abuse and disease.

http://healthguide.com HealthCenter.com presents links to information on mental health and substance abuse topics.

http://www.drugfreeamerica.org This site for the Partnership for a Drug-Free America provides, news, research, resources and advice to children, adolescents, and adults.

http://safety1st.org This site takes a pragmatic approach to drug use, assuming that some adolescents will take—or consider taking—drugs. The focus of this site is on how to stay safe.

Chapter 14

Alcohol and Your College Life
or "I Wonder What Happened in College?"

My roommate and I went to a party, and she got drunk. She hooked up with this guy from the fraternity and had sex with him that night. I couldn't have stopped her because she would have gotten mad. The next day we found out that the guy is seeing someone else and is known all around campus for taking advantage of girls when they're drunk.
— Anonymous respondent, *Binge Drinking on Campus*, Wechsler et al., 1995

> **Test for Self-Awareness**—Before reading further, complete and score the TWEAK on p. A45 (Russell, 1994) and Alcohol: Reasons for Using Scale on p. A47 (Schick, Astor-Stetson, & Beck, 1996). This will help you understand and apply the information in this chapter.

Let's Look at a Few Facts about Drinking….

If someone asked you whether you had ever broken the law, how would you answer? Would you ignore underage drinking when you answer that question? If you are an "average" college student, you are very likely to have consumed alcohol by now. In fact, the average age for first consuming alcohol is 11 for men and 14 for women! According to the nationwide Monitoring the Future Study (Johnston, O'Malley, & Bachman, 1999a), over 80% of high school seniors had tried alcohol at least once, and 31% of them had consumed five or more drinks on at least one occasion (i.e., had engaged in binge drinking) in the past 2 weeks (Johnston, Bachman, & O'Malley, 1998). In comparison, 65% of high school seniors had smoked cigarettes, 49% had used marijuana, and 9% had used cocaine (Johnston, O'Malley, & Bachman, 1996).

We wanted to include the statistics for high school drinking because many people believe that "college causes drinking." Actually, drinking in high school is a major predictor of drinking in college, and those who drank heavily in high school form their college social group from other heavy drinkers. Experts in the field designate *five* drinks on one occasion for a man and *four* drinks for a woman as **binge drinking** (due to physiological differences in the action of alcohol in men and women and how the number of drinks is related to behavioral and health problems). Based on criteria set by the American Psychiatric Association (2000), one in five frequent binge drinkers (binged over two times in 2 weeks) could be classified with alcohol dependence (the most severe alcohol disorder), compared to one of every 20 students in the overall student population (Knight et al., 2002). Unfortunately, college students are very poor at recognizing when a person is intoxicated (Rosenberg & Nevis, 2000), and regularly-heavy drinkers define bingeing as consuming *one drink more for each sex* than do experts in the field (Wechsler & Kuo,

2000). The risk of riding with an impaired driver is only one risk related to these misconceptions. A conservative estimate is that 1,400 college students are killed every year in alcohol-related accidents (CNN, 2002). In addition to motor vehicle fatalities, overdoses, falls, and drownings also occurred (homicide and suicide deaths were not included in the total). Let's look at some consistent findings from nationwide studies of high school and college students (e.g., Reis & Riley, 2000; Knight et al., 2002; Wechsler, Lee, Kuo, & Lee, 2000).

> Men drink more than women, but just barely; women are only slightly more likely to be abstainers than men. Nearly one in 10 college men under age 24 met a 12-month diagnosis of alcohol dependence compared to one in 20 college women under age 24. However, a recent national study of women age 8 to 22 found the gender gap is narrowing between boys' and girls' use of tobacco, alcohol, and other drugs; 45% of high school girls drink alcohol, compared with 49% of boys, and girls outpace boys in the use of prescription drugs (*USA Today*, 2003; also see Morse, 2002).
> Proportionally, White students drink more than members of other ethnic groups.
> Fraternity members outdrink others, with fraternity house dwellers drinking the most.
> Sorority members outdrink other women, again with sorority house dwellers drinking the most (usually at fraternity house parties).
> For all Greeks, 66% are binge drinkers (80%, if they live in Greek housing). (Also see McCourt & Reifman, 2002; Sher, Bartholow, & Nanda, 2001.)
> Men and women on sports teams outdrink non-athletically-involved counterparts.
> Women who are chronic dieters drink more *total*, *weekly,* and *yearly* alcohol and are more likely to binge drink (Stewart, Angelopoulos, Baker, & Boland, 2000).
> Those who drank heavily in high school also drink heavily in college.
> Those who initiate and become "regular" drinkers (even once a month) at an earlier age drink heavier and are more at risk for alcoholism (e.g., Grant & Dawson, 1997).
> Heavy drinking is related to poorer grades.
> Colleges in Northeastern and North Central states have higher drinking rates than in the West and South (over 50% binge drank in the last 2 weeks at a third of schools).
> Students at residential campuses drink more than those at commuter campuses.
> Unmarried and unengaged students drink the most.

You're probably saying, "What's the problem with drinking *a little* at a party or relaxing with *a beer*?" There really isn't much of a problem for *some* people (other than breaking the law and the rules of your university!). But many of your peers can't or won't stop at just "a beer." In fact, a 1999 nationwide survey (Wechsler, Lee, Kuo, & Lee, 2000) found that far too many college students drank enough to get into trouble *and* to bother nondrinkers around them. In this survey, both abstention and frequent bingeing had increased since 1993 (Wechsler, Davenport, Dowdall, Moeykens, & Castillo, 1994). In 1999, about 19% of students abstained from drinking (in 1993 it was 15%), 44% binged at least once in 2 weeks (same as 1993), and 28% (in 1993 it was 23%) binged frequently (on three or more occasions in the last 2 weeks). There were also increases in the proportion of students who, in the last 2 weeks, had been drunk three or more times, had consumed alcohol on 10 or more days, usually binge drank, and drank to get drunk. Sadly, only 6% of 14,000 students at 119 colleges who could be diagnosed with alcohol dependence reported that they had sought treatment (Knight et al., 2002).

Frequent bingers averaged 14.5 drinks a week and drank 68% of the alcohol students reported consuming (Wechsler, Molnar, Davenport, & Baer, 1999). And besides spending more on alcohol than on text books and nonalcoholic drinks, students who drank reported a large number of alcohol-related problems (Wechsler et al., 2000). Overall, occasional binge drinkers (once or twice in the last 2 weeks) reported 5 times as many problems as non-binge drinkers, and frequent bingers were 15 times as likely to have experienced a problem as were non-bingers. Let's look at alcohol-related problems reported by drinking students in this national study (based on 5,063 non-bingers, 2,963 occasional bingers, and 3,135 frequent bingers, in that order):

➤ Missed a class: 9%, 31%, 63%
➤ Got behind in schoolwork: 10%, 26%, 46%
➤ Did something you regretted: 18%, 40%, 62%
➤ Forgot where you were or what you did: 10%, 27%, 54%
➤ Argued with friends: 10%, 23%, 43%
➤ Engaged in unplanned sexual activities: 8%, 22%, 43%
➤ Didn't use protection when you had sex: 4%, 10%, 20%
➤ Damaged property: 2%, 9%, 20%
➤ Got into trouble with campus or local police: 1%, 5%, 13%
➤ Got hurt or injured: 4%, 11%, 27%
➤ Required medical treatment for an alcohol overdose: 0.3%, 0.8%, 0.9%
➤ Drove after drinking alcohol: 19%, 40%, 57%
➤ Had 5 or more different alcohol-related problems: 4%, 17%, 48%
➤ Used other substances during the past year (from Wechsler et al., 1994): marijuana (13%, 31%, 55%), amphetamines (2%, 4%, 10%), LSD (2%, 5%, 11%), chewing tobacco (4%, 12%, 20%), and cigarettes (22%, 42%, 59%)

Another way to look at alcohol-related problems is to categorize them as *careless*, *reckless*, or *authority-related* (Vik, Carrello, Tate, & Field, 2000). These researchers found that 93% of college binge drinkers reported *careless* problems (e.g., argued or fought, got hurt, damaged property, fell behind in schoolwork, missed classes), 60% reported *reckless* problems (e.g., had unplanned sex, didn't use protection, drove drunk), and 34% had *authority-related* problems (e.g., got into trouble with police or the dorm RA, got arrested). These problems were progressive from careless to authority-related, and those with the latter type of problems drank more often, consumed more when drinking, and had begun drinking regularly at an earlier age.

But, wait! Before congratulating yourself for abstinence, *think about how often you have been bothered in some way by a drunken peer.* Studies find that nondrinking students living in dorms or Greek housing can't escape alcohol-related problems. For instance, in Wechsler et al. (2000) abstainers reported being awakened or kept from studying (58%), having to take care of a drunken peer (50%), or having been assaulted, insulted, or humiliated by a drunk student (29%). Relative to students on low-binge drinking campuses, nondrinkers on high rate campuses were *3 times* more likely to report these problems. In a sample of 6,000 college students (Warshaw, 1988), 75% of male assailants were under the influence of alcohol when they committed a sexual assault, and 55% of victims revealed that they too had consumed alcohol prior to being assaulted. In another survey of college women, Frintner and Rubinson (1993) found that 68% of male offenders and 55% of female victims had been drinking when date rape or sexual assault occurred.

Writing Activity 14.1—Write about a time you suffered either from your own or another's drinking. Did you vow not to get into that spot again? If so, how did friends react to your decision? (If this hasn't happened to you, write about the experience of someone you know.)

Why *Do* So Many Students Drink So Much?

Opportunity may knock only once, but temptation leans on the doorbell.
— Anonymous

Students don't always drink for the same reason. Sometime they want to be with friends or go to a party, and they drink because others do. Sometime they drink alone to drown their sorrows (mostly true for men). Sometime they know in advance that drinking is on the evening's menu. They have positive **expectations** for what alcohol will do for them before drinking. Let's look at reasons students give for drinking (Cooper, 1994; Littrell, 1991; Sudol & Schick, 1999).

➤ "I drink to get drunk" (answer given by over 50% of students in several studies).
➤ "It's what you do when you get together with friends" (i.e., drinking and social interaction are seen as *automatically* going together).
➤ "I'll look older and more worldly if I drink" (hold-over from middle and high school).
➤ "It's what we did when I was growing up" (people from "alcoholic families" are more likely to drink because it's how they learned to socialize—they expect *more* pleasure, enhancement of assertiveness, and control in a social situation and *less* impairment).
➤ "It feels good, is exciting, and relieves boredom" (how often have you heard—or said—this one: "There's nothing else to do here").
➤ "It helps me forget (or avoid) problems, relax, get to sleep, or 'drown my sorrows'."
➤ "It helps me forget mistakes, deal with threats to my ego, and have an excuse if I do something embarrassing or against my value system."
➤ "I have courage to talk to strangers, especially those who look really 'interesting'."

No doubt a big reason why students drink is that, along with attending college to gain skills and information necessary for their planned careers, *they just want to have a good time.* Many studies run in the 1990s asked if students thought their own *or* peers' drinking was a problem. *Even frequent bingers and students who met the criteria for alcohol abuse or dependence felt that drinking and getting drunk wasn't a problem* (e.g., Clements, 1999; Wechsler et al., 2000)! But the finding that more students were abstaining suggests that some had withdrawn from the chaotic drinking scene—they could have fun without going to a drunken party where spilled beer and cigarette smoke were the least of their risks! During the past decade nondrinking student housing—and even "dry" Greek houses—have become more prevalent.

Many schools have tried to make the actual drinking attitudes and behaviors on their campus known to all their students, especially in-coming freshmen. They hoped that students wishing to abstain would be more comfortable in the social scene knowing that "everybody" didn't drink. But such efforts have usually been ineffective. Some studies found that students become more realistic in estimating the drinking habits of peers, but drinking usually stayed about the same or *increased* slightly despite this knowledge (e.g., Johnston, O'Malley, & Bachman, 1999b; Werch et al., 2000). Although nondrinkers may be slightly deterred from starting and light drinkers may gain the courage not to binge, the students most at risk academically and physically *and* most likely to harm their peers seem relatively immune to this type of intervention.

Therefore, our suggestion to you is that if you are not a binge drinker, avoid like the plague those places where bingers gather! We also hope that the above statistics will encourage some of you who drink *a lot* to curb your overindulgence—and to realize that it *is* dangerous!

Oh, But *Can* You Stop?

Even though a number of people have tried, no one has yet found a way to drink for a living.
— Jean Kerr

Ok, suppose you decide that it's just part of college life to "party hardy." What happens *after* college? Most young adults do "mature out of" their college habit of drinking heavily by their mid-20s or after marriage (e.g., Chen & Kendel, 1995). However, some people just can't stop (e.g., Zucker, Fitzgerald, & Moses, 1995). Drinking while in college is so common that it is often very difficult to uncover individual differences that predict who will become and remain alcoholic as a result of college habits. Recent studies have solved this problem by adopting one of two tactics—follow drinkers after college to see if they stop or cut back *or* compare graduates with those still in college to see which types of people drink in each situation.

Here are factors related to *inability to control or stop binge drinking after college graduation* (for related studies, see Gotham, Sher, & Wood, 1997).

➢ Being male is related to drinking at all ages nationwide; lifetime alcohol dependence (alcoholism) is 20% for men and 8% for women (Kessler et al., 1994).

➢ Growing up in a family with a history of alcoholism is related to heavy drinking in both high school and college, but a student from an alcoholic family had to *also* be a heavy drinker in college to predict continued heavy alcohol use after graduation.

➢ Not graduating "on time" is related to heavy drinking both in college and following graduation—no surprise there!

➢ Having more positive expectations for drinking (expecting a better time socially or more positive emotions while drinking) predicts heavy drinking in and out of college.

➢ Being an extravert is related to "behavioral under-control" (impulsivity, inability to resist taking a drink or to stop drinking before getting drunk) and to heavy drinking; norms that encourage heavy drinking affect extraverts more than they do introverts.

➢ Being *low* in agreeableness (needing alcohol to "feel good" or "be social") or *low* in conscientiousness are related to heavy drinking (and to other self-destructive actions).

➢ For women, being *high* on openness to experience (e.g., being adventurous) consistently predicts heavy drinking.

A post-graduation role *inconsistent* with heavy drinking has usually been associated with reduced alcohol consumption after college. Here are four such roles (e.g., Sadava & Pak, 1994):

➢ Having a full-time job after college (much more influential for men than for women).

➢ Being in a professional training program following graduation from college.

➢ Marrying within a few years of graduation (e.g., Bachman, Wadsworth, O'Malley, Schulenberg, & Johnston, 1997), *unless* your married social group drinks heavily.

➢ Becoming a parent.

Enabling Behavior — A Little *Too Much* Help for Your Friends

Living apart and at peace with myself, I came to realize more vividly the meaning of the doctrine of acceptance. *To refrain from giving advice, to refrain from meddling in the affairs of others, to refrain, even though the motives be the highest, from tampering with another's way of life—so simple, yet so difficult for an active spirit. Hands off!*
— Henry Miller

How often have you helped a friend because that person had been out late or had a hangover? (This does *not* refer to keeping a drinker safe from harm, which was discussed in Chapter 13.) Have you lied for the affected person? How about loaning the person your notes for a class the person missed? If you have done so, you have engaged in *enabling*. Enabling describes an action taken by a concerned person that removes or softens the effect of harmful consequences for the user. *Any* addictive or self-destructive behavior can be enabled by others (e.g., heavy drinking or using, remaining with a battering partner, having an eating disorders, being academically irresponsible). Because this chapter concerns heavy and alcoholic drinking, we'll stick to talking about enabling a drinker. Enabling prolongs dependency by *hiding* harmful consequences from the person and increases the chances for serious trouble, injury, and death. You may think that enabling is "what a friend *does*" (i.e., help the person). Actually, it only makes the problem worse since the person becomes *more* involved with alcohol. If the person doesn't have to face the consequences of heavy drinking, psychological and physical dependence (alcoholism) has time to develop. Once usage is a chronic habit, many people require extreme effort and often professional help to quit and to return to healthy functioning—and recidivism (returning to maladaptive drinking) is very high for "cured" alcoholics! Right now you are at a turning point in your life, and you will be developing the habits you will use throughout your adult life. So are your friends. If these habits are self-destructive, they will be even harder to change because you have *no well-learned mature* habits to return to!

You may think that you are not enabling another person's addiction. But you may not realize how easy it is to do so! Before you start patting yourself on the back, look at some of the common ways that people enable their friends' or family members' drinking behaviors:

➤ Bailing the person out of jail or loaning money to pay fines.
➤ Giving the person "one more chance," then another, and another (this is especially likely to happen if the person is your romantic partner or a family member).
➤ Ignoring the use because he or she gets defensive when you talk about it (or reminds you about how he or she has helped you in the past).
➤ Drinking with the person, supplying the alcohol, going with the person to try to keep the person sober, or holding the person's money to help cut alcohol consumption. These acts take away *the person's responsibility* for self-control—consequently, the person can blame *you* for overindulging or getting into trouble!).
➤ Loaning the drinker money, notes, clean clothes, food, or anything else that he or she (a) can't afford due to spending money on alcohol or (b) didn't take the time to acquire because of drinking or feeling badly afterwards (e.g., having a hangover, having slept poorly or stayed out too late, having skipped class or going to work).
➤ Joining the person in blaming others for his or her bad feelings (e.g., agreeing that it's not his or her fault that something happened or that he or she feels rotten, or agreeing that he or she deserves to get drunk to escape bad feelings and memories).
➤ Doing school work (or other tasks) for the person because he or she doesn't know how or have the time, or because he or she "feels bad." You should realize at this point that the person feels that *your* work and spare time are unimportant and thinks that you will should—and should!—put his or her needs before your own. Unfortunately, once this cycle of "helping" begins, *your* good habits will suffer.
➤ Lying or making excuses for the person to your friends, family, teachers, bosses, RA, or police (you may even come to *believe* the excuses if you say them often enough!).
➤ Denying to yourself that the person has a problem and justifying his or her actions to others. This includes minimizing the problem, putting off confronting the person, changing your own behavior to accommodate the drinker, and keeping your feelings and thoughts to yourself.
➤ And here are some things you might *not* have thought of as enabling: hiding or getting rid of the person's alcohol (again removing *personal responsibility* from the person) or blaming, lecturing, or threatening the person. He or she will just get defensive, and you will have assumed a "parental" role with the person, further diminishing his or her chances of feeling responsible for his or her actions.

As a person becomes a heavy user of alcohol (and eventually becomes dependent as a result), he or she develops an uncanny ability to *deny the problem*. The person sincerely doesn't believe there is a problem and will readily tell others, "I can quit anytime." Of course, it is *obvious* to you and to others that he or she cannot stop. Be aware that your enabling the person to continue to drink *without consequences* strengthens the denial system of the user.

When you begin helping (enabling), you do so spontaneously and naturally because you *want* to help those close to you. Your hope is that the person will magically realize that he or she is "in trouble" and will then *stop*. Unfortunately, as long as he or she "gets away with it," the pattern of drinking and denying the problem is *strengthened*, not diminished, because you have removed or delayed the inevitable damage that will result from his or her self-destructive behavior. Your enabling behavior is maintained (rewarded) because you don't want the person hurt *right now*. You also fear losing the person's friendship or love, so you "help" and stay silent.

And, guess what! As you continue to "help" the person, **enabling becomes your habit!** You no doubt can look through your life at friends and family members who continue to enable other people's maladaptive behaviors, whether it is reckless spending, heavy drinking, battering, having an explosive temper, or being "helpless" to care for him- or herself. And you may also be able to see how the enabler actually falls into a pattern of choosing friends or romantic interests over and over again who "need" this type of help! The enabler comes to see "helping" as how to give and get love, and the person whose behavior is being enabled helps maintain the habit by being helpless to survive alone and by manipulating the enabler's feelings of guilt, fear, and love (e.g., "if you really love me, you'll…). Do *you* want to fall into this habit??

How to stop enabling

No one ever suggested that it's easy to change a habit—any habit. And one that is maintained in the context of an important relationship is the hardest type of habit to change. Here are some steps to take if you recognize that you have fallen into a pattern of enabling someone's maladaptive behavior.

➢ Talk to your RA *and* then to a professional on campus who understands the problem. Most campuses have an alcohol and other drug office (D.A.W.N., on our campus) with someone professionally trained to deal with such problems. Don't *assume* that a regular counselor has had such training—ask the person! Professional organizations recognize that addiction counseling requires extra training because it requires different skills and approaches! If the person is also certified (e.g., a Certified Addiction Counselor), you are even more likely to get help with this problem.

➢ Get outside help, either from a professional in the community who is trained in addiction counseling or by contacting one of the self-help organizations, such as Alateen, Al-Anon, or Families Anonymous (see Web Sites at end of the chapter).

➢ Go on the Web to *reliable* sources (see the end of the chapter for a few suggestions) or get to the library and read up on your situation and your friend's or family member's problem.

158

➤ Be assertive and take a break from your enabling habit. Don't assume this will be easy to do! Habits aren't easy to break *ever*, you will feel guilty, and the person you are enabling will scream bloody murder about being abandoned! Expect him or her to try to manipulate you into continuing your enabling behaviors! Just remember that you have an "excuse" since you are too busy to help him or her due to school work and other obligations—stay strong in reminding the person how overloaded you are!

➤ Talk to your other friends. There is *almost no chance* they don't know what's going on. Remember that social support is an excellent coping technique for stress, and this is a *very* stressful situation. Any time you feel like you are "losing your resolve," turn to a friend to help you stay strong.

➤ *Keep telling yourself that you owe it to the person and to your relationship to help the person get well instead of helping the person to continue the self-destructive behavior!!*

➤ Be aware that you will "relapse" occasionally. Sometimes the person really does need help to survive! But don't see it as a "failure" on your part. Return immediately to your resolve not to enable and *tell the person* that "this once" doesn't mean a return to the old pattern!

➤ Work really hard to get the person to seek (or accept) professional help. You may believe the old myth that only people who want to stop are successful in treatment. Actually, once in treatment, the person who was *pushed* to get help (by family, friends, work or school officials, or the court) is as likely to recover as the person who *volunteered*! This is especially true if the person goes inpatient for a month!

➤ And, above all, take care of your own health and duties—don't become so involved in running the other person's life that you forget about your own!

Writing Activity 14.2—Have you been pushed into drinking or into enabling someone's self-destructive behavior? Write about *how you felt when you gave in to pressure*. Then write *exactly what you will say the next time you feel pressured* (writing will help you rehearse and will make it easier for you to stand up for yourself).

| |
| |
| |
| |
| |
| |
| |

One reason why I don't drink is because I wish to know when I am having a good time.
— Nancy Astor

Suggested Readings

Clements, R. (1999). Prevalence of alcohol-use disorders and alcohol-related problems in a college student sample. *Journal of American College Health, 48,* 111-119.

Frintner, M. P., & Rubinson, L. (1993). Acquaintance rape: The influence of alcohol, fraternity membership, and sports team membership. *Journal of Sex Education and Therapy, 19,* 272-284.

Gotham, H. J., Sher, K. J., & Wood, P. K. (1997). Predicting stability and change in frequency of intoxication from the college years to beyond: Individual-difference and role transition variables. *Journal of Abnormal Psychology, 106,* 619-629.

Grant, B. F., & Dawson, D. A. (1997). Age of onset of alcohol use and its association with DSM-IV alcohol abuse and dependence: Results from the National Longitudinal Alcohol Epidemiologic Survey. *Journal of Substance Abuse, 9,* 103-110.

Littrell, J. (1991). *Understanding and treating alcoholism. Vol. 2. Biological, psychological, and social aspects of alcohol consumption and abuse.* Hillsdale, NJ: Erlbaum.

Rosenberg, H., & Nevis, S. A. (2000). Assessing and training recognition of intoxication by university students. *Psychology of Addictive Behaviors, 14,* 29-35.

Sher, K. J., Bartholow, B. D., & Nanda, S. (2001). Short- and long- term effects of fraternity and sorority membership on heavy drinking: A social norms perspective. *Psychology of Addictive Behaviors, 15,* 42-51.

Stewart, S. H., Angelopoulos, M., Baker, J. M., & Boland, F. J. (2000). Relations between dietary restraint and patterns of alcohol use in young adult women. *Psychology of Addictive Behaviors, 14,* 77-82.

Vik, P. W., Carrello, P., Tate, S. R., & Field, C. (2000). Progression of consequences among heavy-drinking college students. *Psychology of Addictive Behaviors, 14,* 91-101.

Wechsler, H., Lee, J. E., Kuo, M., & Lee, H. (2000). College binge drinking in the 1990s: A continuing problem. *Journal of American College Health, 48,* 199-211.

Wechsler, H., & Wuethrich, B. (2002). *Dying to drink: Confronting binge drinking on college campuses.* Emmaus, PA: Rodale.

Suggested Web Sites

http://www.checkyourself.com/main.html This site includes quizzes you can take to assess your use of alcohol and other drugs, a chance to interact with other teens who have experienced a "moment of truth," and links to treatment resources.

http://health.org Prevline: Prevention Online has links related to risk prevention.

http://www.hsph.harvard.edu/cas This site has numerous studies on college drinking.

http://www.alcoholandotherdrugs.com/ A Web site for college students.

http://alcoholism.about.com/ This site contains links, chat rooms, articles, and information on alcohol abuse and college student drinking (also see: http://alcoholism.about.com/cs/college/).

http://substanceabuse.about.com/ This site contains links, chat rooms, articles, and other helpful information concerning alcohol abuse.

http://www.miami.edu/ctrada/ See this site for the University of Miami Center for Treatment Research on Adolescent Drug Abuse for treatment programs for adolescent substance abuse.

http://ag.udel.edu/extension/fam/resources/substance_abuse_pr.htm University of Delaware site for resources for all types of substance-abuse prevention; it has extensive access to other sites.

http://www.brad21.org B.R.A.D. (Be Responsible About Drinking, Inc) was founded by the family and friends of Bradley McCue, a Michigan State University Junior who died of alcohol poisoning after celebrating his 21st birthday. Site has information and access to other sites.

http://www.samhsa.gov/publications/publications.html The Substance Abuse and Mental Health Services Administration (SAMHSA) site has a wide variety of information, from statistics on use to treatment facilities. Also see http://health.org/newsroom/ncadiReports.aspx and http://health.org/newsroom/abuseInformation/ .

http://www.cdc.gov This site from the Center for Disease Control and Prevention provides information on a wide variety of public health issues, including substance abuse and disease.

http://www.rwjf.org The Robert Wood Johnson Foundation contains information on alcohol abuse and many other health-related topics.

http://www.ama-assn.org/ama/pub/category/3337.html This site has information on alcohol and other drug policy, research, and related issues of the American Medical Association.

http://www.niaaa.nih.gov/ National Institute on Alcohol Abuse and Alcoholism (NIAAA) is part of the National Institutes of Health of the U.S. Department of Health and Human Services.

http://www.speroandjorgenson.com/SperoD.htm The is the "D" part of "Psychiatric Links on the World Wide Web" with links to many sites related to alcohol use (look under Drug Abuse).

http://www.aa.org/ This is the site for Alcoholics Anonymous

http://www.al-anon.alateen.org/ This site is for Al-Anon and Alateen (specifically for those 12 to 20), which are organizations for people whose lives have been affected by problem drinkers. Call 888-4AL-ANON, Monday through Friday, 8 am to 6 pm ET for meeting information.

http://www.familiesanonymous.org/ This is the site for Families Anonymous, a self help, recovery and fellowship of support groups for relatives and friends of those who have alcohol, drug or behavioral problems. Call (800) 736-9805 from 10:00 am to 4:00 pm, Monday-Thursday and 10:00 am to 2:00 pm on Friday, PST, or e-mail i: famanon@FamiliesAnonymous.org

Chapter 15

When Things Go Wrong — Depression and Suicide

Everyone seems normal until you get to know them.
— Anonymous from the Internet

Case Study—Imagine that a close friend of yours has been going through a difficult time. About a month ago, she ended a long-term relationship with her boyfriend when she discovered that he had been cheating on her. Since that time she has had difficulty sleeping and concentrating on her schoolwork. She often calls you on the telephone crying and stating that she does not know how she can go on. In the last week, she has given you lots of her stuff, stating that she does not want to see it anymore. While you have been worried about her, you hope that it is a temporary phase and that she will eventually move on with her life.

Finally, your friend calls you from home where she has gone for the weekend. She states that she is all alone and has decided that she just cannot go on. Things are just too painful to endure. She thanks you for being a good friend and for listening and asks you not to intervene with the decision that she has made. Crying, she hangs up the telephone.

What do you do?

College: It's "The Real World" Also

People often refer to college as a fantasyland, a place where there are few worries and fewer responsibilities. While this view may be partly correct, it also is true that every problem seen in adulthood is also seen in college students. And while college recruiting brochures show happy students interacting with others in stress-free lives, the difficulties of life are just as evident in this age group. Various forms of maladjustment are common in college students. We have discussed some of these in other chapters, including alcohol abuse, other drug abuse, and sexual difficulties. We will continue discussing in this chapter and the next when and why things go wrong, and we will give you some ideas about what to do about it. We will focus our

162

attention on two disorders that are prevalent in college populations: depression and eating disorders. In both cases, we will consider the symptoms and causes for the disorders and make some recommendations for seeking treatment.

Test for Self-Awareness—Before reading on, complete and score What is Normal? on p. A51 (B. L. Beck, 2001, based on American Psychiatric Association, 2000). See how many of the vignettes you can classify correctly, which will help you distinguish between which characteristics make a behavior normal or abnormal.

Depression

Most students have had experiences with being depressed. These feelings often come in reaction to a poor academic performance, interpersonal difficulties, or family troubles. What separates these normal everyday fluctuations in mood from *major depressive disorder* is the severity of the symptoms and the degree to which they interfere with day-to-day functioning. Symptoms of major depressive disorder are usually divided into five groups, as shown below. (In *adolescents*, you may also see restlessness and acting out.)

Symptoms of Major Depressive Disorder (adapted from APA, 2000)

➢ *Emotional:* sadness, loss of interest and pleasure in daily activities (*anhedonia*)
➢ *Motivational:* lack of response initiation, change in activity level, difficulty in making decisions, trouble concentrating
➢ *Cognitive:* low self-esteem, blame self for troubles (high superego), pessimism about the future, suicidal thoughts
➢ *Somatic:* loss of appetite, sleep disturbances, low libido, fatigue
➢ *Behavioral:* low eye contact, low activity, psychomotor retardation, quiet

---

Fortunately, not all of these symptoms are seen in all individuals who are depressed. Our experiences with college students suggest that trouble concentrating and negative thoughts are very common. Major depressive disorder is one of the most prevalent of all the mental disorders; indeed, it is often called the "common cold" of psychological disorders. Recent estimates (Comer, 2001) suggest that 12% of men and 26% of women will experience the full clinical syndrome at some point during their lives. The emotional and financial costs related to this disorder are staggering.

Test for Self-Awareness—Before reading on, complete and score the Beck Depression Inventory on p. A55 (A. T. Beck, 1967), which is designed to detect the presence of depressive thoughts and behaviors. Answer the questions honestly and assess your current mood with respect to these issues.

Associated features of depression

Depression is often seen in combination with other disorders. It can range in severity from very mild and in reaction to normal life events (e.g., the break-up of a relationship) to life-threatening thoughts that seem to come from nowhere. It would seem that the advice of "Just cheer up!" would help, but this does little to lift the spirits of those who are afflicted.

It is interesting to note that even with our amazing societal affluence (look at how much stuff you have!), we seem to live in an "Age of Melancholy" (Klerman, 1979; Klerman & Weissman, 1992). Since World War II, individuals are significantly more likely to experience major depressive disorder than in the generations prior. When we ask students why this is, they often indicate the stressful nature of their lives and the many decisions they are forced to make. However, try to convince your grandparents or great-grandparents that your life is more stressful than theirs (particularly if they lived through the Great Depression...you know, walked 5 miles to school, uphill—both ways!).

Another curious facet of depression is how it afflicts twice as many women as men. Don't worry, men are over-represented in other wonderful diagnostic areas, such as antisocial behavior and substance abuse. An old clinical adage is that "women cry and men get drunk and blow up bridges." For depression, it certainly is true that it is more acceptable for women to express these emotions and to seek out treatment. However, this does not explain nearly all of the gender difference in prevalence. One must also consider the societal attitudes that keep women in lower positions of power and prestige. They may be depressed because they are oppressed.

Finally, major depression is a very democratic disorder. What this means is that it is seen in all social classes and regardless of socioeconomic status. This is evident when you see individuals who are depressed despite seeming to have everything that a person could want. Later, when we discuss suicide, it may help explain why many powerful and wealthy individuals have taken their own lives. The casual observer would think, "What did that person have to be depressed about?" However, the disorder strikes the rich and famous, as well as the very poor. It also gives some insight into our rising depression rates even though the nation as a whole has rarely been wealthier.

Theories concerning the causes of major depressive disorder

Numerous psychological theories have pointed to various causes of depression (Comer, 2001). While none of them are complete in themselves, they contribute to our understanding of the various facets of the disorder. Better yet, they suggest a number of excellent treatments we will address in the next section. *Psychodynamic theorists* propose that depression is the result of unconscious anger turned inward on the individual. When we are unable to express this anger toward others, it implodes on us, and depressed behavior is the result. *Behavioral theorists* point to the fact that depressed people do not engage in as many pleasing, reinforcing activities. How many things do you currently do that are *just pure fun*? *Cognitive theorists* indicate that our negative thoughts and irrational beliefs lead to our being miserable. They suggest that most depressed people exhibit the negative thoughts of being helpless, hopeless, and worthless. *Existential theorists* purport that depression and anxiety are the result of meaninglessness in one's life and the failure to confront the basic questions of existence (Why am I here? What is my purpose? Where am I going?).

In addition to these areas, **biomedical theorists** have recently contributed immensely to our understanding of the physiology of depression. They have shown that there is some genetic heritability of mood disorders that would partially explain why major depression may run in families. Also, for people for whom depression does not seem to arise in response to environmental events (sometimes called **endogenous depression**), biomedical theorists have contributed to our understanding of depression by alerting us to the improper functioning of the neurotransmitters norepinephrine and serotonin. The problems with these neurotransmitter systems have led to effective medication treatment of the disorder for certain individuals.

Treatment for major depressive disorder

Given the widespread prevalence of major depressive disorder, it is fortunate that it is one of the most treatable of all the psychological disorders (Elkin, 1994). In addition, several equally effective treatment approaches are available, so one often has the option of tailoring a program to individual temperaments and needs. For depression that arises in response to some environmental event, it is often effective to have the person deal with the event and its associated stressors. Psychodynamic therapists might accomplish this task by having the client focus on unresolved loss and anger issues. A behavioral therapist might focus on engaging in more rewarding activities. Existential therapists would confront the client's sense of meaning. All of these approaches can be successful. Cognitive theories have made major strides in treating depression by having clients change their maladaptive thoughts and irrational assumptions. One popular self-help book by David Burns (1981), *Feeling Good: The New Mood Therapy*, simplifies this approach for lay people and can be very successful in treating mild forms of the disorder. Researchers have reported substantial success rates from this type of *bibliotherapy* for depression (e.g., Smith, Floyd, Scogin, & Jamison, 1997).

In addition to the psychological treatments, many individuals have benefited from taking **medication** to improve their mood. Drugs from the general category known as the **selective serotonin reuptake inhibitors** (SSRIs; e.g., Prozac, Zoloft, Paxil, Celexa) have been very popular in the last decade for the treatment of depression and associated disorders. And while news organizations have irresponsibly focused on the few cases in which the drugs have had calamitous results, overall, SSRIs have been found to be very safe and relatively nonaddictive medications. In fact, the SSRIs' popularity has not been due to their treatment success being any greater than the prior generation of antidepressants; rather it has been due to the fact that they are safer to use and have fewer side effects. Be sure to talk with your therapist and/or physician about the safety and usefulness of these medications for you. Don't just buy them off the Internet—they can be dangerous in combination with certain physical conditions and with other medications.

Finally, it should be mentioned that while the overall success rate for the psychological or pharmacological treatment of depression is high, a few individuals do not respond to these approaches. For them, more dramatic treatment approaches are available. The first of these is **electroconvulsive therapy** (ECT), also known as electric shock. ECT has an infamous history as a barbaric treatment that often resulted in significant brain damage and left the patient horribly confused. It was used for punishment in many cases rather than for treatment. Fortunately, today ECT is much more humane and administered only under the strictest ethical safeguards. Current treatment results in little long-term brain damage and has much less of the memory loss and confusion formerly associated with it. Researchers have found that ECT can lead to improvement in 50% to 80% of individuals who were previously unresponsive to medication or psychotherapy (APA, 1993). While relapse is a problem, it may buy some vital time for individuals who are suicidal. In addition, a new technique called **repetitive transcranial magnetic stimulation** (a.k.a. magnetic shock therapy) shows some real initial promise as a substitute for ECT (Berman et al., 2000; Janicak et al., 2002; Post et al., 1999). Early reports suggest similar effectiveness rates without many of the side effects of ECT. Be sure to consult with your therapist and stay tuned for future developments.

For all of these approaches, you need to take special care that individuals are qualified to assess and treat your problems. You should be fully informed as to the strengths and dangers of each intervention. Major depression is a debilitating and potentially dangerous disorder that should not be treated irresponsibly. Similarly, given the effectiveness of current treatment approaches, it seems similarly untenable to stand by and do nothing while a loved one suffers. Arm yourself with information and get help! At the end of this chapter, we give several Internet resources for additional information and support.

A Special Case of Depression — Suicide

Few events have the power to shatter lives as does the suicide of a loved one. The lingering trail of guilt, confusion, frustration, and helplessness are often life-altering events in survivors. Indeed, even for therapists, the suicide of a patient is the number one reason why people leave the profession (Corey, Corey, & Callanan, 1998). Therefore, it is imperative that we learn as much as possible about this behavior that may be the end result of major depressive disorder.

Suicide is a self-inflicted death in which one makes an intentional, direct, and conscious effort to end one's life (Schneidman, 1999). It is one of the leading causes of death in college students and the ninth leading cause of death in Western society (Ash, 1999). There are numerous motivations for considering and attempting suicide. As the suicidal individual may have impaired judgment and not be thinking clearly, it is crucial that we remain alert to cues of potential suicidal behavior in friends and loved ones. If you suspect that a friend or loved one is potentially suicidal, we have one recommendation that supersedes all our other advice:

GET HELP!!!

You are *not* qualified to make important assessments about someone else's mental state. In addition, you are going to need some emotional support when trying to be a helpful friend to this individual. We cannot stress this enough—get help from a qualified mental health professional. Even mental health professionals get peer support and advice when dealing with these difficult cases.

Now that we have you seeking help, we want to sensitize you to potential signs and symptoms of suicidal thinking. These are some of the more common signs that are shown; however, just because a person does not exhibit one or more of the signs or symptoms, does not mean that he or she is not suicidal! Some suicidal individuals give no warning signs at all. These are just some common indicators that should encourage you to watch the individual carefully *and* GET HELP!!!

Signs and Symptoms of Suicide
➢ Depression
➢ Giving away prized possessions
➢ Previous suicide attempts
➢ Recent loss
➢ Social isolation
➢ Alcohol/drug abuse
➢ Family history of suicide
➢ Hints or direct threats of suicide
➢ Sudden apparent peace and calm
➢ Statements about helplessness, hopelessness, and worthlessness

Others find the mnemonic *DANGER*, a useful way of remembering the warning signs for suicide:

DEPRESSED MOOD

ALCOHOL OR DRUG ABUSE

NEGATIVE ATTITUDE

GIVING AWAY POSSESSIONS

ESTRANGEMENT AND ALIENATION

REBELLIOUS BEHAVIOR

Myths about suicide

In addition to knowing these warning signs for potential suicidal behavior, it is important for you to be aware of some of the myths surrounding suicide. The following is a collection of commonly-held beliefs about suicide that are **absolutely _untrue_**.

> ➢ ***People who discuss suicide will not commit the act.*** The fact is that up to 75% of those who take their lives have communicated the intent beforehand—perhaps as a cry for help, perhaps to taunt. On the other hand, the vast majority of people who contemplate suicide do not actually attempt to kill themselves.

> ➢ ***Suicide is committed without warning.*** The falseness of this belief is readily indicated by the preceding statement. The person usually gives many warnings; such as saying the world would be better off without him, or making unexpected and inexplicable gifts to others—often of his most valued possessions.

> ➢ ***Only people of a certain class commit suicide.*** Suicide is actually neither the curse of the poor nor the disease of the rich. People in all classes commit suicide.

> ➢ ***Membership in a particular religious group is a good predictor that a person will not consider suicide.*** It is mistakenly thought that the strong Catholic prohibition against suicide makes the risk that Catholics will take their lives much lower. This is not supported by the evidence, perhaps because an individual's formal religious identification is not always an accurate index of true beliefs.

> ➢ ***The motives for suicide are easily established.*** The truth is that we do not fully understand why people commit suicide. For example, the fact that a severe reverse in finances provides a suicide does not mean that the reversal adequately *explains* the suicide.

> ➢ ***All who commit suicide are depressed.*** This fallacy may account for the tragic fact that signs of impending suicide are overlooked because the person does not act despondently. Many of the people who take their lives are not depressed. In fact, some people appear calm and at peace with themselves after having decided to kill themselves.

> ➢ ***A person with a terminal physical illness is unlikely to commit suicide.*** A person's awareness of impending death does not preclude suicide. Perhaps the wish to end their own suffering or that of their loved ones impels many to choose the time of their death.

> ➢ ***To commit suicide is insane.*** Although most suicidal persons are very unhappy, most do appear to be completely rational and in touch with reality.

- ➤ *A tendency to commit suicide is inherited.* Since suicides often run in families, the assumption is made that the tendency to think in terms of self-annihilation is inherited. There is no evidence for this.

- ➤ *Suicide is influenced by seasons, latitude, weather fronts, barometric pressure, humidity, precipitation, cloudiness, wind speed, temperature, and days of the week.* There are no good data to substantiate any of these myths.

- ➤ *Improvement in the emotional state means lessened risk of suicide.* The fact is that people often commit the act after their spirits begin to rise and their energy level improves; this appears to be especially true of depressed patients.

- ➤ *Suicide is a lonely event.* Although the debate whether to commit suicide is waged within the individual's head, deep immersion in a frustrating, hurtful relationship with another person—a spouse, a child, a lover, a colleague—may be a principal cause.

- ➤ *Suicidal people clearly want to die.* Most people who commit suicide appear to be ambivalent about their own deaths.

Suicide: Crisis intervention

Finally, it is important to have some idea of how to respond in these situations. Students often ask, "What am I to do if someone I know becomes suicidal?" While you should rely on a qualified psychotherapist, practical constraints or the suicidal person's reluctance may prevent you from immediately arranging a visit for the person to a therapist. The following guidelines (adapted from Altrocchi, 1980), used in suicide crisis-intervention centers, may be helpful.

- ➤ *Keep alert to suicide clues.* Among these the most obvious, besides previous suicide attempts, are suicidal statements, such as, "The world would be better off without me," or "You won't have to put up with me much longer." Being perceived as a burden is strongly related to suicide potential (Joiner et al., 2002). Another powerful clue is any sign of hopelessness or depression, whether it is the person's statements, sighs, or facial expressions. The person contemplating suicide may begin to make plans for death, as, for example, by making a will or giving away his or her prized possessions. Or such a person may give evidence of extreme concern with his or her health or of increasing alienation from others. Finally, you should be alert to a person's reactions to the loss of someone close or of something important, such as a job, a symbol of status, or the like.

  Never be fooled into believing that the suicidal statements are simply a manipulation, a means of gaining attention, or a cry for help. You are not qualified to make this judgment. Even if manipulative, they are a desperate method of involving others and should be taken seriously.

169

➢ **Ask directly.** If you have any suspicion, *however remote*, that a person is thinking of suicide, ask the person about his or her thoughts or intentions straightforwardly, with concern, and without negative suggestions.

A sample series of useful questions is: "Have you ever wondered whether going on living was worthwhile?" "Are you thinking of killing yourself?" (Do *not* say "hurting yourself"; many methods, like pills or a bullet through the head, do not hurt at all.) "How close are you to doing it?" "Exactly how would you do it?"

An example of a possibly harmful, negatively suggestive question is: "You are not thinking of doing something foolish, are you?" The person who asks this question really means, "Thinking of suicide is foolish, and if you are thinking about it, I do not want to hear about it."

It is a common myth that people who discuss suicide will not commit the act. In addition, it is untrue that talking about suicide will cause the person to commit the act. Many suicidal people are relieved that someone is willing to listen to these frightening ideas.

➢ **Unhesitatingly demonstrate genuine interest, concern, and caring for the person.** This is the central feature of helping a person who is contemplating suicide. If you do not already have a close relationship with the person in trouble, establish and develop one—it may become a temporary lifeline. Everyone has a particular way of forming a relationship; use you own style, spontaneously. Listen very carefully and be patient, interested, and honest. People in distress often see through hypocrisy and feel betrayed. Be self-assured, knowledgeable, and hopeful. This general approach is justified if you do not carry it too far, as for example, by giving false reassurances, such as "I am sure he loves you," or "I am sure everything will turn out well." You cannot be sure!

Be careful not to abandon the person when you see an improvement in his or her emotional state. Often the suicidal person will commit the act following a lift in his or her spirits (this may partially be due to a relief from conflicting feelings after making the final decision to kill oneself). Stay with the person.

➢ **Assess lethality.** The best evidence of lethality can be obtained from answers to the questions suggested before. If the person says "yes" to any of them and describes a carefully worked-out plan for committing suicide that he or she proposes to carry out immediately or very soon, you should assume that the situation is lethal. Other information that may be helpful in assessing lethality—the severity of hopelessness, depression, or irrational, uncontrolled thinking or behavior; a history of one or more previous suicide attempts; and any current heavy use of alcohol or other drugs. The more potentially lethal the situation is, the more vigorous and prompt your action must be.

➤ ***Determine the person's internal and external strengths and resources.*** You can build on disclosures the person makes, such as love for his or her children or of music, or on his or her close relationships with others. Everyone has some strengths and resources, no matter what he or she says, and reminding the person of them may help.

➤ ***Identify and clarify the focal problem.*** Suicidal individuals are usually distraught and not thinking in a fully coherent, let alone a creative, problem-solving fashion. In their chaos and confusion, they may be unable to concentrate on any one problem, but tend to get lost in all of them. Help the person to become as clear as possible about the problems and about what he or she has tried to do or thought about doing to resolve them.

➤ ***Help the person formulate a plan of action.*** The person often has "tunnel vision"; you may be able to help evolve some alternatives other than the one or two the person is using at the time. Here you need to be quite active because the person feels helpless. You must be authoritative (reasoning with), but not authoritarian (demanding), because the person is not sure what to do and you do know some things that would, and some that would not, be helpful.

Involving others—especially family members, friends, or people who can be counted on to be helpful—in order to combat alienation and create more enduring lifelines can be crucial. For example, in one case a crisis-call volunteer persuaded a man to postpone his deadline for killing himself while another volunteer tracked down the man's minister, who went to the man's home and persuaded the man to accompany him on the rest of his day's house calls and social functions. At the end of the day the man was back on an even keel. The minister kept in close touch with him.

➤ ***Contact a mental health professional as soon as possible.*** This person can see the suicidal person for counseling, as well as offer help and suggestions for you. ***You should call the police if the person indicates serious suicidal intent and you do not have a way to prevent a suicide attempt.*** Believe it or not, it is illegal to commit suicide in many states.

We hope these ideas give you some information and support in dealing with what is invariably a difficult and anxiety-provoking situation. ***Again, even with all our suggestions, our number one recommendation is to get help.*** Below are some Internet resources that might be helpful with the general topic of mood disorders, as well as the specific area of suicide resources and information. Good luck!

Too often we underestimate the power of a touch, a smile, a kind word,
a listening ear, an honest compliment, or the smallest act of caring —
all of which have the potential to turn a life around. — Dr. Leo Buscaglia

Suggested Readings

Burns, D.'D. (1981). *Feeling good: The new mood therapy*. New York: Penguin Books.

Comer, R. J. (2001). *Abnormal psychology* (4th ed.). New York: Worth.

Janicak, P. G., Dowd, S. M., Martis, B., Alam, D., Beedle, D., Krasuki, J., et al. (2002). Repetitive transcranial magnetic stimulation versus electroconvulsive therapy for major depression: Preliminary results of a randomized trials. *Biological Psychiatry, 51*, 659-667.

Joiner, T. E., Pettit, J. W., Walker, R. L., Voelz, Z. R., Cruz, J., Rudd, M. D., et al. (2002). Perceived burdensomeness and suicidality: Two studies on the suicide notes of those attempting and those completing suicide. *Journal of Social and Clinical Psychology, 21*, 531-545.

Klerman, G. L. (1979). The age of melancholy? *Psychology Today, 12*, 36-42, 88.

Smith, N. M., Floyd, M. R., Scogin, F., & Jamison, C. S. (1997). Three-year follow-up of bibliotherapy for depression. *Journal of Consulting and Clinical Psychology, 65*, 324-327.

Suggested Web Sites

http://www.psycom.net/depression.central.html This site, entitled Dr. Ivan's Depression Central, has substantial information on depression and several other mood disorders.

http://www.pendulum.org/index.html This is an excellent site for information on another mood disorder often found in students—bipolar disorder. It includes information on assessment, therapies, and support groups for the disorder.

http://www.mentalhealth.com/book/p40-sad.html On this site you will find a detailed account of Seasonal Affective Disorder (SAD). Symptoms of SAD are similar to those of major depressive disorder but only occur in seasonal cycles (i.e., winter).

http://psychcentral.com/helpme.htm Dr. Grohol's excellent PsychCentral mental health page is a comprehensive resource for the assessment and treatment of all psychological disorders. This particular link, Suicide Resources, lists resources and ideas for suicide survivors on coping.

http://www.mhsource.com The Mental Health Infosource is a more generic resource for information on psychological disorders and their treatment. Of particular interest are the sites on schizophrenia and bipolar disorder and a locator for a mental health person near you.

http://www.psychwatch.com/ This site contains information on all areas of psychology and access to other web sites of interest.

http://www.unc.edu/depts/unc_caps/resources.htm The University of North Carolina's Counseling And Psychological Services presents practical information on many topics, including eating disorders, substance abuse, depression, sleep, grief, stress management, assertiveness, and helping a friend. You can access other sites from this page too.

http://www.save.org/ This site contains information on suicide prevention and for suicide survivors.

Chapter 16

When Things Go Wrong — Eating Disorders

Families are like fudge–mostly sweet but also a few nuts.
— Anonymous from the Internet

Case Study: *Jennifer*—Your female friend, Jennifer, is constantly seeking companionship. She tells you that she would have more guys interested in her if she could just lose 5-10 more pounds. You wonder about this because, if anything, she is a little thin. To accomplish her goals, Jennifer heads to the gym about an hour a day and is very particular about the foods she eats. You also notice that she frequently excuses herself in the middle of a meal, saying she has to "go to the bathroom." Also, you note that she has taken to wearing baggy, long-sleeve shirts and turtleneck sweaters even though the weather has been fairly mild.

As time goes on, you and your friends become increasingly concerned about Jennifer. Everyone notices that she has lost a lot of weight recently and has become more secretive about her activities. Along with the body thinness, you notice that Jennifer's hair, skin, and teeth just don't look good. You and your friends become convinced that Jennifer has an eating disorder. Either she is throwing up during meals or she is restricting her intake of food to the point of anorexia. You ask for help from one of your professors, who suggests that you and your friends confront Jennifer about her behavior. When your group does so, she becomes quite angry. She denies having a problem, states that it is none of your business, and adamantly refuses to seek treatment. Worse, she isolates herself from all of her friends, and her behavior appears to be getting worse.

What do you do?

Pathological eating behavior has become an all-too-common aspect of Western culture, particularly among college students. Its prevalence is evident in everything from discussions at orientation activities to guest lectures in classrooms to student support groups. It is unusual to make it through a discussion of the problem without students sharing personal experiences or those of friends. In addition, most students can give you a rough outline of some of the major causes of these disorders, including issues of family control and societal influences. Yet, with all this information, the problem of eating disorders continues to be one of the most frequent difficulties seen in student counseling centers. In this chapter, we will take a look at some of the attitudes that sustain eating disorders, consider the etiology (or causes) of it, and give suggestions and resources for seeking treatment.

Writing Activity 16.1—Do you believe that the problem of eating disorders in college students is improving or getting worse? What evidence do you have that supports your belief? Do you think your generation will make any strides in conquering them? What major changes will be needed to accomplish these goals?

Body Image

The following is a simple, non-technical **Exercise** on *body image*. It requires three people, a rubber band, a piece of string, masking tape, and a flashlight (it works better with an overhead projector). Give it a try—it will give you a good introduction to this topic.

Exercise—*Body Image*. In this **Exercise**, all three of you will demonstrate your body image by estimating the size of your cheeks, waist, hips, and thighs. You will do this by using a projected image on a blank wall or screen. One person will serve as the subject or estimator, one person will manipulate the image, and one person will do the measuring.

When ready, the person with the flashlight (or overhead projector) and the rubber band will project the image of the rubber band on the blank wall or screen at about the height of the subject's head. The person will stretch the rubber band with two hands until the subject agrees that it is about the width of his or her face at the cheeks. The person doing the measuring can mark this width on the wall with two pieces of masking tape or a pencil. They will repeat this procedure at the level of the subject's waist, then hips, then thighs.

You should also rotate among individuals to ensure that everyone gets to participate as the subject. After the marks are all made, the person doing the measuring will take a piece of string and measure the *actual* size of the subject's cheeks, waist, hips, and thighs. The actual measurement should be compared to the subject's perceived image marked on the wall.

How accurate were your estimates?

Was your perceived body image larger or smaller than its actual size?

Which body area was misperceived the most?

Were there any gender differences (if possible) in your group?

Do you think these differences would be found in another culture?

Why do you think individuals misperceived the size of their bodies?

Prior research in this area (e.g., Thompson, 1986) has revealed some fascinating results. It has been found that 95% of women, free of eating disorders, overestimate the size of their bodies. On the average, women overestimate their body image by 25%. Men, in contrast, overestimate their body image by 13%. Women overestimate the size of their cheeks the most, followed by their waist, thighs, and hips. Two women out of five overestimate at least one body part to be 50% larger than it is this.

It is instructive to consider the reasons for these distortions. Could it be that our weight-obsessed society has caused us to misperceive and exaggerate how big we really are? And remember, these results were found in individuals with *no* history of eating disorders. What happens when our poor body image interacts with our eating behaviors in a culture obsessed with thinness?

Anorexia Nervosa

Case History—Mary S., aged 16.5 years, grew disgusted with a close friend who began to put on weight by eating candy. The two girls agreed to go on a reducing diet, although Mary weighed only 114 pounds. A year later she graduated from high school and obtained a job as a stenographer. She began to lead a very busy life, working every day and going dancing at night with a young man who paid her attention. As her activities increased, her weight loss became more apparent, and soon her menses disappeared. Up to this time her dieting had been a voluntary control of eating, but now her appetite failed. Some months later one of the patient's sisters lured her boyfriend from her, Mary began to feel tired and had to force herself to keep active. The onset of dizzy spells caused her to consult a doctor, who suggested a tonsillectomy. After the operation she refused to eat, but continued her active pace, including dancing every night. She now weighed 71 pounds. Two months later she became so dizzy and weak that she could no longer walk, and was finally brought to the hospital weighing 63 pounds. In three days, 2.5 years after beginning her diet, Mary S. was dead of bronchopneumonia (Nemiah, 1961).

Anorexia Nervosa is a serious, life-threatening disorder. It is estimated that 2% to 6% of anorectic women die, and another 25% continue in the chronic course of the disorder (Comer, 2001). The disorder typically begins in adolescence with a diet that gets out of hand. For various reasons and often following a stressful event, the individual (usually a young girl) slowly begins to starve herself. The following are the primary symptoms of anorexia nervosa, from the DSM-IV-TR (American Psychiatric Association, 2000), the most commonly used manual for diagnosing mental disorders in United States.

Symptoms of Anorexia Nervosa
➤ Refusal to maintain body weight above a minimally normal weight for age and height (e.g., weight loss leading to a maintenance of body weight 15% below that expected)
➤ Intense fear of gaining weight, even though underweight
➤ Disturbance in body perception, undue influence of weight or shape on self-evaluation, or denial of the seriousness of the current low weight
➤ In post-menarcheal women, absence of at least 3 consecutive menstrual cycles

Historically, Anorexia Nervosa has been found disproportionately in middle- and upper-class women in Western industrialized nations. Unfortunately, with improved global communications and exposure to Western culture, the incidence of Anorexia has been rising in other societies. In one study done in parts of the Fiji Islands and the South Pacific following the introduction of satellite TV, it was found that girls who watched a lot of this television were more likely to suffer from a poor body image and engage in dangerous dieting behaviors

(Becker, 1999). We found similar distortions in body image and self-esteem in middle-school students who were exposed to heavy doses of television and magazines (Beck, Jara, Astor-Stetson, Zarecky, & Starks, 1998).

Bulimia Nervosa

Case History—Gary R., a 27 year-old White male, came to the county clinic in late October. He was somewhat sloppily dressed, but spoke well and quickly launched into a vivid description of his current problems. At the time Gary entered therapy, his life seemed to be coming apart at the seams. He was moderately depressed, low in self-esteem, and had even thought of suicide. During the first session, he explained that his most pressing problem was staying out of jail, a real enough threat considering the 20 or so bad checks he had written in the last few weeks. To cover these checks, Gary explained that he had taken several advances on his salary, had borrowed money from close family and friends, and had furthered his indebtedness by borrowing from high interest, short-term lending institutions. All of this resulted in outstanding debts totaling $12,000. The possibility of borrowing additional funds to cover the checks was bleak.

Supermarket, restaurant, and fast food purchases were responsible for Gary's financial predicament. During the course of a weekday, he would spend between $20 and $50 on groceries and prepared foods. On weekends the figure would rise to upwards of $100 in a single day. Gary explained that the vast quantities of foodstuffs were quickly consumed, usually at home, but sometimes at restaurants or in his automobile. He was able to eat all of this food only by regurgitating several times during a "meal."

Further details concerning these gastronomical binges were discussed in later therapy sessions. On weekdays, trying to conserve money, Gary would not eat anything until lunchtime. Lunch might consist of a dozen McDonald's hamburgers, five jumbo orders of French fries, four chocolate shakes, and several single-portion apple pies. If time permitted, Gary said that the more enjoyable lunches were leisurely ones at "all you can eat" restaurants offering spreads of unlimited pastas, salad, fried fish, or chicken. These meals could easily last for 2 hours during which several pizza pies, many orders of fish or chicken, or plate upon plate of pasta were consumed. Several trips to the bathroom, during which he would vomit, allowed him to consume these vast quantities of food. Perhaps fortunately for Gary, although to his dismay, these "all-you-can-eat establishments" recognized his voracious appetite; many banned him from partaking of their specials.

Gary's compensatory behavior at dinner was even worse. His bingeing behavior necessitated between 5 and 15 trips to the bathroom to throw up. This binge and purge cycle consumed his every waking moment, and he had little time left for a social life. Gary also compensated for his binges by excessive swimming. If time allowed, he would swim upwards of 85 laps twice a day (adapted from Neale, Oltmanns, & Davison, 1982).

People with *Bulimia Nervosa*, also known as the binge-purge syndrome, engage in frequent episodes of binge eating. These binges involve the consumption of large amounts of high-calorie food in a relatively brief period of time. Following these episodes of binge eating, the person will engage in some form of compensatory behavior; for example, vomiting, laxatives, diuretics, and excessive exercise. The following are the primary symptoms of Bulimia Nervosa from the DSM-IV-TR (APA, 2000).

Symptoms of Bulimia Nervosa
➢ Recurrent episodes of binge eating ➢ Recurrent, inappropriate compensatory behavior in order to prevent weight gain (e.g., vomiting, laxatives, diuretics, exercise) ➢ Symptoms continuing, on average, at least twice a week for 3 months ➢ Undue influence of weight or shape on self-evaluation

It is estimated that 13% to 20% of college women suffer from this disorder. Depression is a common condition for individuals with this diagnosis. Although cases of Bulimia Nervosa are much more commonly seen in women, the rate of the disorder has begun to rise in men (Gilbert, 1996). This is more commonly seen in individuals for whom weight is a requirement for their job or for sports (e.g., jockeys, wrestlers, bodybuilders). It has yet to be determined whether the precipitating factors for the disorder for men are the same as those for women.

Individuals with Bulimia Nervosa tend to be very concerned with body image and attractiveness. Unfortunately, these purging behaviors are destined to fail. For example, with vomiting, one-third of the calories of the purged food are absorbed, and the vomiting disrupts the mechanisms that let you know you are no longer hungry. Laxatives and diuretics only result in very temporary reductions and no long-term weight loss. Numerous adverse physical effects (e.g., nutritional deficiencies, destruction of tooth enamel, irritation of the esophagus) are found with these purging behaviors (Comer, 2001).

Again, we must wonder about the cultural norms that would lead to such destructive behaviors. When one of the authors was in graduate school, he was told by several members of a sorority how they trained new pledges in bulimic behavior. The pledges would be told to eat a meal beginning with green beans. Then, they would eat large quantities of high-calorie food (e.g., ice cream, doughnuts, chocolates). Then, the new sorority members would be instructed to stick their fingers down their throats and *throw up until they could feel the green beans coming out!* This story was told as if it were a normal part of one's daily life, much as one would describe how to start a car or buy groceries. Whether this worked or not, the author was horrified and wondered what social forces could lead to such aberrant behavior.

Test for Self-Awareness—Before reading further, complete and score the Eating Attitudes Test (EAT-26) on p. A59 (Garner, Olmsted, Bohr, & Garfinkel, 1982). The EAT-26 assesses thoughts and symptomatic behaviors frequently associated with eating disorders. You can use your scores to better understand the material in this chapter and as information on your level of risk for experiencing an eating disorder.

Causes Of Eating Disorders

While Anorexia Nervosa and Bulimia Nervosa are distinct disorders, there is some overlap, particularly in what causes individuals to engage in these behaviors. Possible causes have included cognitive disturbances, mood disorders, biological factors, and family issues. Of particular interest here is how *societal pressures* have contributed to the increased incidence of eating disorders. Anorexia was a rare disorder prior to 1950 with about one in 2000 young women showing the behavior. Today, that number has risen to almost one in 100, a dramatic increase (APA, 2000). So, what societal changes have been associated with this increase? In general, the standard for beauty has gotten much thinner. Our standards of beauty, for example, women in Playboy magazine and Miss America contestants, have become thinner while the population as a whole has gotten larger (Garner, Garfinkel, Schwartz, & Thompson, 1980; Rubinstein & Caballero, 2000). Correspondingly, longitudinal research on body image has shown that people have become more dissatisfied with the size of their bodies with each passing decade (Garner, Cooke, & Marano, 1997).

Interestingly, eating disorders and body image dissatisfaction have historically been found in young White women. This was believed to be due to the messages that were sent specifically to this group. However, with increased media exposure, it is feared that the disorder will become more prevalent in African-American women and young boys (Williamson, 1998).

Treating Eating Disorders

The good news is that, even though the attitudes that sustain eating disorders are pervasive in our society, there are successful treatments available (Comer, 2001; Wilfley et al., 2002). In some cases, particularly with Anorexia Nervosa, the disorder may be at such an advanced stage that hospitalization is necessary. In most cases, however, outpatient treatment is sufficient. Normal treatment for eating disorders involves ascertaining how to stop the maladaptive eating while challenging the thoughts that sustain it. Doing so is often accompanied by individual, group, and family therapy that both deals with the issues and provides some support. In some cases of eating disorders, medication can be a useful additional approach.

In all cases, individuals and families should seek out the help of a qualified mental health professional. Please be diligent in your search for help. ***Eating disorders typically do not go away by themselves.*** Treating an eating disorder takes a concerted effort on the part of family, friends, and professionals. Seek assistance and support during this process, particularly from professors you trust (including us!) and your college counseling center. In addition, listed below are two excellent Web sites with resources on information and treatment. Good luck!

Suggested Readings

Becker, A. (1999, May 31). Fat-phobia in the Fijis: TV-thin is in. *Newsweek*, 70.

Comer, R. J. (2001). *Abnormal psychology* (4th ed.). New York: Worth.

Garner, D. M., Cooke, A. K., & Marano, H. E. (1997, February). The 1997 body image survey results. *Psychology Today*, 30-44. (Available: http://www.psychologytoday.com/htdocs/prod/ptoarticle/pto-19970201-000023.asp)

Gilbert, S. (1996, July 28). More men may seek eating-disorder help. *New York Times*.

Rubinstein, S., & Caballero, B. (2000). Is Miss America an undernourished role model? *Journal of the American Medical Association, 283*, 1569.

Thompson, J. K. (1986). Larger than life. *Psychology Today, 20*, 38-44.

Thompson, J. K. (1996). *Body image, eating disorders, and obesity.* Washington, DC: American Psychological Association.

Wilfley, D. E., Welch, R. R., Stein, R. I., Spurrell, E. B., Cohen, L. R., Saelens, B. E., et al. (2002). A randomized comparison of group cognitive-behavioral therapy and group interpersonal psychotherapy for the treatment of overweight individuals with binge-eating disorder. *Archives of General Psychiatry, 59*, 713-721.

Williamson, L. (1998). Eating disorders and the cultural forces behind the drive for thinness: Are African-American women really protected? *Social Work Health Care, 28*, 61-73.

Suggested Web Sites

http://www.something-fishy.org/ - From the oddly-named "Something Fishy" (we always tell students it is a real organization!), this is an excellent Web site for information about all the major forms of eating disorders. It includes a chat link for support from professional therapists, a treatment center locator, and even music!

http://www.anad.org The site of the National Association of Anorexia Nervosa and Associated Disorders. It has information about warning signs, symptoms, and therapies for eating disorders. Even better, it gives ideas about how to confront an individual with an eating disorder.

Chapter 17

In Hot Pursuit of Happiness

Happiness is a butterfly, which, when pursued, is always just beyond your grasp,
but which, if you will sit down quietly, may alight upon you. — Nathaniel Hawthorne

The Constitution only gives people the right to pursue happiness.
You have to catch it yourself. — Ben Franklin

Pause, take a deep breath, and *circle the number* corresponding to your feelings about the following question: ***How satisfied are you with your life as a whole these days?***

```
/ 0 / 1 / 2 / 3 / 4 / 5 / 6 / 7 / 8 / 9 / 10 /
```
Completely   Neutral   Completely
Dissatisfied   Satisfied

What did you put? Do you think you are about average in life satisfaction? Are you about the same as your friends? What about other college students? What about people worldwide? Do you think pre-college adolescents would give the same ratings?

This question has actually been asked of individuals many times in a multitude of situations across diverse backgrounds. Two investigators of happiness, David Myers and Ed Diener (1996), combined data from 916 surveys of 1.1 million people in 45 nations representing most of the world. They found the *average* individual's rating of satisfaction was *6.75*. We found virtually the same scores in our research involving college students (Starks, Astor-Stetson, Beck, Jara, & Zarecky, 1998), high school students (Beck & Scott, 1996), and middle school students (Beck, Jara, Astor-Stetson, Zarecky, & Starks, 1998; Beck, Zarecky, Astor-Stetson, Jara, & Starks, 1998).

Surprised? It seems that most people think that others are less happy than they really are. The nightly news shows many unhappy people in horrible circumstances. Is that an accurate reflection of society? If we can believe what people say, it appears that it is not. From published reports (e.g., Myers, 2000), more than 90% of individuals indicate that they are somewhat or very happy. So what is responsible for all this happiness? What are the characteristics and situations that lead to happy lives? Before continuing, complete the scale in the Appendix and the following writing assignment on what it takes to be really happy.

Test for Self-Awareness—Complete and score the Satisfaction with Life Scale on p. A61 (Pavot & Diener, 1993).

Writing Activity 17.1—*Key questions to ask yourself about how to be really happy.*
Answer each question about how you *personally* feel.

What are you doing when *"time flies"*?

What would you *do if money were no object*? Would you do this for *a short time* or *permanently*? Why?

How would you feel in 5 years if you were doing *exactly* the same things you are doing right now? What is *the one thing* you would most like to be different 5 years from now?

What kind of people bring out "the best" in you—make you feel good about the situation *and yourself*?

Right now *and* on a day-to-day basis, how can you get more pleasant activities and more stimulating people into your life? What would be your *first* step toward this change?

For you, what would characterize a depressed, unfulfilling life? A fulfilling, exciting life?

What would be a *first* step to make your life more fulfilling and exciting *right now*?

What is *really* possible for you to become? What are *your* real expectations for yourself? How high a price are you willing to pay for what you want to become? What are you *not* willing to "pay" or give up?

Core Dimensions of Happiness

Any insights? What does it take to be truly happy and satisfied with one's life? There has been a recent movement toward the scientific understanding of life satisfaction and happiness (also known as ***subjective well-being***). Some of the findings from this research may surprise you. When we ask students what they think brings happiness, they often respond, *"Health and Wealth!"* Sounds reasonable, but is this accurate? Scientific results suggest that the answer is *"NO!"* For example, when we reported at the first of the chapter that most people around the world were happy (Myers & Diener, 1996), this actually included many who were poor, unemployed, elderly, or disabled. For example, Diener and Diener (1996) found that people with spinal cord injuries were only slightly less satisfied with life than others and that over 90% of individuals with spinal cord injuries said they were happy to be alive.

Maybe *money* is the key to happiness. Wouldn't it be great to win that big lottery or inherit a fortune so that life would be easy and stress-free? Wealthy people must be happier than the average person—what do they have to worry about? Interestingly, a study of the richest people in America (Diener, Sandvik, Seidlitz, & Diener, 1993) showed that they are only slightly happier than the average person. In addition, Myers (2000) reports that today's college-aged individuals are much wealthier than their grandparents. Has this resulted in increased levels of happiness? As a matter of fact, it has not. If anything, today's college students have a slightly *decreased* level of happiness and a much greater risk of depression and other psychological problems. *Stunning!* We are not saying that it is great to be poor. Extreme poverty is associated with lower levels of happiness and with more life difficulties. However, the research literature suggests that once your basic needs are met, money has very little correlation with happiness.

So, what *is* the key? Many people from various disciplines have weighed in on this question. In fact, entire books have been written on happiness. We don't want to force entire books on you; we think that might be associated with unhappiness! However, we do want to give you some things to think about and inspire you to do some research on your own. A nice framework on happiness has been provided by the psychologist Carol D. Ryff (1995). From reading the research literature, she has identified *six core dimensions of subjective well-being*. These are *self-acceptance, positive relations with other people, autonomy, environmental mastery, purpose in life*, and *personal growth*. Let's explore each area in greater detail.

Self-Acceptance

In terms of happiness, accepting yourself for who you are is very important. This is easier said than done. This does not mean that you don't continue to strive for additional learning or self-improvement; rather you need to realize you are a worthy person just because you are a human being. And as a human being, you realize that you are continually in the process of realizing your potential. ***Self-acceptance*** *refers to owning all your qualities, good and bad.* You are aware of negative aspects of yourself and don't have to vehemently deny them to others. You are okay with being less than perfect. You are okay with past experiences. The next **Activity** is related to the idea of "fooling yourself." See if you can find times in the past when you have done this and assess whether you are comfortable with your poor judgment.

Now read some actual reports of such incidents from students in our courses.

Response number one. "My senior year in high school, I met my first boyfriend. He
was my complete opposite. He did not go to high school anymore because he was kicked out for
hitting a teacher. He also drank and dealt drugs, which I had never even been related to. He was
sweet to me and eventually said the three magical words, I love you. I was hooked for some
reason. We thought we would be together forever, and I thought I could change his ways. I was
way off on that one. I stuck by him for too long. It was so hard for me to break up with him
because I thought I loved him and I thought I could change him. However, it was me in the end
that was hurt the most. I fell head over heels for him. When we broke up, I swore I would never
love anyone ever again. I would never let myself get hurt like that again. After my first
semester at college, I was completely convinced that all men were jerks. I cannot state that more
emphatically. I hated men in a relationship. I turned down a few guys who could have been
good guys, but I would not even give them the chance. I was bitter. Even though my father is a
wonderful man, I still found flaws that supported my feelings toward men. I swore I would
make my own money and live the single life. I was never interested in children, especially
having my own. So my life was set. I was going to work and make lots of money. I would be
an aunt to my sister's children once she settled down. Not until my second semester junior year
did I allow myself to have another boyfriend. He was a good friend of mine. We started seeing
each other casually. I was enjoying myself. I had dates to my date parties and hayrides. I still
did not want to let myself get too close to him. It was like that for a while. We both just liked
hanging out with each other. Before I realized it, I actually had feelings for him. I was angry

with myself for caring too much. Before long, I realized this guy is a good guy. What can I say but I fell in love with him. He's my best friend and my confidant. I would like to have his children one day. I know he would be a great father. Whether we take our relationship to the next stage of getting engaged or not, I still do not worry about it. I realized that I cannot rely on wishes. I take this relationship day by day. Whether he's 'the one' or not, I now know there are good guys out there. Men are not all bad. I am glad I realized this and that I was wrong."

Response number two. "Well, being a person who is rarely wrong (ha, ha), it is not often that I fool myself into thinking otherwise. Seriously, I tend to look at the world in a fairly realistic manner. Everyday, usual occurrences I tend to deal with very well. In female/male relationships, on the other hand, I have often had a problem seeing what is right in front of me. The incidence that is freshest in my mind is the situation that brought about my marriage. My spouse previously was a co-worker of mine. I had recently gotten out of a horrible relationship. (I use the word 'horrible' because certain expletives are inappropriate to use in a paper that is to be handed in to a professor. I will simply say I was lucky to get away with my life.) This person I worked with was the most supportive, most wonderful, most anything I have ever known. He became my best friend, and we spent much time together. He proposed that we take our relationship to another level. I felt slightly uncomfortable about that, so much so that I cut off ties with this person. He was in love with me. I rationalized the ideas I had of what I wanted, who he was, and what I was to do. I am very good at rationalizing. I told myself that this individual has all of the qualities of the individual you want to marry—he is honorable, trustworthy, loving, romantic...I could go on and on. I do not want you to puke or anything, so I will stop now. Coming to this realization, I cut all ties with him for a period of five months! Then, one day it struck me. I love this person. I want to be with him. I will be with him. After all those months of denying how I felt and what I wanted, I realized, virtually in seconds, what I was going to do. It was like this incredible weight was lifted off of my shoulders. I knew what I needed to do. I did it. I am now married to the most wonderful person in the world."

Response number three. "The most recent 'fooling myself' episode I had was the 'unwanted, but needed' break up with my boyfriend. Have you ever had a friend that you knew deserved better, but was just hanging on to a relationship for security's sake? Well, that friend was me. Deep down inside I knew that I deserved better, but was not doing anything about it. I kept telling myself and everyone else, 'No, it will get better; he really does love me.' All the signs of a terrible relationship were right in my face: the mistrust (I didn't trust him), the extreme selfishness on his part, and the emotional abuse. Then finally one day my 'knowing' self came into contact with my 'reality' self and all things I knew in my head filled my heart too. It was like a barrier from my head to my heart was finally broken. I finally admitted to myself that he didn't really care because if he did, he would not be treating me this way and I would not always feel so awful about the relationship. And finally I ended it, and it actually felt good. Sometimes reality does feel good."

So how about it? Were you able to identify situations in which you "fooled yourself?" Looking back on it, are you able to *accept* your errors in judgment? Could you *accept* the errors made by the students in the vignettes? Part of happiness is giving up the irrational need to be perfect. We all are fallible human beings who make many errors and grow personally from hard life experiences. *Come join the rest of us morons!*

Positive relations with others

A friend is one who knows us, but loves us anyway. — Fr. Jerome Cummings

The importance of close friends is an idea that goes back through history. In recent scientific research, few variables have proved as powerful in alleviating the effects of stressful events and aiding psychological well-being as has social support from others. All three authors have performed numerous research studies in which social support was investigated to see if it served as a buffer for negative life events. *The variable has been important every single time!* One of the authors had an amusing interaction with a psychologist at a national convention. The psychologist said she thought she had run the only study in history in which social support was found unimportant. *It is just that powerful!*

Happy, healthy people cultivate friendships. In these interactions they can experience trust, respect, admiration, affection, and regard. The noted psychologist Irv Yalom (1985) stated that friends help us experience ***universality***—the idea that we are all experiencing the same issues in life. Myers (2000) provided substantial experimental support for the idea that having friends is one of the biggest predictors of individual well-being. If you don't believe us, take this **Quiz**, currently circulating on the Internet, on the importance of friends.

Friendship Quiz

This isn't like other quizzes, so don't bother getting a pen and paper...just read:

> ➤ Name the five wealthiest people in the world.
> ➤ Name the last five Heisman trophy winners.
> ➤ Name the last five winners of the Miss America contest.
> ➤ Name ten people who have won the Nobel or Pulitzer prize.
> ➤ Name the last half dozen Academy Award winners for Best Actor and Actress.
> ➤ Name the last decade's worth of World Series Winners.

How did you do? The point is, none of us remembers the headliners of yesterday. These are no second-rate achievers. They're the best in their fields. But the applause dies. Awards tarnish. Achievements are forgotten. Accolades and certificates are buried with their owners. Now, here are some more questions. See how you do on them:

> ➤ List a few teachers who aided your journey through school.
> ➤ Name three friends who have helped you through a difficult time.
> ➤ Name five people who have taught you something worthwhile.
> ➤ Think of a few people who have made you feel appreciated and special.
> ➤ Think of five people you enjoy spending time with.
> ➤ Name a half dozen "heroes" whose stories have inspired you.

Easier?

The lesson? The people who make a difference in our lives aren't the ones with the most credentials, the most money, or the most awards. They are our friends and others who care.

Intimate Relationships with Others

Our students often ask us the secrets about romantic, intimate relationships with others. How do you find, maintain, and manage that relationship with a special someone? This certainly has a correlation with happiness, doesn't it? Of course, it does! In fact, most of the art, music, and literature of our civilization has been devoted to this topic. So, we don't hold any delusions that we are going to give you the ultimate answers in a couple of pages. We thought it might be helpful to give you some advice from people with four years of experience in college relationships—our senior teaching assistants. Here is advice from our TA's on relationships.

Senior TA's Dish the Dirt on Relationships

Initiating a Relationship

- Go to activities on and off campus.
- Talk to other people in your classes.
- Get to know other people on your floor in your dorm.
- Practice: "Don't I know you from General Psychology?"
- Don't try too hard and be wary of bars.
- Share commonalities and join clubs (e.g., major, interests).
- Use basic flirting and flattery.
- Stay alert for opportunities (e.g., laundry, grocery store, gym, Wal-Mart).
- Introduce yourself to as many people as possible (particularly if you are shy!).

Maintaining a Relationship

- Don't spend all of your time together!
- Keep your own interests and hobbies.
- Do something other than having sex.
- Plan fun outings (e.g., skiing, picnics, concerts, hikes).
- Be realistic in your expectations, say what you mean, and don't be dramatic.
- Keep communicating so you can deal with inevitable conflicts.
- Be unpredictable (but not too much so); appreciate the other person (and say so!).
- Cook dinner together; study together.
- Maintain a sense of humor about things.
- Sometimes you need to walk away when you are angry.
- Try to see problems from the other person's point of view.

Ending a Relationship

- Don't keep calling the other person.
- Be honest (every TA said this!).
- Tell them immediately and give an adequate explanation for why.

The Web site for the Student Counseling and Resource Center at the University of Chicago (cited at the end of this chapter) has many more ideas for each of these situations.

Autonomy

Thoughts from the Internet—Happy people are usually happy throughout life. As discussed earlier, neither age nor debilitating illness nor disability predicts degree of happiness over time. Here is a message circulating on the Internet that illustrates the attitude of a happy person.

"The 92-year-old well-poised and proud woman, who, despite her being legally blind, is dressed each morning by 8:00 with her hair fashionably coifed and makeup perfectly applied, moved to a nursing home today. Her husband of 70 years recently passed away, making the move necessary. After many hours of waiting patiently in the lobby, she smiled sweetly when told her room was ready. As she maneuvered her walker to the elevator, the nurse provided a visual description of her tiny room, including the eyelet sheets that had been hung on her window.
"I love it," she stated with the enthusiasm of an 8-year-old having just been presented with a new puppy.
"Mrs. Jones, you haven't seen the room—just wait."
"That doesn't have anything to do with it," she replied. "Happiness is something you decide on ahead of time. Whether I like my room or not doesn't depend on how the furniture is arranged. It's how I arrange my mind. I already decided to love it. It's a decision I make every morning when I wake up. I have a choice; I can spend the day in bed recounting the difficulty I have with the parts of my body that no longer work or get out of bed and be thankful for the ones that do. Each day is a gift, and as long as my eyes open, I'll focus on the new day and all the happy memories I've stored away—just for this time in my life. Old age is like a bank account—you withdraw from what you've put in."

Students often say to us, "Isn't happiness just about being lucky enough to have good things happening to you?" In other words, is it more the good fortune of avoiding environmental disasters? Well, interestingly enough, there is little evidence to suggest that positive life events are a major force related to depression. We mentioned earlier the fact that most people who suffered debilitating injuries or were disabled reported that they were happy. Although people's happiness or unhappiness is disrupted by positive and negative life events (e.g., marriage, widowhood), both formerly happy and unhappy people rebound toward their prior level of happiness (e.g., Lucas, Clark, Georgellis, & Diener, 2003; Suh, Diener, & Fujita, 1996).

If good fortune isn't the answer, what is? Well, it seems that independently choosing one's activities and goals is partly the answer. *Happy people are self-directed and autonomous.* They are not easily swayed by what is politically correct at the time or by current trends. While not exactly arrogant, they do have a good sense of their values and are not easily influenced to follow the opinions of the group. Once they act, they take ownership for their behavior. Consider the following guidelines and *assess how autonomous you are in your decision-making.*

I Am Responsible for the Choices in My Life

➤ Your past is PAST—don't moan about what "might have been." You are who you are *right now*, including the coping skills developed through the experiences.

➤ Develop a complex self-concept—don't be a "one-trick pony." Value yourself for *all* your skills and characteristics—you won't be as disappointed when you aren't doing well in one area because you can still see how well you are progressing in another! Such a complex self-concept helps you cope better with stressful events, *and* you will be less likely to get bored since you have many interests and abilities.

➤ Avoid excusing, blaming, or punishing yourself—use positive self-talk instead.

➤ But remember to be *realistic* about why an event occurred—don't blame another person or the situation if YOU were responsible—this includes the *mood* you are in (e.g., "you make me angry" is really "I get angry when you…").

➤ Respect yourself and your opinions—*but* remain open-minded to new information from *all* sources. Self-confidence reduces a tendency to be defensive!

➤ *Be enthusiastic!* —not only will you find you are more motivated in *any* situation—you will also be *more attractive* to other people!

➤ Know your strengths, abilities, possibilities, and preferences *before* you enter a new situation—and stay focused on them when you become frustrated (and you will!).

➤ Frustration is a sign of "work in progress" and that you may have overestimated your skill-level or the difficulty of the task. You may become frustrated because you went into the task unmotivated or pessimistic. If so, use positive self-talk to get yourself back on task! Think of a situation in which you worked hard for extended periods of time—a sport? a hobby?—and you will realize the power of motivation!

➤ Remember the self-fulfilling prophecy—if you believe you can, you will work harder to make it happen. If you believe you can't, your motivation will be compromised.

➤ It is also important to admit your weaknesses, unpracticed and unlearned skills, and nonmotivating situations because they will guide you in your life choices, show you what still needs to be worked on in your development, and alert you about situations during which you need to be more patient with yourself and ask for help!

➤ Regardless of circumstances, it is the way you look at a situation that affects how hard you try and what you say to yourself about both your effort and its outcomes.

➤ Remember that your thoughts and emotions are your most powerful assets—and they are the only things in a situation that you can always control!

Environmental mastery

Happy people do have some skills in coping with environmental difficulties. Sometimes, however, it is not so much that they are so accomplished in problem-solving, but rather they set the situation so that they are more likely to succeed. We are amused at the students who come to us to discuss their plans to make changes in their lives. They confidently assert that they are going to quit smoking, lose weight, get along better with their parents, and study more *ALL AT THE SAME TIME!* And they tend to want to see results by the end of the week! This is just a recipe for failure (think: New Year's Resolution!). Happy people are much better at choosing *realistic* goals and actually accomplishing them. *This is what makes them happy!* One of the best boosters to self-esteem is actually accomplishing something. It doesn't help much that people try to comfort you by telling you what a good person you are—it helps to be able to *do* something! ***Happy people are much better at structuring the situation to ensure success.***

Along with showing environmental mastery, ***happy people are able to manipulate their internal voices to turn obstacles into opportunities.*** That is, they are able to appraise the situation as a *challenge* rather than another chance for failure. Below, we have examples of the types of self-talk that differentiate happy people from the rest.

Self-Talk: It *Will* Affect Your Motivation

HELPLESSNESS	POWER
I can't (or shouldn't).	I won't.
I should (or must)…	I could, but don't have to…
It's not my fault.	I'm responsible for…
It's a problem.	It's hard, but it's an opportunity.
Why can't I just be satisfied? It's safer to stick with my old habits and roles.	I'm curious—I want to learn and grow.
Life is a struggle and often out of my control.	Life is an adventure—a chance to explore, to try out new roles.
I hope (or wish) it would happen.	I will work toward…
If only *things* had gone differently…	Next time *I* will…
Oh, what can I do?	I can handle it—I can stand it.
It's terrible! I can't stand it!	I have a chance to learn.
Oh, poor me!	It's OK to be disappointed.

Purpose in life

> *Happiness…proceeds from the achievement of one's values.* — Ayn Rand

A strong indicator of happiness is whether one has a purpose in life—a sense of meaning about the past, present, and future. Myers (2000) presented some interesting data from 6.5 million U. S. college students on this variable. Since 1965, the percentage of college students reporting that it is "very important" or "essential" to "develop a meaningful philosophy of life" has dropped from over 80% to roughly 40%. At the same time, the percentage of college students reporting that it is "very important" or "essential" to "be very well off financially" has risen from about 40% in 1965 to 74% in 1998. *For happiness, this is disastrous.* We discussed earlier that money is very minimally associated with happiness—and remember that putting financial well-being ahead of friends/family, helping the world, and self-knowledge is related to maladjustment (Kasser & Ryan, 1993). However, our culture's rampant focus on material goods has convinced many young people that this must be the path to well-being. In addition, what seems to have been sacrificed is the idea of the importance of developing a *sense of purpose* in one's life. Research suggests that they may pay a high price for these misaligned priorities.

Myers (2000) found ***a number of correlations of well-being with active religiosity.*** Active religiosity is not merely identifying with a religion; rather, it is frequently participating in it. Actively religious people are less likely to experience common mental health problems. They tend to be physically healthier and live longer. They report *higher levels of happiness*. Finally, they tend to bounce back better after suffering negative life events, such as, unemployment, divorce, serious illness, or loss of a loved one. While the mechanism for this resilience is not exactly clear, we certainly could speculate that actively religious people receive a high degree of social support and have a stronger sense of purpose in life.

> ***How About You?*** Close your eyes for a minute and think about what your purpose in life is. What are your *top two or three goals*? Then, look at your daily activities for the past week. *Are they consistent with these life goals?* Keeping your daily rituals in line with your overall purpose can go a long way toward increasing your happiness!

Personal growth

> *Freedom is what you do with what's been done to you.* — Jean-Paul Sartre

Finally, happy people see themselves as continually growing and expanding. As mentioned earlier, they have a sense of self-acceptance about their present and past. But they also have an orientation toward the future. ***Happy people interpret life's experiences as an opportunity for learning and personal growth.*** They also take active steps toward ensuring that their lives, values, and relationships are not stagnant. The following are some suggestions for how to facilitate personal growth in your own life, along with some common fears that inhibit this growth. While reading these items, honestly assess your capacities and tendencies in each area. Then, we encourage you to set some realistic goals for improvement.

You Are a Work in Progress:
Suggestions for Getting There!

Adventure isn't hanging on a rope off the side of a mountain. Adventure is an attitude that we must apply to the day-to-day obstacles of life: facing new challenges, seizing new opportunities, testing our resources against the unknown, and, in the process, discovering our own unique potential.
— John Amatt, Organizer of /participant in Canada's first successful expedition up Mt. Everest

When making *any* change (a new relationship, a new major or job, a life-style change), you will face self-doubts and remarks from even those with your "best interest" in mind. Here are some common reactions to expect. After these, we offer ideas to help you *go for it.*

External factors that may be hindering your choices for or attempts to change:

- ➢ family obligations, real or imagined
- ➢ stereotyping others hold about you (e.g., age, gender, ethnicity, personality)
- ➢ financial obligations or limitations
- ➢ regional limitations (partly due to unwillingness to leave family or friends)

Internal factors that may be limiting your possibilities for change:

> ➤ lack of skills, education, or credentials (e.g., degrees, licenses)
> ➤ lack of willingness to ask for or accept help
> ➤ lack of knowledge of how to work with others (interpersonal skills)
> ➤ limiting your choices due to your own stereotypes of yourself (may include false beliefs about what a choice requires—how hard it will be, what skills are required)
> ➤ beliefs that your personality, motivation, temperament, or past limit your choices
> ➤ lack of knowledge of available choices (e.g., what a major or career really is, how to find out about options or careers, where to get information, how to get started)

Some common fears that may be "roadblocks" for you:

> ➤ fear of change
> ➤ fear of failure
> ➤ fear of making a "wrong" choice
> ➤ fear of not having enough confidence, motivation, or skill to pursue a choice
> ➤ fear of adverse impact on present relationships (e.g., loss due to move, time pressures, "growing apart")
> ➤ fear of rejection, disapproval, or ridicule
> ➤ fear that it really won't make life better—or that things aren't better anywhere else
> ➤ fear of making a fool of yourself or of embarrassment while learning a new path
> ➤ fear of losing security—of abandoning a "safe," familiar behavior, situation, or person

Ideas for coping with real or imagined fears or limitations

> ➤ *Take one step at a time* (break large steps into smaller ones *or* ask for help!).
> ➤ Minimize risk by taking a "practice tour" of a choice you *might* make. Sample rather than making a complete change—*reality test* rather than burning that bridge!
> ➤ Sometimes you think you need change when you're just bored! Examine your current life. Would a small change do the trick? Could an acquaintance become a friend? Could a friend become a romantic interest? Could your major or job be enhanced or redirected?
> ➤ Realize that feeling shaky and uncertain about change is *normal*—fear occurs *naturally* when making a choice and when experiencing change:
>   - Fear is what any *sensible* person feels—you *don't* know what will happen, if you can *handle* it, if the *costs* will be too large. Talk back to negative, derogatory self-talk.
>   - Being nervous is a sign you are *aroused*—*not* that you are "chicken." It is a *survival state*, energizing your body—our ancestors wouldn't have lived long enough to reproduce if they hadn't had this feeling in their more physically dangerous world!
>   - Don't try to *suppress* your arousal—these attempts take too much effort (one reason why the shakes and headaches often occur *after* an emergency passes).
>   - If you get overaroused facing change (e.g., nausea, hyperventilation, weakness), use a relaxation technique to help you "tone down" the arousal (see Chapter 9).

192

> For major or long-term changes, self-help groups can be very useful. You can also look on the internet, and some self-help books can help with ideas and techniques.

> If you can, talk to someone who has already made the change you are planning. Get advice and ask about pitfalls so you can anticipate and prepare for them. If the change is a skill, watch a model perform the behavior. Self-help groups (or books) may also be helpful.

> Role models can provide tips on how to proceed, but *do not* measure your current state against the success they have already reached or think it was "easy" for them! (See Chapter 3 on *upward social comparison*, that can make you feel frustrated, impatient, clumsy, or guilty for being "inadequate"—*and may make you give up*.)

> *Visualize* yourself coping successfully with the next step of your "project." Picturing yourself actually *doing* what you have chosen to do will help you "practice" how to proceed *and* increase motivation. Try rehearsing in front of a mirror or with a friend too.

> Use positive self-talk—"psych" yourself up, be optimistic. Remember, you have control over *how you react mentally*, even if you can't control the situation! Look for the good side of situations—but don't deny *real* costs and pitfalls.

> Avoid self-limiting talk (…too old…too young…too shy…too unlovable…too afraid… too inexperienced). Creative, enthusiastic people change and grow throughout life.

> Realize you have *many* options and choices available—even if things initially look bleak or too difficult. Expect *gradual* change toward a goal—and occasional road blocks. Keep your eye on your goal during difficulties and times of frustration.

> Redefine change as an *evolving life-style*—some of the changes will be unpleasant but will *lead to* pleasant goals you are working toward. Don't always choose the "easy" way. Try to see the harmony and coherence of your life. Don't feel "at the mercy of" life.

> Allow time for change to become "natural." Any new behavior or situation feels strange at first, even if you don't have to learn how to do it—it will disrupt the pattern of your day, whether the change is adding or subtracting something from your life. Be patient and the change will become a habit—as natural as the old one you chose to leave behind.

> Realize that *persistence* is more useful than *mere confidence* when making changes! Change attempts are often abandoned because of frustration and lack of a skill. Think of something that was very hard for you to learn to do, *but* that you worked on until you "got it right." Remind yourself of that experience when your spirit lags.

> Realize that life is sometimes boring. And stimulation and excitement are stressful—but welcomed—changes *at times*. Balancing between too much security and too much adventure will make you happier than striving for just one of these all the time!

> Don't undertake changes you do not "own." Doing something just because others want you to or because you won't make the effort to explore other options will end either in failure due to lack of motivation or unhappiness because of not following a path you love.

➢ A further warning—thinking you can accomplish *anything* by working hard enough is a myth! Some people won't like you no matter how nice you are, some won't love you even if you dedicate your life to them, and some careers and behaviors just don't fit you due to physical, mental, emotional, or temperament limitations! There is no *one, perfect* friend, lover, career, or job for you—there are *many* that can lead to your being a happy, contented person! *Make choices with your dreams, abilities, and limitations in mind!*

➢ When making changes, be honest about the costs *and* rewards for a change. Giving up smoking is a *very* costly change—but the rewards easily outweigh the costs! However, "winning" some friendships, lovers, grades, or jobs may tempt you to endure costs far beyond the rewards you will reap. *Don't compromise your values and self-worth!*

➢ Rewards from others are *least likely* early in a life-style change or new activity.
  ▪ Even if the change was their idea or had their blessing, they will worry that a change will threaten their place and power in your life! Their fears may lead them to punish, or attempt to sabotage, your efforts. Especially beware if the person has been possessive or overprotective of you in the past (see Chapter 14 on enabling).
  ▪ Recognize that external sources of recognition, security, and reward are fickle—learn to reinforce yourself for making the changes you know are best for you.
  ▪ Forming or joining a support group of others currently changing will give you social support when motivation lags—and you can celebrate their small victories too!
  ▪ Cultivate friends, a mentor, or a counselor to cheer progress and soften setbacks.

➢ In times of stress and negative events, promise yourself that you will work *at least one* good experience or reward into each day—you deserve a reward for coping!

➢ Beware of **entrapment**, the tendency to think you must continue toward a selected goal *just because you have invested so much and worked so hard to get this far.* You have a right to change your mind—the goal may turn out to be unsuitable or too costly, you may have changed in ways that make the goal less appealing, or you may have found a more attractive or currently available goal. Keep in mind that the more you have *invested* in the process, the stronger will be the feeling that you *must* continue—that it *must* be a "good" project for you to have invested so much effort. Needs and interests change.

➢ Confronting a challenge or working for change will increase your self-worth and the skills you will need to cope with future stressors. This is true *regardless* of whether you meet your original or an altered goal—or stop short of what you originally defined as "success." The *process* can be more important than the product! You learn tolerance for change and more about your life goals, current skill levels, *and* limitations. This insight will help you make *better* choices and *better* plans for accomplishing them in the future.

Once you make a decision, the universe conspires to make it happen.
— Ralph Waldo Emerson

An Ending That is Really a Beginning

The doors we open and close each day decide the lives we live. — Flora Whittemore

We've given you a lot of information about ways to live your life to *maximize* your chances for happiness and *minimize* choices that won't be particularly fulfilling. *It is your job to take this information and make modifications in your daily rituals that will let you reach your goals and win that pursuit of happiness.* We thought we would finish this chapter by reminding you of a song from that happiness sage, Bobby McFerrin. Surely you remember the words and tune from his classic song, "Don't Worry, Be Happy!" We hope it runs happily through your head all day long!

Suggested Readings

Kasser, T., & Ryan, R. M. (1993). A dark side of the American dream: Correlates of financial success as a central life aspiration. *Journal of Personality and Social Psychology, 65,* 410-422.

Diener, E., & Diener, C. (1996). Most people are happy. *Psychological Science, 7,* 181-185.

Diener, E., Sandvik, E., Seidlitz, L., & Diener, M. (1993). The relationship between income and subjective well-being: Relative or absolute? *Social Indicators Research, 28,* 195-223.

Myers, D. G. (2000). The funds, friends, and faith of happy people. *American Psychologist, 55,* 56-67.

Myers, D. G., & Diener, E. (1996, May). The pursuit of happiness. *Scientific American, 274,* 54-56.

Ryff, C. D. (1995). Psychological well-being in adult life. *Current Directions in Psychological Science, 4,* 99-103.

Suggested Web Site

www.psych.upenn.edu/seligman/teachinghighschool.htm Site for Positive Psychology.

http://www.psych.uiuc.edu/~ediener/index.html This is Dr. Ed Diener's home page. It contains links to information on subjective well-being (happiness).

http://counseling.uchicago.edu/vpc The site for the Student Counseling and Resource Center at the University of Chicago. They have excellent virtual pamphlets on dealing with relationships.

Chapter 18

*Diversity in the *University*

I hope my roommates don't think I know all about tractor pulls and tipping cows.
— worried student from a rural area about to start college in Philadelphia.

The young woman quoted above lives outside a little town of 5,000 people. She guesses that within 15 miles of her house there are fifteen Italian restaurants, five Chinese restaurants, five Mexican restaurants, one Indian restaurant, one Thai restaurant, and a bagel shop. There is also the "country cooking" place with a huge model cow on the roof. And another place where local bands play country music at open mike night every Wednesday to the delight of the people line dancing. Contrary to what some people might think, this young woman does not know about tractors and cows. *However, she can order desserts from apple pie to zabaglione.* She is familiar with many types of wonderful food. She has met people from all over the world.

Do all towns of 5,000 people have such a wide selection of restaurants? Do the residents of most small towns include people from many nations? If there is a university or two in the area, they might. Universities value diversity. They value the ideas, outlooks and cultures of other people. When many types of people are welcome in an area, they will come bringing their food, music, art, and other ethnic enrichments. And everyone can benefit from this.

Combining "diversity" and "university" may seem like an oxymoron. That is, the two words preclude each other (kind of like jumbo shrimp!). The word "university" comes from the Latin word "universus" meaning entire or whole (http://dictionaries.travlang.com/LatinEnglish/, Feb. 28, 2003). "University", then, includes everyone, implying some kind of unity. In contrast, "diversity" focuses on differences, on the distinctions between individuals. Putting them together, diversity in the university involves difference and unity, individuality and sameness. These qualities seem contradictory, but they are not truly incompatible.

Universities as Communities

Perhaps one way to approach this seeming contradiction is to look at the university as a community. According to psychologists (e.g., Dalton, Elias, & Wandersman, 2001), people feel they are members of a community when they are aware of belonging to a group, when they feel they and the group influence each other, when they feel they share values with other members of the group, and when they have some emotional bond with the group. When you are a member of a community, you can accept someone else as a community member even if you do not personally know that individual.

Certainly universities meet the definition of community. Students identify themselves as community members as soon as they say they are a student at a particular college. In completing assignments, students allow the university to influence their behavior. By participating in class, student government, campus jobs, (and even by paying their bills!), students can impact the university. Given that students attend universities to be educated—and the primary goal of faculty and staff is to educate students, the members of a university share values. Finally, it is difficult to avoid having some emotional relationship with an institution where you spend many hours a week and where you have friends and acquaintances. Does this mean that all the members of a community must be the same? Of course not. Many communities, including universities, consist of people who vary in many respects.

Writing Activity 18.1—List 10 characteristics that describe *you*.

| |
| |
| |
| |
| |
| |
| |
| |
| |
| |

Number the characteristics from the most important to you to the least important to you. Did you include physical traits like hair color? Did you include your race? Ethnic background? Religion? Sexual preference? Major? Gender? Which types of traits (e.g., athletic, friendly) did you indicate were *most* important? Which were *least* important?

Dalton, et al. (2001) proposed that the most important ways in which people vary include race, culture, religion, social class, ability/disability, sexual preference, age, and ethnicity. The students, faculty and staff of a university include people differing in all of these attributes. Based on their backgrounds, each member of the university community brings with them different values and goals. They also bring different expectations about the university and about other people. But they are still members of the college community. To demonstrate this, think about the exercise above. What where the most important traits that you listed about yourself? How might these be the same or different for you roommate? Your best friend? Your classmates? Your professors?

Community Members are *NOT* all the Same

The truth will not penetrate a preoccupied mind.
— Charles Darwin

If students look at the people in their classes they will probably be able to identify people older or younger than themselves, people of different races, both males and females, and individuals with varying abilities or disabilities. Other differences between people, such as ethnicity, religion, or sexual preference, may not be obvious, but will still exist. Have you ever thought about the values and expectations these other people bring to the university? For example, does the woman with children who attends your Anthropology class have the same expectations for the course that you have? Does the deaf young man in your General Psychology class have the same questions about how babies learn language that you have? Does the student from China have the same expectations about friendships that American students have?

Writing Activity 18.2—Write down all the ways in which students in your classes vary. For example, are there students of different races, genders, majors, etc? In what ways may their view of class differ from yours?
The next time you go to class, observe the other students. Were there any differences you students. Were there any differences you did *not* list? List them here.

Adult students returning to school may share more similar goals with each other than with traditionally aged students. Deaf students may share a culture that does not include hearing students. Students from foreign countries may look more to each other for friendship than they look to American students. It is not surprising that students with traits in common may wish to form groups based on these traits. These subgroups within the college community may be sub-communities. In addition, student groups based on religion, race, and ethnicity may be sub-communities. Students in social groups may form sub-communities. Even students in a particular major may form a sub-community.

Are sub-communities bad? Again, of course not. All the individuals in these sub-groups bring something unique to the university. It makes the university a richer environment. It allows the members of the university to broaden their perspectives and exposes them to ideas they might not otherwise have had the opportunity to experience. Further, the individuals in each of these sub-communities still recognize themselves—and members of other sub-communities—as belonging to the greater university community. Despite the fact that they all bring with them their own goals and values, they also attend the university to acquire the skills and values offered by the university. Some of the skills sought by students in the university overlap (e.g., the ability to think critically). Other skills sought differ between students. For example, some people are studying chemistry while others study art. But what about values? Are there values shared by the university community as a whole?

Universities Are Communities

Education is the ability to listen to almost anything without losing your temper.
— Robert Frost

Acceptance of diversity

Although there is not one standard list of the values of the university, there are issues on which most faulty and staff would agree. Of course, universities value knowledge and education. The majority of universities require students to take classes in a variety of areas, as well as classes in their major. This helps ensure students are broadly educated as well as focused on a discipline. Universities also value intellectual honesty. This covers a variety of topics. It includes acknowledging when you gained an idea or information from someone else, rather than presenting it as your own. It means accurately reporting scientific data rather than inventing findings. It also includes admitting the mistakes you make and assuming responsibility for your work. Universities also value respect for others, including their opinions, ideas and interests. *As you have probably realized, all of these indicate that the university values diversity.* Universities provide diversity in the areas of study that students can pursue. Universities encourage diversity through sharing varied ideas and opinions. Universities demand acceptance of diversity by requiring individuals to respect other people.

What does acceptance of diversity mean on an individual level? What does it mean for you? It can mean *your acceptance of people who are in some way different from you.* Acceptance of diversity can also mean *other people's acceptance of you despite your difference from them.* All of us can be the person who is different given the right context. The young woman in the example that started this chapter was worried about her differences from her roommates, who were from New York and Philadelphia. Being from a rural area made the young woman different. She worried she would seem unsophisticated and undereducated. Her roommates had their own traits that set them apart. One was African American and another was in recovery from drug abuse. Certainly these young women also felt concerns about the willingness of others to accept and respect them for whom they are.

Writing Activity 18.3—Have you ever been the person who was different? List some times you were the person who stood out. How did you feel? What did people do that made you feel more comfortable? What did they do that made you feel worse?

How may individuals demonstrate their acceptance of diversity? A single, simple answer to this does not exist. However, several straightforward steps may be helpful (e.g., Dalton, et al., 2001). First, people must be aware that their own life experiences are not shared by all other people. Therefore, one person's view of the world will be different than another person's. Second, people must accept that no one perspective is right or wrong: different views are just different. Third, individuals must be willing to learn about the experiences and views of people whose backgrounds are different from their own.

Writing Activity 18.4—Hanna (2003), lists 3 questions people may ask themselves to assess their acceptance of people different from themselves: "Is my thinking reasonable and rational?" "Am I being fair?" "Am I basing my impressions on knowledge of the individual as a person or only as a representative of a group?" (p. 243). How does your thinking reflect these questions?

A great many people think they are thinking when they are
merely rearranging their prejudices. — William James

On being the same—but still being unique

When thinking about starting college did you think about whether other people would like you? Were you concerned about how easy it would be to make friends or to find romantic partners? Did you wonder whether you would fit in? Almost all students would answer "yes" to some of these questions. Most students hope that other people with accept them as individuals. Universities, in valuing diversity, promote the acceptance of the unique characteristics that individuals bring to the institution. This value is consistent with the main function of the university: to educate students. Surely, there would be a lot less to learn, and the university would be a lot less valuable, if we were all the same.

Only the educated are free.
— Epictetus

Suggested Readings

Hanna, S. L. (2003). *Person to person: Positive relationships don't just happen.* Upper Saddle River, NJ: Prentice Hall.

Suggested Web Sites

http://www.diversityweb.org/. This site provides information on encouraging acceptance of diversity in universities.

http://www.forbetterlife.org/ The Foundation for A Better Life is dedicated to supporting beliefs that value the individual and the community.

http://dictionaries.travlang.com/LatinEnglish/ This site helps travelers and potential travelers translate, search for lodging, chat, and look up currency exchange rates.

http://www.apa.org/ed/biblio.html This APA web page contains an annotated bibliography on diversity in psychology prepared by the Task Force on Diversity Issues at the Precollege and Undergraduate Levels of Education in Psychology.

Chapter 19

When Your Child Leaves for College:
This Chapter is for Parents

I saw my son once the first semester he was gone, and we didn't phone each other at all.
— father of a college freshman

Now that I'm a junior, I don't call my parents much—only 3 or 4 times a week.
— said with no irony by a female student

How do children and their parents respond to the child's starting college? Only one thing is sure—the responses are VERY variable. Some adolescents are racing for independence. They are eager to live without direct parental supervision; they are eager to make their own decisions. Other adolescents are much more hesitant. They are not yet comfortable with too much independence. They want parental involvement in many aspects of their lives. Parental responses also vary. Some parents calmly watch their children leave for college with the expectation that their involvement in the child's life will now be limited at best, dictated mainly by the child's desire to maintain contact. Other parents expect they will still be an active part of their child's life.

Regardless of what characterizes your family, there are some issues that most parents of college students must face. This chapter will address some of these topics and will offer suggestions for how to address them. Issues facing both the parents of students who are going away to college and issues facing the parents of commuting students will be discussed. First addressed are the concerns facing parents of students who will be living away from home. These include family reactions when children first leave for college, how to maintain contact with students, when to get involved in students' campus life, and what are some warning signs that should not be ignored. Following this, situations which parents of commuting students might confront are presented.

Please keep in mind that what is offered in this chapter are *suggestions*, not rules. Because there are such large differences between individuals, there are no "right ways" to behave. Just as parents of babies are often told that they need to do what feels right for them, parents of college students can often follow the same advice. Most parents know their child better than anyone else does. Parents know best what they themselves are comfortable with. Most parents will probably do best making decisions consistent with their own feelings.

Before reading on, you can use the following **Activity** to consider the concerns you and your child have about college life.

Writing Activity 19.1—Parental Concerns vs. Student Concerns. Both parents and students have some issues about which they are concerned or anxious or worried. List the *five* most problematic issues *you* believe your child will face.

Now list the *five* issues that *your child* is most concerned about.

Are the issues you listed as your concerns the same as the issues you listed for your child? Why do you think they are or are not the same? If you asked your child to complete this **Activity**, do you think your child would answer exactly as you did? Where might the differences occur?

How to Say Goodbye

Parents learn a lot from their children about coping with life. — Muriel Spark

For students living away from home, saying goodbye might be traumatic or joyful. And which it is might be different for students, their siblings, and their parents. This can lead to a lot of stress for parents—how do they coordinate their own feelings with what is best for the student, and what is best for any other children that might be involved? Although there are no set answers for this, several guidelines may make this easier.

First, acknowledge that it is okay for everyone in the family to have their own reaction, as long as it is polite and decorous. If it's accepted that everyone will react in his or her own way, then no one can be accused of acting in an incorrect manner. Everyone will know that his or her feelings are legitimate. If they want to, they will be able to talk about these feelings. A common scene on move-in day is a college student holding the hand of a teary-eyed younger sibling. Equally common are younger siblings plotting their take-over of previously shared space in closets, bedrooms, bathrooms, etc. Both types of reactions are normal, healthy, and frequently found in the same person!

Second, parents need to pay attention to their student's reactions. They need to take their cues for how to act from the student. Some students are eager for their parents to help them move in and then leave. In fact, the student may say things like, "Are you ready to go home yet?" This does not mean they do not love their parents. It does not mean that they hated their home life. It just means the student is ready for a new adventure. Parents probably should respect this. Other students may clearly be more anxious. They may need more help saying good-bye. In cases like this, parents may have to initiate the leave taking. This is okay, too.

Third, parents should not ignore their own feelings. However, parents should be sensitive about how they express these feelings. Some individuals, and families, are very demonstrative; laughing, hugging, even the occasional tears are expected. Other individuals, and families, are more reserved. For example, some adolescents do not wish to kiss their parents in any place that may be deemed public. Parents need to find an acceptable blend of their own needs and those of their children. In general, moderation works. It is not acceptable for parents to weep copiously as their child unpacks the car. On the other hand, if the parents would really like a good-bye kiss, that is not an unreasonable request.

Finally, because there is no single right way to say good-bye, there is no real way to do it right and no real way to do it wrong. Some parents feel guilty after leave-taking because they are afraid they did not do enough, or they did too much, or they said the wrong thing, or they did not say what they should have said. Some parents feel angry for the same reasons. But there is no right or wrong thing to say or do. And besides, you can always phone later or come back for a visit. Which nicely leads in to the next issue:

Maintaining Contact With Your College Student

Of course, there are no set rules for how to do this, either. Basically, parents should not hobble their children, but parents should not cast off their children either. As is demonstrated by the quotes introducing this chapter, there are a lot of differences in peoples' responses. How children become independent and how their parents allow it are variable.

Some people believe that students should initiate all contact. In this way the students can directly control the amount of interaction they have with their families, seeking more interaction when they need family support and less interaction when they are confident on their own. Although this view has merit, it ignores the needs of the rest of the family. It also puts a lot of pressure on the students. Students who may want to call may feel they are weak or juvenile if they call too much. Others may feel guilty if they suspect they are ignoring their families. Having set guidelines for contact that were made considering both the needs of the student and the needs of the family may alleviate some of these problems.

It may be a good idea for parents to discuss how and when they will make contact with their children before the children actually leave for college. The immediate stress of leaving may make this kind of decision difficult to deal with. Discussing the issue in advance, when everyone is calm, may make decisions easier and everyone happier. Of course, if the guidelines developed do not work for either the student or the family, the guidelines can always be changed.

What, then, are some specific issues that may be considered when thinking about how and when parents should contact their college student children? First, it helps to consider all the means by which people can communicate: phone calls, e-mail, regular mail, visits, etc. The young woman in the example introducing this chapter clearly wanted contact by phone. She later stated quite explicitly that she wanted to *talk* to her parents. The father and student described in the example did not need phone contact. What the example does not include, however, is that this father and son e-mailed each other every day! The students and their families were satisfied—but what worked for one family clearly would not have worked for the other. Think about the strategies that would work for your family. You might consider daily e-mail, weekly phone calls scheduled at a particular day and time, regularly sent mail, scheduled visits, etc. Some families prefer not to schedule any of these. Rather they plan to contact each other on an "as needed" basis. Other families find weekly contact too infrequent. Be willing to try things out and see what works for the student and the family.

One form of mail people sometimes seem to forget in this electronic age is regular mail. However, college students seem to LOVE finding letters, postcards, and packages in their mailboxes. The mail is a way to maintain contact without demanding time when the student does not have it. It is also cheap and easy. If you do not like to write letters, there are many cute cards you can send. Even postcards can be used to send warm wishes or short funny stories. And it is the rare college student who is disappointed opening an envelop that contains even a small check! In honesty, however, it does not seem that most college students frequently contact their families using the mail.

A final issue that might be addressed here is visiting. Again, how often families expect to visit and how often students expect visits is not consistent. This is influenced in part by how far from home the college is. If the child is in school hundreds of miles from home, visits are going to be infrequent. If the child is an hour from home, visits may or may not be frequent. Some children in school close to home expect to see their families regularly, either by going home themselves or having the family come to see them. Other students in school close to home do not hold these expectations. There are students who live an hour from home who see their parents 3 times a semester. Again, there is no right answer. What is right is what works for each family. However, there are a few guidelines to keep in mind. Except in exceptional situations, parents should not expect to visit if that will interfere with their child's studies. A student's primary work in college is education. On the other hand, students do not want to feel deserted. Many students want to know they can go home when they need to and that they will be welcomed.

Writing Activity 19.2—Mail, E-mail, or Phone. Although you may not really know what is going to work, some misunderstandings might be avoided if parents and children consider the following issues.

What forms of communication are you comfortable using?

With which of these is your child comfortable?

How often do you think you would like to talk with your child on the phone?

Ask your child how often he/she would like to talk?

If your preference and your child's are different, can you work out a compromise? What would it be?

How often do you expect to e-mail each other?

How often do you expect to send mail or receive mail?

How often do you expect to visit your child? How often do you expect your child to come home?

When the Children Come Home from College:
Some Unexpected Changes

No man knows his true character until he has run out of gas,
purchased something on the installment plan, and raised an adolescent.
— Mercelene Cox

Many students feel that, although they look forward to going home from college, they experience a lot of conflict with their parents once they get there. Often, this is true. Parents frequently expect their children to resume the same roles in the household that they had before going to college. Parents may hold expectations about curfews, bedtimes, household chores, etc. However, the students have been living on their own. They have had no curfew. They have gone to bed whenever they wished. Their room is as clean, or as messy, as they (or their roommate) allows. The difference in expectations between the students and their parents often leads to some kind of conflict.

Can the conflict be avoided? Probably not entirely. However, it might be decreased. Parents and students need to clearly communicate with each other about what they expect. And both sides probably need to make some compromises. Some parents decide that college students need no curfews—but still request that their children let the rest of the family know where they are going and when they will be back. Other families allow their college students more freedom, but still expect them to participate in household chores. Most of the time, the conflicts are worked out. Many students report that by their sophomore year things are much more harmonious. Communication between family members and treating each other courteously, seem to be key ingredients to successfully resolving conflicts.

When to Get Involved in Your College Student's Campus Life, and When Not To

Parents of elementary and high school students are expected to be involved with their children's school. Parents are expected to attend parent-teacher conferences. Parents are often invited by the teachers to call the school if they feel their child needs help or is having problems. Is this kind of involvement expected in college? The answer is emphatically "**NO**." College students are expected to handle most of the problems that they face concerning school by themselves.

When students are having academic difficulties, it is their responsibility to discuss this with their professors. Professors do not expect parents to call and inquire about their child's grades or study skills or attendance. If students must miss class for some reason, professors expect the student to make contact, provide documentation of why he or she is missing class, and arrange to make up the work.

The expectation that students will handle problems themselves applies to nonacademic aspects of student life as well. If a student is having difficulty with a roommate, it is up the student to address this problem. If a student is having other kinds of housing difficulties, he or she should contact the appropriate authority to address the problem. Parents are not expected to immediately get involved in students' housing crises.

Does this mean, then, that parents should never get involved? The answer to that is also "**NO**." When, then, should parents get involved? One situation in which parental involvement is clearly warranted is when there is a serious family crisis, for example, severe illness or death in the family. It may well be appropriate for a parent to inform the office concerned with student life that a family crisis has occurred. In many situations, the student life office will then contact the student's professors. If parents are unsure which office to call in order to inform the school about the situation, they should pick any office that seems reasonable; if it is the wrong one, the people in that office will simply redirect the parents to the correct place.

Other situations that may call for parental involvement include those that involve the safety of the student or harassment of the student. If a parent feels that some aspect of the student's living situation is unsafe, it may be appropriate to contact officials. For example, if a female student studies late at the library, is there an escort service available so she can be walked back to her dorm? If not, parents may wish to point this out. Similarly, if parents have evidence that their child is being harassed based on group membership (for example, gender, sexual orientation, religion, or ethnic background) it may be appropriate for parents to become involved. However, even in the situations presented here, it is appropriate for the child to make the first contact with college authorities about these problems. Only if nothing is done, or the situation gets beyond the student's ability to cope with, should parents become involved.

Writing Activity 19.3—When to Get Involved. For each of the following situations, consider when you *would or would not* become involved with your child's campus life.

1. Your daughter calls home and says her psychology professor is awful and she is going to fail the class.

2. During a visit home your daughter discusses how weird her roommate is.

3. The dorm bathroom on your son's floor has overflowed into your son's room and ruined some of his possessions. The housing office tells him there is nothing that can be done about it.

4. Your son says he spoke with his calculus professor, but he is still going to get a "C" in the class.

5. Your daughter feels that one of the professors is touching her inappropriately.

Although there are, as usual, no specifically right answers for these situations, most professors would agree that parents have *no* reason to get involved in situations 1, 2, and 4. These are the kinds of occurrences that students should be able to address on their own. Situation 3 is less clear because the student has tried to handle the problem but has gotten nowhere. The student should probably go to the Dean in charge of housing and see if that is effective. If it is not, then it may be appropriate for parents to start calling. Situation 5 is most problematic. On most campuses there is an office or an individual who is officially designated as the contact for individuals who feel they are being harassed. The student in this example should be encouraged to contact that individual or office. If such an office does not exist, the student should probably contact another member of the university: the department chairperson of the professor in question, the dean, or even a vice president.

Warning Signs:
When Parents Need to Pay Attention

Many college students face some problems in adjusting to college: students express homesickness, stress, sadness, etc. Usually these reactions are not too intense, are fairly short-term, and may be tied to a specific situation like finishing a major paper. Just as parents should not become overly involved in a student's campus life, parents should not be overly controlling of students' daily activities, including the ways in which the student handles stress. There are times, however, when things go wrong. Students may be facing intense emotional problems. Students may also face health problems without being aware of it. What are some warning signs that your child is facing more than the normal degrees of adjustment problems?

Weight changes

Some change in their weight is normal for college students. In fact, the "freshman 15" is legendary. Many students gain a noticeable amount of weight their freshman year. However, parents may be concerned if the change in weight seems very extreme, whether their child is losing weight or gaining weight. Extreme weight change can be an indication of eating disorders, depression, chronic stress, drug/alcohol use, physical illness, or other situations. (See Chapters 9, 13, 14, 15, and 16 for in-depth discussions of many of these problems.)

If a college student does exhibit a large change in weight, parents may first wish to have the child have a medical exam. Illnesses the child may be ignoring, like mononucleosis, can result in weight loss. If the child is ill, then treatment can begin. If the child is not ill, other possibilities need to be considered.

Anorexia Nervosa, an eating disorder, is characterized by failure to maintain a normal body weight. This is a very severe disorder that can result in the death of the individual. It is best if it is identified quickly and the person is given physical and psychological therapy.

Drug or alcohol use can also result in changes in weight. Determining that your child is using drugs or alcohol is generally not easy to do—and weight loss alone is not a clear indication of substance abuse. Other kinds of information can give clues to students' use of substances. However, it is difficult to know what substances a child is using without actually finding the drugs.

Depression

When college students are depressed they often talk about feeling sad or worthless. Their sleeping and eating habits may be disrupted. They may have no energy. Some students, especially males, may express their depression with anger. Depression, like any illness, needs to be treated. As was the case for weight loss, if a student seems depressed, it is a good idea to first have them get a medical exam. If physical illness is ruled out as a cause of the problem, then depression can be addressed. Depression can also be related to other problems the student may have. Drug use, academic problems, and social problems can all be related to depression.

Identifying Depression in Teens— In recent nation-wide interviews with adolescents' parents and other care givers (Sawyer, 2000), about 5% of their 13- to 17-year-old adolescents were reported to suffer from clinical depression. However, 12% of adolescents reported they were depressed. That wasn't the only disagreement—88% of these adolescents were *not* identified as depressed by their parents, whereas 74% of adolescents reported as depressed by parents didn't say they were.

Even worse, "…only 40% of adolescents identified by parents as depressed had attended a professional service for help with their problems in the previous 6 months…. Only 18.5% of adolescents who reported themselves as depressed had attended a service for help," according to Dr. Michael Sawyer, Associate Professor in the Department of Psychiatry at Adelaide University and one of the authors of *The Mental Health of Young People in Australia*. Although this study was not conducted in the U.S., the countries are very similar, so we can expect that a study here would yield very similar results.

Once depression is diagnosed, modern treatments is very effective, but adolescents with problems have to be identified *and* taken to see a mental health professional. As this study warns, you *cannot* diagnose depression yourself. But keeping the channels of communication open and taking your teen for help are important first steps. Clinical depression is a *serious* problem and is related to development of substance abuse, eating disorders, disruptive behaviors, and suicide.

We urge you to read more about this and other problems in other chapters in the book, including those on Depression, Alcohol, Drugs, Eating Disorders, Assertiveness, and Stress.

Social Isolation

Happy, well-adjusted people have friends. They may not have lots of friends, but they have some people with whom they spend time or to whom they are close. If a college student does not have any friends, there is probably a problem. If the parents of a college student see their child is isolated, with no friends, the parent may wish to talk to a counselor about what steps to take.

Feedback from others

The people a college student lives with come to know the student well. Most students are also usually hesitant to tell parents or authority figures that one of their acquaintances is having problems (see discussion of *enabling* in Chapter 14). Therefore, if a roommate, classmate, or friend of a student tells that student's parents there is a problem, this should probably not be dismissed. Of course, the person might be mistaken. But the person might also be right.

This is hardly a complete list of the warning signs parents should note. However, most parents can rely on their common sense. If things seem to be wrong with the student, it is probably a good idea to look into it.

Issues Facing Parents of Commuting Students

Some of the issues discussed above are clearly relevant for parents regardless of whether their students are living on campus or living at home. When parents should become involved in a student's academic life and the warning signs of problems are concerns of parents regardless of where their child resides. Other issues discussed above are not relevant; since commuting students are still living at home, there is no big goodbye. However, there is still a transition. This transition can be both academic and social.

Because college students tend to have fewer activities and fewer hours of class than high school students, parents may expect their children to be home at least as much as they were in high school. However, college is generally far more academically challenging than high school. Because of this, college students may spend time on campus outside of class doing research or studying or working on projects. In order to get their academic work done, they may go to sleep far later than their parents think healthy. Some students describe how they must demand time away from home because their parents expect more home involvement that the student can comfortably give. Other students describe how their parents would like them to go to sleep at regular hours—but when a major assignment is due, the student may be up to the wee hours completing it.

Similarly, the amount and kind of social freedom expected by college students is often different from that expected by high school students. Parents may expect their children home by 11:00 on weeknights. College students may just be finishing studying then. They may then expect to participate in some social activity. The fact that commuting students study and socialize with residential students may exacerbate differences between students and parents. The students living on campus have no parents immediately available that they have to please. These students have no curfews and no one directly monitoring them. The commuting students who socialize with the resident students may expect the same type of freedom.

Clearly, there is a lot of potential for conflict between parents and their children commuting to college. Parents and students need to develop realistic expectations. The student needs time to study—but at the same time, the student is a member of a household and so has household responsibilities. The student is a young adult and should be granted the freedoms appropriate for young adulthood. But students are still members of their parents' household and should treat their parents with appropriate respect. How can a balance between parental demands and student demands be reached? Open communication, clear rules, flexibility, and mutual respect are keys.

As a parent, you just hang on for the ride. — Robert Wagner

Enjoy Your Child's Journey Through College

This chapter had no hard and fast rules about how parents should treat their college students. Why? Because there *are* no hard and fast rules. Parents need to be there for their students without smothering them. What the means for doing are will vary from family to family. Remember, parents probably know their children better than anyone else does. Do what feels right for you. Listen to your child. Be flexible and make changes when it is necessary. College can be a wonderful adventure—for both the student and the parents.

Suggested Readings

Coburn, K. L., & Treeger, M. L. (1997). *Letting go* (3rd ed.). New York: HarperCollins.

Suggested Web Sites

http://www.apa.org/psychnet/ Psychnet, which has all kinds of information for the general public, is part of the American Psychological Association's Web site.

http://www.aacap.org/publications/factsfam/index.htm Web site for the American Academy of Child and Adolescent Psychiatry.

http://www.thesemester.com/ Tips on how to successfully complete the semester are offered.

http://www.collegefreshmen.net/ This site presents advice for the challenges faced by college freshmen.

http://www.pflag.org Information is presented for gay and lesbian individuals and their families and friends.

http://www.psychwatch.com/ This site is one of the best we've found to contain information on all areas of psychology and to give you access to other Web sites of interest. Sign up to receive a free newsletter every Friday, containing links to releases on research and books for that week. You can search the archives for earlier news releases, and there are tutorials on many topics.

Chapter 20

Mike and Lauren Revisited:
Survivors of the Semester

The end of all exploring
Will be to arrive where we started
And know the place for the first time.
— T. S. Eliot

Mike and Lauren just reached a milestone: they completed their first semester in college and are pleased with their grades! Of course, they have already made the "New Year's resolutions of college life": next semester they will be more organized, start earlier on assignments, set up a study schedule and keep it, and…oh, yes…party just a little less and a little more wisely. While they realize they still have a long way to go before they have truly mastered being a college student, they feel that they have matured in many ways—not just academically, but also in terms of autonomy, self-control, and their social relationship skills.

We are confident that you too have learned a lot about yourself during this semester and have begun to feel more like an "expert" than just a "hanger-on." We especially hope that our book has made your transition into college easier. We have a few final suggestions to help you stay more organized and less stressed out. When next semester begins, we recommend that you develop the habit of writing notes as reminders for the details in your busy life. Even before the semester, you can begin constructing (and then regularly update) a semester calendar, which will encourage you to break up large tasks into edible pieces and will save you from nasty surprises.

And finally, we urge you to continue writing about your feelings and the events in your life—not just next semester, but throughout your life. You will find that keeping a journal—or just writing during times of stress and change—can be good for both your mental and physical health. As discussed earlier in the book, writing about traumatic situations—and everyday experiences—helps you put everything into perspective and understand yourself better. In fact, talking or writing about and seeking insight into confusing or stressful situations was found to be associated with improved health and better functioning of the individual's immune system (Pennebaker, Kiecolt-Glaser, & Glaser, 1988; Pennebaker & Susman, 1988; Petrie, Booth, Pennebaker, Davison, & Thomas, 1995). And, as discussed in Chapter 2, knowing about both your good and bad characteristics boosts self-worth and feelings of being in control of your own destiny (Baumgardner, 1990). Self-certainty lets you predict what you can and cannot do well, which is helpful when you are making serious decisions, picking a major, selecting courses for the next semester, and choosing a career.

The information we have included in this book was designed not just to help you during your first semester in college, but also to make your journey through college and later life go more smoothly. In the future, we urge you to read what you have written throughout the book, especially in those sections that apply specifically to situations you are confronting. The information we have provided and your personal writings will facilitate your problem solving and help you cope with circumstances you cannot change. Here's one last writing assignment to give you closure on this semester's adventures.

Writing Activity 20.1—Think about how you feel *right now* about your journey so far through college. What have you learned about yourself and about college life that you didn't know when you began the semester? What is the major "New Year's resolution of college life" that you have made for next semester?

We would appreciate receiving feedback from you about which parts of this book were especially useful to you. We would also like to receive suggestions for new topics or information you think would be beneficial for incoming college students. Indeed, this edition has incorporated ideas we received from past students. We have provided a sheet at the end of the book that you can complete and send to us, or you can write us on your own paper.

We hope the rest of your college years—and the rest of your life—meet the goals you set for yourself. Just remember, if you decide to change yourself *or* your goals, you have the skills and the commitment to do so. And when you question yourself, return to the chapters in this book *and* your own writings to help you answer back! ***You are your own best project in life***—and only you can choose the path and the techniques to get you to your goals. Go for it!

How much better to know that we have dared to live our dreams
than to live our lives in a lethargy of regret. — Gilbert Caplin

We all live in suspense from day to day; in other words,
you are the hero of your own story. — Mary McCarthy

Suggested Readings

Baumgardner, A. H. (1990). To know oneself is to like oneself: Self-certainty and self-affect. *Journal of Personality and Social Psychology, 58,* 1062-1072.
Pennebaker, J. W., Kiecolt-Glaser, J. K. & Glaser, R. (1988). Disclosure of trauma and immune function: Health implications for psychotherapy. *Journal of Consulting and Clinical Psychology, 56,* 239-245.
Postman, N., & Weingartner, C. (1973). *The school book.* New York: Delacorte.

Suggested Web Sites

Look back to the end of Chapter 1 for Web sites that will be equally useful at this point in your journey. And if you run into a particular roadblock or pothole in your path, return to the end of the appropriate chapter for readings and Web sites that can help you out. We wish you interesting days!

Bibliography

Albaili, M. A. (1998). Goal orientations, cognitive strategies and academic achievement among United Arab Emirates college students. *Educational Psychology, 18,* 195-203.

Alexander, T. (2000). *Adjustment and human relationships.* Upper Saddle River, NJ: Prentice Hall.

Alpert, R., & Haber, R. N. (1960). Anxiety in academic achievement situations. *Journal of Abnormal and Social Psychology, 61,* 207-215.

Altrocchi, J. (1980). *Abnormal behavior.* New York: Harcourt Brace.

Amabile, T. M., Hill, K. G., Hennessey, B. A., & Tighe, E. M. (1994). The Work Preference Inventory: Assessing intrinsic and extrinsic motivational orientations. *Journal of Personality and Social Psychology,* 66, 950-967.

American Psychiatric Association. (2000). *Diagnostic and statistical manual of mental disorders* (4th ed. text revision). Washington, DC: Author.

American Psychological Association. (1993). *Practice guidelines for major depressive disorder in adults.* Washington, DC: Author

Ames, C. (1992). Classrooms: Goals, structures, and student motivation. *Journal of Educational Psychology, 84,* 261-271.

Ames, C., & Archer, J. (1988). Achievement goals in the classroom: Student learning strategies and motivation processes. *Journal of Educational Psychology, 80,* 260-267.

Arkin, R. M., & Baumgardner, A. H. (1985). Self-handicapping. In J. H. Harvey & G. Weary (Eds.), *Attribution: Basic issues and applications* (pp. 169-202). New York: Academic Press.

Ash, R. (1999). *Fantastic book of 1001 facts.* New York: DK Publishing.

Bachman, J. G., Wadsworth, K. N., O'Malley, P. M., Schulenberg, J., & Johnston, L. D. (1997). Marriage, divorce, and parenthood during the transition to young adulthood: Impacts on drug use and abuse. In J. Schulenberg, J. L Maggs, & K. Hurrelmann (Eds.), *Health risks and developmental transitions during adolescence* (pp. 246-279). New York: Cambridge University Press.

Bandura, A. (1989). Human agency in social cognitive theory. *American Psychologist, 44,* 1175-1184.

Bartholomew, K., & Horowitz, L. M. (1991). Attachment styles among young adults: A test of a four-category model. *Journal of Personality and Social Psychology, 61,* 226-244.

Baum, A., & Fleming, I. (1993). Implications of psychological research on stress and technological accidents. *American Psychologist, 48,* 665-672.

Baumgardner, A. H. (1990). To know oneself is to like oneself: Self-certainty and self-affect. *Journal of Personality and Social Psychology, 58,* 1062-1072.

Baumgardner, A. H. (1991). Claiming depressive symptoms as a self-handicap: A protective self-presentation strategy. *Basic and Applied Social Psychology, 12,* 97-113.

Baumgardner, A. H., Lake, E. A., & Arkin, R. M. (1985). Claiming mood as a self-handicap: The influence of spoiled and unspoiled public identities. *Personality and Social Psychology Bulletin, 11,* 349-357.

Beck, A. T. (1967). *Depression: Causes and treatment.* Philadelphia: University of Pennsylvania Press.

Beck, A. T., Ward, C. H., Mendelson, M., Mock, J. E., & Erbaugh, J. K. (1961). An inventory for measuring depression. *Archives of General Psychiatry, 4,* 561-570.

Beck, B. L., Jara, D., Astor-Stetson, E., Zarecky, A., & Starks, M. (1998). *The effects of body image, social support, and media sensitivity on self-esteem, psychological well-being, and restrained eating in middle school students.* Poster session presented at the meeting of the Eastern Psychological Association, Boston.

Beck, B. L., Koons, S. R., & Milgrim, D. L. (2000). Correlates and consequences of behavioral procrastination: The effects of academic procrastination, self-consciousness, self-esteem and self-handicapping. *Journal of Social Behavior and Personality, 15*(5), 3-13.

Beck, B. L., & Scott, L. D. (1996). *It's all in the family: The effects of friend, significant other, and family social support on self-esteem, psychological well-being, self-handicapping, the impostor phenomenon, and locus of control.* Poster session presented at the meeting of the Eastern Psychological Association, Philadelphia.

Beck, B. L., Zarecky, A., Astor-Stetson, E., Jara, D., & Starks, M. (1998). *The effects of age, sex, grade level, body image, and family involvement on self-esteem, psychological well-being, and depression in middle school students.* Poster session presented at the meeting of the Eastern Psychological Association, Boston.

Becker, A. (1999, May 31). Fat-phobia in the Fijis: TV-thin is in. *Newsweek,* 70.

Benson, H. (1992). *The relaxation response.* New York: Avon.

Berglas, S., & Jones, E. E. (1978). Drug choice as a self-handicapping strategy in response to noncontingent success. *Journal of Personality and Social Psychology, 36,* 405-417.

Berman, R. M., Narasimhan, M., Sanacora, G., Miano, A. P., Hoffman, R. E., Hu, X. S., Charney, D. S., & Boutros, N. N. (2000). A randomized clinical trial of repetitive transcranial magnetic stimulation in the treatment of major depression. *Biological Psychiatry, 47,* 332-337.

Blakeslee, S. (2000). "Sleep on it" may be a lesson worth heeding. *Milwaukee Journal Sentinel,* May 1. (Available: http://www.jsonline.com/alive/news/apr00/sleep01043000.asp)

Blumenfeld, P. C. (1992). Classroom learning and motivation: Clarifying and expanding goal theory. *Journal of Educational Psychology, 84,* 272-281.

Bognatz, G., & Schick, C. (1996, March). *Relationships among attachment style, Type A behavior pattern, and perfectionism in teenage college students.* Poster session presented at the meeting of the Eastern Psychological Association, Philadelphia.

Buehler, R., Griffin, D., & Ross, M. (1994). Exploring the "planning fallacy": Why people underestimate their task completion times. *Journal of Personality and Social Psychology, 67,* 366-381.

Burke, R. J., & Weir, T. (1980). The Type A experience: Occupational and life demands, satisfaction and well-being. *Journal of Human Stress, 6,* 28-38.

Burns, D. D. (1980, November). The perfectionist's script for self-defeat. *Psychology Today,* pp. 34-52.

Burns, D. D. (1981). *Feeling good: The new mood therapy.* New York: Penguin Books.

Butler, R. (1987). Task-involving and ego-involving properties of evaluation: Effects of different feedback conditions on motivational perceptions, interest and performance. *Journal of Educational Psychology, 79,* 474-482.

Butler, R. (1988). Enhancing and undermining intrinsic motivation: The effects of task-involving evaluation on interest and performance. *British Journal of Educational Psychology, 58,* 1-14.

Buunk, B P., Collins, R. L., Taylor, S. E., VanYperen, N. W., & Dakof, G. A. (1990). The affective consequences of social comparison: Either direction has its ups and downs. *Journal of Personality and Social Psychology, 59,* 1238-1249.

Carver, C. S., Scheier, M. F., & Weintraub, J. K. (1989). Assessing coping strategies: A theoretically based approach. *Journal of Personality and Social Psychology, 56,* 267-283.

Centers for Disease Control and Prevention. (Sept. 27, 1996). Youth risk behavior surveillance—United States, 1995. *Morbidity and Mortality Weekly Report, 45* (No. SS-4).

Chen, K., & Kendel, D. B. (1995). The natural history of drug use from adolescence to the mid-thirties in a general population sample. *American Journal of Public Health, 85,* 41-47.

Clements, R. (1999). Prevalence of alcohol-use disorders and alcohol-related problems in a college student sample. *Journal of American College Health, 48,* 111-119.

CNN. (2002, April 9). *Study: College drinking in 1,400 deaths..* (Available: http://www.cnn.com/2002/fyi/teachers.ednews/04/09/us.college.drinking.ap/index.html)

Coburn, K. L., & Treeger, M. L. (1997). *Letting go* (3rd ed.). New York: HarperCollins.

Cohen, S., Frank, E., Doyle, W. J., Skoner, D. P., Rabin, B. S., & Gwaltney, J. M. (1998). Types of stressors that increase susceptibility to the common cold in healthy adults. *Health Psychology, 17,* 214-223.

Comer, R. J. (2001). *Abnormal psychology* (4th ed.). New York: Worth.

Cooper, L. M. (1994). Motivations for alcohol use among adolescents: Development and validation of a four-factor model. *Psychological Assessment, 2,* 117-128.

Coren, S. (1996). *The sleep thieves: An eye-opening exploration into the science and mysteries of sleep.* New York: Free Press.

Corey, G., Corey, M., & Callanan, P. (1998). *Issues and ethics in the helping professions* (5th ed.). Pacific Grove, CA: Brooks/Cole.

Covington, M. V. (1998). *The will to learn: A guide for motivating young people.* New York: Cambridge University Press.

Covington, M. V. (2000). Intrinsic versus extrinsic motivation in schools: A reconciliation. *Current Directions in Psychological Science, 9(1),* 22-25.

Dalton, J., Elias, M., & Wandersman, A. (2001). *Community psychology: Linking individuals and communities.* Stamford, CT: Wadsworth

Deaux, K., & Emsmiller, T. (1974). Explanations of successful performance on sex-linked tasks: What is skill for the male is luck for the female. *Journal of Personality and Social Psychology, 29,* 80-85.

Deci, E. L., Koestner, R., & Ryan, R. M. (1999). A meta-analytic review of experiments examining the effects of extrinsic rewards on intrinsic motivation. *Psychological Bulletin, 125,* 627-668.

Diener, E. (1984). Subjective well-being. *Psychological Bulletin, 95,* 242-273.

Diener, E., & Diener, C. (1996). Most people are happy. *Psychological Science, 7,* 181-185.

Diener, E., Emmons, R. A., Larsen, R. J., & Griffin, S. (1985). The Satisfaction with Life Scale. *Journal of Personality Assessment, 49.*

Diener, E., Sandvik, E., Seidlitz, L., & Diener, M. (1993). The relationship between income and subjective well-being: Relative or absolute? *Social Indicators Research, 28,* 195-223.

Doebler, T. C., Schick, C., Beck, B. L., & Astor-Stetson, E. (2000). Ego protection: The effects of perfectionism and gender on acquired and claimed self-handicapping and self-esteem. *College Student Journal, 34,* 524-536.

Dohrenwend, B., Pearlin, L., Clayton, P., Hamburg, B., Dohrenwend, B. P., Riley, M., & Rose, R. (1982). Report on stress and life events. In G. R. Elliott & C. Eisdorfer (Eds.), *Stress and human health: Analysis and implications of research.* New York: Springer.

Donnerstein, E. (1998, January). *Why do we have those new ratings on television?* Invited address presented at the annual meeting of the National Institute on the Teaching of Psychology, St. Petersburg Beach, FL.

Dweck, C. S. (1986). Motivational processes affecting learning. *American Psychologist, 41,* 1040-1048.

Dweck, C. S., & Leggett, E. S. (1988). A social-cognitive approach to motivation and personality. *Psychological Review, 95,* 256-273.

D'Zurella, T. J., & Goldfried, M. R. (1971). Problem solving and behavior modification. *Journal of Abnormal Psychology, 78,* 107-126.

Eisenberger, R., & Cameron, J. (1996). Detrimental effects of rewards: Reality or myth? *American Psychologist, 51,* 1153-1166.

Elkin, I. (1994). The NIMH Treatment of Depression Collaborative Research Program: Where we began and where we are. In A. E. Bergin & S. L. Garfield (Eds.), *Handbook of psychotherapy and behavior change* (4th ed.). New York: Wiley.

Elliot, A. (1996, January 18). Personal communication with Nielsen Media Research Director of Communications via e-mail (Anne_Elliot@tvratings.com). Cited in D. G. Myers, *Psychology* (6th ed.), p. 670. New York: Worth.

Ellis, A., & Harper, R. A. (1978). *A new guide to rational living.* N. Hollywood: Wilshire.

Ellis, A., & Knause, W. T. (1977). *Overcoming procrastination.* New York: Signet Books.

Fairlie, P., Flett, G. L., & Hewitt, P. L. (1993, August). *Perfectionism and perfectionistic self-presentation in dimensions of self-esteem, anxiety, and depression.* Poster session presented at the annual meeting of the American Psychological Association, Toronto, Ontario, Canada.

Ferrari, J. R., & Beck, B. L. (1998). Affective responses before and after fraudulent excuses by academic procrastinators. *Education, 118,* 529-537.

Festinger, L. (1954). A theory of social comparison processes. *Human Relations, 7,* 117-140.

Flett, G. L., & Hewitt, P. L. (1992, June). *Perfectionism in anxiety and depression: An investigation with the Perfectionism Cognitions Inventory.* Paper presented at the World Congress of Cognitive Therapy, Toronto, Ontario.

Flett, G. L., Hewitt, P. L., Blankstein, K. R., & Mosher, S. W. (1991). Perfectionism, self-actualization, and personal adjustment. *Journal of Social Behavior and Personality, 6,* 147-160. (Special issue: Handbook of self-actualization.)

Friant, P., Astor-Stetson, E., & Beck, B. (1996). *A comparison of the safe sex behaviors of a college community and an adult homosexual community.* Poster session presented at the meeting of the Eastern Psychological Association, Philadelphia, PA.

Frintner, M. P., & Rubinson, L. (1993). Acquaintance rape: The influence of alcohol, fraternity membership, and sports team membership. *Journal of Sex Education and Therapy, 19,* 272-284.

Friedman, H. S. (Ed.). (1992). *Hostility, coping, & health.* Washington, DC: American Psychological Association.

Friedman, M., & Rosenman, R. H. (1974). *Type A behavior and your heart.* New York: Knopf.

Friedman, M., & Ulmer, D. (1984). *Treating Type A behavior and your heart.* New York: Fawcett.

Gambrill, E., & Richey, C. A. (1975). An assertion inventory for use in assessment and research. *Behavior Therapy, 6,* 547-549.

Gambrill, E. D., & Richey, C. A. (1976). *It's up to you: Developing assertive social skills* (pp. 158-159). Millbrae, CA: Les Femmes.

Gambrill, E., & Richey, C. A. (1985). *Taking charge of your social life.* Belmont, CA: Wadsworth.

Garner, D. M. (1997). Psychoeducational principles in treatment. In: D. M. Garner & P. E. Garfinkel (Eds.), *Handbook of treatment for eating disorders.* New York: Guilford Press.

Garner, D. M., Cooke, A. K., & Marano, H. E. (1997, February). The 1997 body image survey results. *Psychology Today,* 30-44. (Available: http://www.psychologytoday.com/htdocs/prod/ptoarticle/pto-19970201-000023.asp)

Garner, D. M., Garfinkel, P. E., Schwartz, D., & Thompson, M. (1980). Cultural expectations of thinness in women. *Psychological Reports, 47,* 483-491.

Garner, D. M., Olmsted, M. P., Bohr, Y., & Garfinkel, P. E. (1982). The Eating Attitudes Test: Psychometric features and clinical correlates. *Psychological Medicine, 12,* 871-878.

Gibbons, F. X., & Gaeddert, W. P. (1984). Focus of attention and placebo utility. *Journal of Experimental Social Psychology, 20,* 159-176.

Gilbert, S. (1996, July 28). More men may seek eating-disorder help. *New York Times.*

Goethals, G. R. (1986). Social comparison theory: Psychology from the lost and found. *Personality and Social Psychology Bulletin, 12,* 261-278.

Gotham, H. J., Sher, K. J., & Wood, P. K. (1997). Predicting stability and change in frequency of intoxication from the college years to beyond: Individual-difference and role transition variables. *Journal of Abnormal Psychology, 106,* 619-629.

Grant, B. F., & Dawson, D. A. (1997). Age of onset of alcohol use and its association with DSM-IV alcohol abuse and dependence: Results from the National Longitudinal Alcohol Epidemiologic Survey. *Journal of Substance Abuse, 9,* 103-110.

Greenberg, J. S. (1996). *Comprehensive stress management* (5th ed.). Madison, WI: Brown & Benchmark.

Greene, B. A. & Miller, R. B. (1996). Influences on achievement: Goals, perceived ability, and cognitive engagement. *Contemporary Educational Psychology, 21,* 181-192.

Gross, J. J., & Levenson, R. W. (1997). Hiding feelings: The acute effects of inhibiting negative and positive emotion. *Journal of Abnormal Psychology, 106,* 95-103.

Hanna, S. L. (2003). *Person to person: Positive relationships don't just happen.* Upper Saddle River, NJ: Prentice Hall.

Harris, R. N., & Snyder, C. R. (1986). The role of uncertain self-esteem in self-handicapping. *Journal of Personality and Social Psychology, 51,* 451-458.

Hatfield, E., & Walster, G. W. (1981). *A new look at love.* Reading, MA: Addison-Wesley.

Hazan, C., & Shaver, P. (1987). Romantic love conceptualized as an attachment process. *Journal of Personality and Social Psychology, 52,* 511-524.

A Health Self-Test. National Health Information Clearinghouse, P.O. Box 1133, Washington, D.C. 20013

Heiby, E. M. (1983). Assessment of frequency of self-reinforcement. *Journal of Personality and Social Psychology, 44,* 1304-1307.

Hewitt, P. L., & Flett, G. L. (1991). Perfectionism in the self and social contexts: Conceptualization, assessment, and association with psychopathology. *Journal of Personality and Social Psychology, 60,* 456-470.

Hewitt, P. L., Flett, G. L. , & Turnbull-Donovan, W. (1992). Perfectionism and suicide potential. *British Journal of Clinical Psychology, 31,* 181-190.

Hewitt, P. L., Flett, G. L., Turnbull-Donovan, W., & Mikail, S. F. (1991). The Multidimensional Perfectionism Scale: Reliability, validity, and psychometric properties in psychiatric samples. *Psychological Assessment, 3,* 464-468.

Hewitt, P. L., & Genest, M. (1990). The ideal self: Schematic processing of perfectionistic content in dysphoric university students. *Journal of Personality and Social Psychology, 59,* 802-808.

Higgins, R. L., Snyder, C. R., & Berglas, S. (1990). *Self-handicapping: The paradox that isn't.* New York: Plenum.

Hill, M. B., Hill, D. A., Chabot, A. E., & Barrall, J. F. (1978). A survey of college faculty and student procrastination. *College Student Journal, 12,* 256-262.

Hirt, E. R., McCrea, S. M., & Kimble, C. E. (2000). Public self-focus and sex differences in behavioral self-handicapping: Does increasing self-threat still make it "just a man's game"? *Personality and Social Psychology Bulletin, 26,* 1131-1141.

Janicak, P. G., Dowd, S. M., Martis, B., Alam, D., Beedle, D., Krasuki, J., et al. (2002). Repetitive transcranial magnetic stimulation versus electroconvulsive therapy for major depression: Preliminary results of a randomized trials. *Biological Psychiatry, 51,* 659-667.

Johnston, L. D., Bachman, J. G., & O'Malley, P. M. (1998*). National survey results on drug use from the Monitoring the Future study, 1995-1997.* (NIH Publication No. 98-4345). Rockville, MD: National Institute on Drug Abuse.

Johnston, L. D., O'Malley, P. M., & Bachman, J. G. (1996*). National survey results on drug use from the Monitoring the Future study, 1975-1994; Volume II: College Students and Young Adults.* Rockville, MD: National Institute on Drug Abuse.

Johnston, L. D., O'Malley, P. M., & Bachman, J. G. (1999a). *National survey results on drug use from the Monitoring the Future study, 1975-1998; Volume I: Secondary School Students.* Rockville, MD: National Institute on Drug Abuse.

Johnston, L. D., O'Malley, P. M., & Bachman, J. G. (1999b). *National survey results on drug use from the Monitoring the Future study, 1975-1998; Volume II: College Students and Young Adults.* Rockville, MD: National Institute on Drug Abuse.

Joiner, T. E., Pettit, J. W., Walker, R. L., Voelz, Z. R., Cruz, J., Rudd, M. D., et al. (2002). Perceived burdensomeness and suicidality: Two studies on the suicide notes of those attempting and those completing suicide. *Journal of Social and Clinical Psychology, 21,* 531-545.

Jones, E. E., & Rhodewalt, F. (1982). *Self-Handicapping Scale.* Available from the authors (E. E. Jones, Department of Psychology, Princeton University, or Frederick Rhodewalt, Department of Psychology, University of Utah, Salt Lake City, UT 84112).

Kaplan, B. H. (1992). Social health and the forgiving heart: The Type B story. *Journal of Behavioral Medicine, 15,* 3-14.

Kasser, T., & Ryan, R. M. (1993). A dark side of the American dream: Correlates of financial success as a central life aspiration. *Journal of Personality and Social Psychology, 65,* 410-422.

Kasser, T. & Ryan, R. M. (1996). Further examining the American dream: Differential correlates of intrinsic and extrinsic goals. *Personality and Social Psychology Bulletin, 22,* 80-87.

Kelly, K. E., & Houston, B. K. (1985). Type A behavior in employed women: Relation to work, marital, and leisure variables, social support, stress, tension, and health. *Journal of Personality and Social Psychology, 48,* 1067-1079.

Kessler, R. C., McGonagle, K. A., Zhao, S., Nelson, C. B., Hughes, M., Eshleman, S., Wittchen, H-U., & Kendler, K. S. (1994). Lifetime and 12-month prevalence of DSM-III-R psychiatric disorders in the United States. *Archives of General Psychiatry, 51,* 8-19.

Kim, Y., Pilkonis, P., Frank, E., Thase, M., & Reynolds, C. (2002). Differential functioning of the Beck Depression Inventory in late-life patients; Use of item response theory. *Psychology and Aging, 17,* 379-391.

Klerman, G. L. (1979). The age of melancholy? *Psychology Today, 12,* 36-42, 88.

Klerman, G. L., & Weissman, M. M. (1992). Interpersonal psychotherapy. In E. S. Paykel (Ed.), *Handbook of affective disorders.* New York: Guilford.

Knight, J. R., Wechsler, H., Kuo, M., Seibring, M., Weitzman, E. R., & Schuckit, M. A. (2002). Alcohol Abuse and dependence among U.S. college students. *Journal of Studies on Alcohol, 63,* 263-270. (Available: http://www.hsph.harvard.edu/cas)

Kobasa, S. O. (1984, September). How much stress can you survive? *American Health,* pp. 64, 66-68, 70-74, 76, 77.

Kobasa, S. O., Maddi, S. R., & Kahn, S. (1982). Hardiness and health: A prospective study. *Journal of Personality and Social Psychology, 42,* 168-177.

Kong, C. & Hau, K. (1996). Students' achievement goals and approaches to learning: The relationship between emphasis on self-improvement and thorough understanding. *Research in Education, 55,* 74-85.

Kuhn, C., Swartzwelder, S., & Wilson, W. (1998). *Buzzed.* New York: Norton.

Labott, S. M., & Martin, R. B. (1987). The stress-moderating effects of weeping and humor. *Journal of Human Stress, 13,* 159-164.

Lawler, K. A., & Armstead, C. A. (1991). Type A behavior and intrinsic vs. extrinsic motivational orientation in male college students. *Psychological Record, 41,* 335-343.

Lay, C. H., Edwards, J. M., Parker, J. D. A., & Endler, N. S. (1989). An assessment of appraisal, anxiety, coping, and procrastination during an examination period. *European Journal of Personality, 3,*195-208.

LeDoux, J. (1996). *The emotional brain.* Touchstone Books.

Littrell, J. (1991). *Understanding and treating alcoholism. Volume 2. Biological, psychological, and social aspects of alcohol consumption and abuse.* Hillsdale, NJ: Lawrence Erlbaum.

Lucas, R. E., Clark, A. E., Georgellis, Y., & Diener, E. (2003). Reexamining adaptation and the set point model of happiness: Reactions to change in marital status. *Journal of Personality and Social Psychology, 84,* 527-539.

Luginbuhl, J., & Palmer, R. (1991). Impression management aspects of self-handicapping: Positive and negative effects. *Personality and Social Psychology Bulletin, 17,* 655-662.

Martin, G., & Pear, J. (1996). *Behavior modification: What it is and how to do it* (5th ed.). Upper Saddle River, NJ: Prentice Hall.

McCourt, A., & Reifman, A. (2002, August). Social connectedness and mental health in college students. Poster session presented at the annual meeting of the American Psychological Association, Chicago. (Available: http://www.hs.ttu.edu/research/reifman/apa2002.htm)

McKim, W. (1997). *Drugs and Behavior: An Introduction to Behavioral Pharmacology* (3rd ed.). Upper Saddle River, NJ: Prentice Hall.

Meece, J. L., Blumenfeld, P. C., & Hoyle, R. K. (1988). Students' goal orientations and cognitive engagement in classroom activities. *Journal of Educational Psychology, 88,* 514-523.

Miller, R. B., Beherens, J. T., Greene, B. A. & Newman, D. (1993). Goals and perceived ability: Impact on student's valuing, self-regulation, and persistence. *Contemporary Educational Psychology, 18,* 2-14.

Morse, J. (2002). *Women On a Binge: Many teen girls are drinking as much as boys. More college women regularly get drunk. Is this a case of girl power gone awry?* (Available: http://www.time.com/2002/wdrinking/story.html

Morton, J.C., Richey, C.A., & Kellett, M. (1981). *Building assertive skills A practical guide to professional development for allied dental health providers.* Mosby.

Mueller, C. M., & Dweck, C. S. (1998). Praise for intelligence can undermine children's motivation and performance. *Journal of Personality and Social Psychology, 75,* 33-52.

Myers, D. G. (2000). The funds, friends, and faith of happy people. *American Psychologist, 55,* 56-67.

Myers, D. G., & Diener, E. (1995). Who is happy? *Psychological Science, 6*(1).

Myers, D. G., & Diener, E. (1996, May). The pursuit of happiness. *Scientific American, 274,* 54-56.

Neale, J. M., Oltmanns, T. F., & Davison, G. C. (1982). *Case studies in abnormal psychology.* New York: Wiley.

Nemiah, J. C. (1961). The case of Mary S. In *Foundations of psychopathology.* Oxford: Oxford University Press.

Nolen, S. B. (1988). Reasons for studying: Motivational orientations and study strategies. *Cognition and Instruction, 5,* 269-287.

Olson, J. M., Herman, C. P., & Zanna, M. P. (1986). *Relative deprivation and social comparison: The Ontario symposium* (Vol. 4). Hillsdale, NJ: Erlbaum.

Osborn, A. F. (1963). *Applied imagination: Principles and procedures of creative problem solving* (3rd ed.). New York: Scribner's.

Parillo, K., & Schick, C. (1998, February*). Effect of Hypermasculinity/femininity, gender, and type of video seen on beliefs about, justifications for, and political views and statistics on date rape.* Poster session presented at the meeting of the Eastern Psychological Association, Boston.

Partnership for a Drug Free America. (2003, February). Partnership study: Teen ecstasy use levels, but most see scant risk in trying "X". *Partnership Bulletin,* p. 1.

Pauk, W. (2000). *How to study in college* (7th ed.). Boston: Houghton Mifflin.

Paulus, P. B., Larey, T. S., Putman, V. L., & Leggett, K. L. (1996). Social influence processes in computer brainstorming. *Basic and Applied Social Psychology, 18,* 3-14.

Pavot, W., & Diener, E. (1993). Review of the Satisfaction with Life Scale. *Psychological Assessment, 5,* 164-172.

Pennebaker, J. (1993). Putting stress into words: Health, linguistic, and therapeutic implications. *Behavioral Research Therapy, 31,* 539-548.

Pennebaker, J. & Francis, M. (1996). Cognitive, emotional, and language processes in disclosure. *Cognition and Emotion, 10,* 601-626.

Pennebaker, J. W., Kiecolt-Glaser, J. K. & Glaser, R. (1988). Disclosure of trauma and immune function: Health implications for psychotherapy. *Journal of Consulting and Clinical Psychology, 56,* 239-245.

Pennebaker, J. W., & Susman, J. R. (1988). Disclosure of trauma and psychosomatic processes. *Social Science and Medicine, 26,* 327-332.

Persing, C. R., & Schick, C. (1999, April). *Development of a Multidimensional Self-Destructiveness Questionnaire for young adults.* Poster session presented at the meeting of the Eastern Psychological Association, Providence, RI.

Persing, C. R., & Schick, C. (2000, March). *Validation of the Multidimensional Self-Destructiveness Scale (MSS) for young adults.* Poster session presented at the meeting of the Eastern Psychological Association, Baltimore. Contact either author: C. R. Persing, Lehigh University, Department of Psychology, 17 Memorial Drive, Bethlehem, PA 18105, capf@lehigh.edu *or* Dr. Connie Schick, Bloomsburg University, Department of Psychology, 400 East 2nd Street, Bloomsburg, PA 17815, cjschi@bloomu.edu or cjschick@uplink.net

Petrie, K. J., Booth, R. J., Pennebaker, J. W., Davison, K. P. & Thomas, M. G. (1995). Disclosure of trauma and immune response to a hepatitis vaccination program. *Journal of Consulting and Clinical Psychology, 63,* 787-792.

Pintrich, P. R., & De Groot, E. (1990). Motivational and self-regulated learning components of classroom academic performance. *Journal of Educational Psychology, 82,* 33-40.

Post, R. M., Kimbrell, T. A., McCann, U. D., Dunn, R. T., Osuch, E. A., Speer, A. M., & Weiss, S. R. B. (1999). Repetitive transcranial magnetic stimulation as a neuropsychiatric tool: Present status and future potential. *Journal of ECT, 15,* 39-59.

Postman, N., & Weingartner, C. (1973). *The school book.* New York: Delacorte.

Price, V. A. (1982). *Type A behavior pattern: A model for research and practice.* New York: Academic Press.

Ptacek, J. T., Smith, R. E. & Zanas, J. (1992). Gender, appraisal, and coping: A longitudinal analysis. *Journal of Personality, 60,* 747-770.

Reis, J., & Riley, W. L. (2000). Predictors of college students' alcohol consumption: Implications for student education. *Journal of Genetic Psychology, 161,* 282-292.

Rhodewalt, F. (1994). Conceptions of ability, achievement goals, and individual differences in self-handicapping behavior: On the application of implicit theories. *Journal of Personality, 62,* 67-85.

Rhodewalt, F., & Davison, J., Jr. (1986). Self-handicapping and subsequent performance: Role of outcome valence and attributional certainty. *Basic and Applied Social Psychology, 7,* 307-323.

Robinson, V. M. (1983). Humor and health. In P. E. Mcghee & J. H. Goldstein (Eds.), *Handbook of humor research.* New York: Springer-Verlag.

Roedel, T. D., Schraw, G., & Plake, B. (1994). Validation of a measure of learning and performance goal orientations. *Educational & Psychological Measurement, 54,* 1013-1021.

Roig, M., & DeTommasso, L. (1995). Are college cheating and plagiarism related to academic procrastination? *Psychological Reports, 77,* 691-698.

Rosenberg, H., & Nevis, S. A. (2000). Assessing and training recognition of intoxication by university students. *Psychology of Addictive Behaviors, 14,* 29-35.

Rosenman, R. (1978). The interview method of assessment of the coronary-prone behavior pattern. In T. M. Dembroski, S. M. Weiss, J. L. Shields, S. G. Haynes, & M. Feinleib (Eds.), *Coronary-prone behavior* (pp. 55-69). New York: Springer-Verlag.

Roy, M. C., Gauvin, S., & Limayem, M. (1996). Electronic group brainstorming: The role of feedback on productivity. *Small Group Research, 27,* 215-247.

Rubinstein, S., & Caballero, B. (2000). Is Miss America an undernourished role model? *Journal of the American Medical Association, 283,* 1569.

Russell, M. (1994). New assessment tools for risk drinking during pregnancy: T-ACE, TWEAK, and others. *Alcohol Health & Research World, 18,* 55-61.

Russell, M., Czarnecki, D. M., Cowan, R., McPherson, E., & Mudar, P. (1991). Measures of maternal alcohol use as predictors of development in early childhood. *Alcoholism: Clinical and Experimental Research, 15,* 991-1000.

Russell, M., Martier, S. S., Sokol, R. J., Mudar, P., Bottoms, S., Jacobson, S., & Jacobson, J. (1994). Screening for pregnancy risk-drinking. *Alcoholism: Clinical and Experimental Research, 18,* 1156-1161.

Russell, M., & Skinner, J. B. (1988). Early measures of maternal alcohol misuse as predictors of adverse pregnancy outcomes. *Alcoholism: Clinical and Experimental Research, 12,* 824-830.

Ryff, C. D. (1995). Psychological well-being in adult life. *Current Directions in Psychological Science, 4,* 99-103.

Sadava, S. W., & Pak, A. W. (1994). Problem drinking and close relationships during the third decade of life. *Psychology of Addictive Behaviors, 8,* 251-258.

Sawyer, M. G., Arney, F. M., Baghurst, P. A., Clark, J. J., Graetz, B. W., Kosky, R. J., Nurcombe, B., Patton, G. C., Prior, M. R., Raphael, B., Rey, J., Whaites, L. C., & Zubrick, S. R. (2000). *The mental health of young people in Australia: Child and adolescent component of the National Survey of Mental Health and Wellbeing.* Canberra: Australian Government Publishing Service. (Available: http://www.mentalhealth.gov.au; go to Publications & Resources and look under the heading National Survey of Mental Health and Wellbeing, and The Mental Health of Young People.)

Sax, L. J., Astin, A. W., Korn, W. S., & Mahoney, K. M. (1999). *The American freshman: National norms for fall 1999.* Los Angeles: Higher Education Research Institute, UCLA.

Sax, L. J., Lindholm, J. A., Astin, A. W., Korn, W. S., & Mahoney, K. M. (2001). *The American freshman: National norms for fall 2001.* Los Angeles: Higher Education Research Institute, UCLA. (more information at http://www.gseis.ucla.edu/heri/heri.html and http://www.usatoday.com/news/education/2003-01-26-frosh-usat_x.htm)

Schachter, S., & Singer, J. E. (1962). Cognitive, social and physiological determinants of emotional state. *Psychological Review, 69,* 379-399.

Scheier, M., & Carver, C. (1993). On the power of positive thinking: The benefits of being optimistic. *Current Directions in Psychological Science, 2,* 26-30.

Schick, C., Astor-Stetson, E., & Beck, B. L. (1996). *Alcohol: Reasons for Use test.* Unpublished test, Bloomsburg University. (Dept of Psychology, 400 East 2nd St., Bloomsburg, PA 17815; cjschi@bloomu.edu)

Schneidman, E. S. (1999). Perturbation and lethality: A psychological approach to assessment and intervention. In D. G. Jacobs et al. (Eds.), *The Harvard Medical School guide to suicide assessment and intervention.* San Francisco: Jossey-Bass.

Schraw, G., Horn, C., Thorndike-Christ, T., & Bruning, R. (1995). Academic goal orientation and students classroom achievement. *Contemporary Educational Psychology, 20,* 359-368.

Schunk, D. H. (1996). Goal and self-evaluative influences during children's cognitive skill learning. *American Educational Research Journal, 33,* 359-382.

Seligman, M. E. P. (1991). *Learned optimism.* New York: Knopf.

Selyé, H. (1976). *The stress of life.* New York: McGraw-Hill.

Sher, K. J., Bartholow, B. D., & Nanda, S. (2001). Short- and long- term effects of fraternity and sorority membership on heavy drinking: A social norms perspective. *Psychology of Addictive Behaviors, 15,* 42-51.

Sherer, M., Maddux, J. E., Mercandante, B., Prentice-Dunn, S., Jacobs, B., & Rogers, R. W. (1982). The Self-Efficacy Scale: Construction and validation. *Psychological Reports, 51,* 663-671.

Silverstein, B., Perdue, L., Peterson, B., & Kelly, E. (1986). The role of the mass media in promoting a thin standard of bodily attractiveness for women. *Sex Roles, 14,* 519-532.

Singh, S., & Darroch, J. (1999). Trends in sexual activity among adolescent women: 1982-1995. *Family Planning Perspectives, 31,* 212-219.

Sirois, F. M., & Pychyl, T. A. (2002, August). Academic procrastination: Costs to health and well-being. In *Academic procrastination: A common event that's not commonly understood.* Symposium conducted at the meeting of the American Psychological Association, Chicago, Illinois. (Available: http://www.carleton.ca/~tpychyl/prg/conferences/apa2002/apaslides2002/sld001.htm)

Smith, M. J. (1975). *When I say no, I feel guilty.* New York: Bantam.

Smith, N. M., Floyd, M. R., Scogin, F., & Jamison, C. S. (1997). Three-year follow-up of bibliotherapy for depression. *Journal of Consulting and Clinical Psychology, 65,* 324-327.

Smith, T. W., Snyder, C. R., & Handelsman, M. M. (1982). On the self-serving function of an academic wooden leg: Test anxiety as a self-handicapping strategy. *Journal of Personality and Social Psychology, 42,* 314-321.

Smith, T. W., Snyder, C. R., & Perkins, S. C. (1983). The self-serving function of hypochondriacal complaints: Physical symptoms as self-handicapping strategies. *Journal of Personality and Social Psychology, 44,* 787-797.

Smyth, J. M. (1998). Written emotional expression: Effect sizes, outcome types, and moderating variables. *Journal of Consulting and Clinical Psychology, 66,* 174-184.

Solomon, L. J., & Rothblum, E. D. (1984). Academic procrastination: Frequency and cognitive-behavioral correlates. *Journal of Counseling Psychology, 31,* 503-509.

Starks, M., Astor-Stetson, E., Beck, B. L., Jara, D., & Zarecky, A. (1998). *The effects of family control, family acceptance, and social support on self-esteem and psychological well-being.* Poster session presented at the meeting of the Eastern Psychological Association, Boston.

Stewart, S. H., Angelopoulos, M., Baker, J. M., & Boland, F. J. (2000). Relations between dietary restraint and patterns of alcohol use in young adult women. *Psychology of Addictive Behaviors, 14,* 77-82.

Strube, M. J. (1986). An analysis of the Self-Handicapping Scale. *Basic and Applied Social Psychology, 7,* 211-224.

Strube, M. J., Berry, J. M., Goza, B. K., & Fennimore, D. (1985). Type A behavior, age, and psychological well being. *Journal or Personality and Social Psychology, 49,* 203-218.

Substance Abuse and Mental Health Services Administration. (2000). *1999 National Household Survey on Drug Abuse*. (On-line). Retrieved September 10, 2000.

Sudol, K. Y., & Schick, C. (1999, April). *Relationship of attachment style and parental drinking to background, sexual and drinking beliefs and behaviors, reasons for drinking, and alcoholism in teenage college students*. Poster session presented at the meeting of the Eastern Psychological Association, Providence, RI.

Suh, E., Diener, E., & Fujita. F. (1996). Events and subjective well-being: Only recent events matter. *Journal of Personality and Social Psychology, 70,* 1091-1102.

Suls, J., & Mullen, B. (1982). From the cradle to the grave: Comparison and self-evaluation across the life-span. In J. Suls (Ed.), *Psychological perspectives on the self* (Vol. 1). Hillsdale, NJ: Erlbaum.

Tallmer, J., Scherwitz, L, Chesney, M., Hecker, M., Hunkeler, E., Serwitz, S., & Hughes, G. (1990). Selection, training, and quality control of Type A interviewers in a prospective study of young adults. *Journal of Behavioral Medicine, 13,* 449-466

Taylor, S. E., Klein, L. C., Lewis, B. R., Gruenewald, T. L., Gurung, T. L., & Updegraff, J. A. (2000). Biobehavioral responses to stress in females: Tend-and-befriend, not fight-or-flight. *Psychological Review, 107,* 411-429.

Thompson, J. K. (1986). Larger than life. *Psychology Today, 20,* 38-44.

Thompson, J. K. (1996). *Body image, eating disorders, and obesity.* Washington, DC: American Psychological Association.

Thoresen, C. E., & Pattillo, J. R. (1988). Exploring the Type A behavior pattern in children and adolescents. In B. K. Houston & C. R. Snyder (Eds.), *Type A behavior pattern: Research, theory, and intervention* (pp. 98-145). New York: John Wiley & Sons.

Tice, D. M., & Baumeister, R. F. (1997). Longitudinal study of procrastination, performance, stress, and health: The costs and benefits of dawdling. *Psychological Science, 8,* 454-458.

Trauger, H., Schick, C., Astor-Stetson, E., & Beck, B. L. (1998, February). *Billy Joel was wrong: Relationship of attachment style, religion, and alcohol use to college students' sexual and intimacy-related beliefs, behaviors, and traits.* Poster session presented at the meeting of the Eastern Psychological Association, Boston.

Tucker, J. A., Vuchinich, R., & Sobel, M. (1981). Alcohol consumption as a self-handicapping strategy. *Journal of Abnormal Psychology, 90,* 220-230.

UC Berkeley Wellness Letter. (1995, August). *The sleepy teen years,* p. 7.

Uchino, B. N., Cacioppo, J. T., & Kiecolt-Glaser, J. K. (1996). The relationship between social support and physiological processes: A review with emphasis on underlying mechanisms and implications for health. *Psychological Bulletin, 119,* 488-531.

USA Today. (2003, February). *Study finds girls more easily addicted. Study of gender differences in reasons for using substances.* (Available: http://www.usatoday.com/news/health/2003-02-05-girl-addicts_x.htm)

Valacich, J. S., Dennis, A. R., & Connolly, T. (1994). Idea generation in computer-based groups: A new ending to an old story. *Organizational Behavior and Human Decision Processes, 57,* 448-467.

van der Kolk, B. (1994). The body keeps the score: Memory and the evolving psychobiology of posttraumatic stress. *Harvard Review of Psychiatry, 1,* 253-265.

Vik, P. W., Carrello, P., Tate, S. R., & Field, C. (2000). Progression of consequences among heavy-drinking college students. *Psychology of Addictive Behaviors, 14,* 91-101.

Warshaw, R. (1988). *I never called it rape.* New York: Harper & Row.

Wechsler, H., Davenport, A., Dowdall, G., Moeykens, B., & Castillo, S. (1994). Health and behavioral consequences of binge drinking in college: A national survey of students at 140 campuses. *Journal of the American Medical Association, 272,* 1672-1677.

Wechsler, H., Dowdall, G. W., Davenport, A., & DeJong, W. (1995). *Binge drinking on campus: Results of a national study* (Publication No. ED/OPE95-8). Newton, MA: The Higher Education Center for Alcohol and Other Drug Prevention. (On-line). Retrieved May 10, 2001. (Available: http://www.edc.org/hec/pubs/binge.htm)

Wechsler, H., & Kuo, M. (2000). College students define binge drinking and estimate its prevalence: Results of a national survey. *Journal of American College Health, 49,* 57-65.

Wechsler, H., Lee, J. E., Kuo, M., & Lee, H. (2000). College binge drinking in the 1990s: A continuing problem. *Journal of American College Health, 48,* 199-211.

Wechsler, H., Molnar, B., Davenport, A., & Baer, J. (1999). College alcohol use: A full or empty glass? *Journal of American College Health, 47,* 247-252.

Wechsler, H., & Wuethrich, B. (2002). *Dying to drink: Confronting binge drinking on college campuses.* Emmaus, PA: Rodale.

Weinstein, N. D. (1984). Why it won't happen to me: Perceptions of risk factors and susceptibility. *Health Psychology, 3,* 431-457.

Weinstein, N. D., & Klein, W. M. (1996). Unrealistic optimism: Present and future. *Journal of Social and Clinical Psychology, 15,* 1-8.

Werch, C. E., Pappas, D. M., Carlson, J. M., DiClemente, C. C., Chally, P. S., & Sinder, J. A. (2000). Results of a social norm intervention to prevent binge drinking among first-year residential college students. *Journal of American College Health, 49,* 85-93.

Wilfley, D. E., Welch, R. R., Stein, R. I., Spurrell, E. B., Cohen, L. R., Saelens, B. E., et al. (2002). A randomized comparison of group cognitive-behavioral therapy and group interpersonal psychotherapy for the treatment of overweight individuals with binge-eating disorder. *Archives of General Psychiatry, 59,* 713-721.

Williams, R. L., & Eggert, A. (2003). Notetaking predictors of test performance. *Teaching of Psychology, 29,* 234-237.

Williamson, L. (1998). Eating disorders and the cultural forces behind the drive for thinness: Are African-American women really protected? *Social Work Health Care, 28,* 61-73.

Wood, J. V., Taylor, S. E., & Lichtman, R. R. (1985). Social comparison in adjustment to breast cancer. *Journal of Personality and Social Psychology, 49,* 1169-1183.

Yalom, I. (1985). *The theory and practice of group psychotherapy* (3rd ed.). New York: Basic Books.

Zucker, R. A., Fitzgerald, H. E., & Moses, H. D. (1995). Emergence of alcohol problems and the several alcoholisms: A developmental perspective on etiologic theory and life course trajectory. In D. Cicchetti & D. J. Cohen (Eds.), *Developmental psychopathology: Vol. 2. Risk, disorder, and adaptation* (pp. 677-711). New York: Wiley.

Appendix:
Scales to Aid Your Journey Toward Self-Discovery

This scale assesses your motivation when approaching tasks. Knowing your tendencies will help you to understand and apply the information in this book, beginning in Chapter 1.

The Work Preference Inventory

Respond to each item using a scale going from 1 to 4:

       1 = never or almost never true of me
       4 = always or almost always true of me

____ 1. I am not concerned about what other people think of me.
____ 2. I prefer having someone set clear goals for me in my work.
____ 3. The more difficult the problem, the more I enjoy trying to solve it.
____ 4. I am keenly aware of the goals I have for getting good grades.
____ 5. I want my work to provide me with opportunities for increasing my knowledge and skills.
____ 6. To me, success means doing better than other people.
____ 7. I prefer to figure things out for myself.
____ 8. No matter what the outcome of a project, I am satisfied if I feel I gained a new experience.
____ 9. I enjoy relatively simple, straightforward tasks.
____ 10. I am keenly aware of the GPA (grade point average) goals I have for myself.
____ 11. Curiosity is the driving force behind much of what I do.
____ 12. I am less concerned with what work I do than what I get for it.
____ 13. I enjoy tackling problems that are completely new to me.
____ 14. I prefer work I know I can do well over work that stretches my abilities.
____ 15. I'm concerned about how other people are going to react to my ideas.
____ 16. I seldom think about grades and awards.
____ 17. I'm more comfortable when I get to set my own goals.
____ 18. I believe there is no point in doing a good job if nobody else knows about it.
____ 19. I am strongly motivated by the grades I can earn.
____ 20. It is important for me to be able to do what I most enjoy.
____ 21. I prefer working on projects with clearly specified procedures.
____ 22. As long as I can do what I enjoy, I'm not that concerned about exactly what grades or awards I can earn.
____ 23. I enjoy doing work that is so absorbing that I forget about everything else.
____ 24. I am strongly motivated by the recognition I can earn from other people.
____ 25. I have to feel that I'm earning something for what I do.
____ 26. I enjoy trying to solve complex problems.
____ 27. It is important for me to have an outlet for self-expression.
____ 28. I want to find out how good I really can be at my work.
____ 29. I want other people to find out how good I really can be at my work.
____ 30. What matters most to me is enjoying what I do.

Scoring. To compute your intrinsic and extrinsic motivation scores, follow these instructions:

➤ ***For intrinsic motivation:*** using *reversed* scores (1 = 4, 2 = 3, 3 = 2, 4 = 1) for <u>9</u> and <u>14</u>, add scores for 3, 5, 7, 8, <u>9</u>, 11, 13, <u>14</u>, 17, 20, 23, 26, 27, 28, 30 = ____

➤ ***For extrinsic motivation:*** using reversed scores (1 = 4, 2 = 3, 3 = 2, 4 = 1) for items <u>1</u>, <u>16</u>, and <u>22</u>, add scores for <u>1</u>, 2, 4, 6, 10, 12, 15, <u>16</u>, 18, 19, 21, <u>22</u>, 24, 25, 29 = ____

➤ A higher score reflects greater intrinsic and extrinsic motivation, respectively, and there is little correlation between scores on the two subscales.

➤ Mean scores for both male and female students were about 45 and 39 on intrinsic and extrinsic measures, respectively.

Computing the following parts of each of the scales will help you understand the specific types of goals you wish to meet (remember to use reversed score for underlined items):

➤ ***Orientation toward challenging tasks:*** add 3, 5, <u>9</u>, 11, 13, <u>14</u>, 26 = ____

➤ ***Orientation toward enjoyment in one's work:*** 7, 8, 17, 20, 23, 27, 28, 30 = ____

➤ ***Outward orientation toward the recognition and dictates of others:*** <u>1</u>, 2, 6, 12, 15, 18, 21, 24, 25, 29 = ____

➤ ***Concern with compensation:*** 4, 10, <u>16</u>, 19, <u>22</u> = ____

The Work Preference Inventory (Amabile, Hill, Hennessey, & Tighe, 1994) assesses the degree to which you perceive yourself to be intrinsically and extrinsically motivated toward your tasks. In this study, intrinsic motivation correlated positively with need for cognition (enjoyment of figuring out difficult things and doing puzzles), academic comfort (feeling comfortable doing academic activities), interest in scientific pursuits, creativity, adult playfulness, and cognitive curiosity. Extrinsic motivation was negatively related to the need for cognition, and on the Myers-Briggs Type Inventory, extrinsically-oriented individuals were more likely to be ESTJ types (Extraverted, Sensing, Thinking, and Judging). ESTJ types have been found to prefer business marketing and management careers, to emphasize economic values, and to describe themselves as conscientious with a preference for order.

Source for this scale:
Amabile, T. M., Hill, K. G., Hennessey, B. A., & Tighe, E. M. (1994). The Work Preference Inventory: Assessing intrinsic and extrinsic motivational orientations. *Journal of Personality and Social Psychology, 66,* 950-967.

This scale measures your beliefs in your ability to accomplish tasks and your willingness to continue working even when faced with adversity. Knowing your score will help you understand and apply the information in Chapter 1 and in Chapters 5-7 on self-management and academic skills.

Self-Efficacy Scale

For each item, place you score in the space provided using this scale:

1	2	3	4	5	6	7
STRONGLY DISAGREE			NEITHER AGREE NOR DISAGREE			STRONGLY AGREE

_____ 1. When I make plans, I am certain I can make them work.

_____ 2. One of my problems is that I cannot get down to work when I should.

_____ 3. If I can't do a job the first time, I keep trying until I can.

_____ 4. When I set important goals for myself, I rarely achieve them.

_____ 5. I give up on things before completing them.

_____ 6. I avoid facing difficulties.

_____ 7. If something looks too complicated, I will not even bother to try it.

_____ 8. When I have something unpleasant to do, I stick to it until I finish it.

_____ 9. When I decide to do something, I go right to work on it.

_____ 10. When trying to learn something new, I soon give up if I am not initially successful.

_____ 11. When unexpected problems occur, I don't handle them well.

_____ 12. I avoid trying to learn new things when they look too difficult for me.

_____ 13. Failure just makes me try harder.

_____ 14. I feel insecure about my ability to do things.

_____ 15. I am a self-reliant person.

_____ 16. I give up easily.

_____ 17. I do not seem capable of dealing with most problems that come up in life.

_____ 18. It is difficult for me to make new friends.

_____ 19. If I see someone I would like to meet, I go to that person instead of waiting for him or her to come to me.

_____ 20. If I meet someone interesting who is hard to make friends with, I'll soon stop trying to make friends with that person.

_____ 21. When I'm trying to become friends with someone who seems uninterested at first, I give up easily.

_____ 22. I do not handle myself well in social gatherings.

_____ 23. I have acquired my friends through my personal abilities at making friends.

Reprinted with permission of authors and publisher from: Sherer, M., Maddux, J. E., Mercandante, B., Prentice-Dunn, S., Jacobs, B., & Rogers, R. W. The Self-efficacy Scale: construction and validation. *Psychological Reports,* 1982, 51, 663-671. © Psychological Reports 1982.

Scoring. There are two factors for this scale: *General Self-Efficacy* and *Social Self-Efficacy*.

> ***General Self-Efficacy:*** First, ***reverse the scores*** for the following items (if you answered an item with 1, change it to 7; 2 to 6; etc.): 2, 4, 5, 6, 7, 10, 11, 12, 14, 16, 17. Next, add up the scores for items 1 through 17 (using reversed scores for the items you reversed). General self-efficacy contains items related to initiation or persistence on a task and willingness to continue a task when face with difficulty or adversity.

> ***Social Self-Efficacy:*** First, ***reverse the scores*** for the following items: 18, 20, 22. Then, add up the scores for items 18 through 23 (using reversed scores for items you reversed).

Self-efficacy is a belief that you can accomplish a task successfully and that your success is due to effort and skill rather than to chance. It is related to your tendency to take on a behavior or task, put forth effort to complete it, and be willing to persist when a task is difficult or long or when it interferes with other tasks (perhaps ones that seem more interesting, pressing, or easier).

The ***General Self-Efficacy*** factor was found to correlate with ***locus of control*** (LOC) scores, belief in personal control scores, interpersonal competency scores, self-esteem, and successes in academic, vocational, and military settings. (***Locus of control*** measures your beliefs about whether *your own efforts* or *those of powerful others or chance* cause things to happen in your life—***internal*** LOC is your belief that your actions are important in determining your future, while ***external*** LOC is your belief that your future is at the mercy of powerful other people, fate, or chance.) ***Social Self-Efficacy*** was related to interpersonal competency and number of times hired and fired, but not to academic, vocational, or military successes.

Source for this scale:

Sherer, M., Maddux, J. E., Mercandante, B., Prentice-Dunn, S., Jacobs, B., & Rogers, R. W. (1982). The Self-Efficacy Scale: Construction and validation. *Psychological Reports, 51,* 663-671.

Rate the following **reasons** on the 5-point scale below indicating **how much it reflects why you procrastinated at the time.** Put your answer for each item in the space provided.

Not at all reflects why I procrastinated		Somewhat reflects		Definitely reflects why I procrastinated
1	2	3	4	5

_____ 1. You were concerned the professor wouldn't like your work.

_____ 2. You had a hard time knowing what to include and what not to include in your paper.

_____ 3. You waited until a classmate did his or hers, so that he/she could give you some advice.

_____ 4. You had too many other things to do.

_____ 5. There's some information you needed to ask the professor, but you felt uncomfortable approaching him/her.

_____ 6. You were worried you would get a bad grade.

_____ 7. You resented having to do things assigned to others.

_____ 8. You didn't think you knew enough to write the paper.

_____ 9. You really disliked writing term papers.

_____ 10. You felt overwhelmed by the task.

_____ 11. You had difficulty requesting information from other people.

_____ 12. You looked forward to the excitement of doing this task at the last minute.

_____ 13. You couldn't choose among all the topics.

_____ 14. You were concerned that if you did well, your classmates would resent you.

_____ 15. You didn't trust yourself to do a good job.

_____ 16. You didn't have enough energy to do a good job.

_____ 17. You felt it just takes too long to write a term paper.

_____ 18. You liked the challenge of waiting until the deadline.

_____ 19. You knew that your classmates hadn't started the paper either.

_____ 20. You resented people setting deadlines for you.

_____ 21. You were concerned that you wouldn't meet your own expectations.

_____ 22. You were concerned that if you got a good grade, people would have higher expectations of you in the future.

_____ 23. You waited to see if the professor would give you some more information about the paper.

_____ 24. You set very high standards for yourself and you worried that you wouldn't be able to meet those standards.

_____ 25. You just felt too lazy to write a term paper.

_____ 26. Your friends were pressuring you to do other things.

Scoring: For the 6 **academic activities** on which you may procrastinate (pp. A5-A6), add your answers for the first 2 of the 3 questions for _each activity_ (i.e., add up your answers for 1, 2, 4, 5, 7, 8, 10, 11, 13, 14, 16, 17). **Your academic procrastination score =** _____
Your answer to the _last_ item for each of the 6 _academic activities_ shows which ones you are most willing and eager to attack now to reduce your procrastination.

Most students involved in the developmental study for this scale were freshmen. Here are percentages for those saying they "nearly always" or "always" procrastinated in each area.

> *46.0% procrastinated on writing a term paper.*
> *27.6% procrastinated on studying for exams.*
> *30.1% procrastinated on reading their weekly assignments.*
> *23.0% procrastinated on attendance tasks.*
> *10.6% procrastinated on administrative tasks.*
> *10.2% procrastinated on school activities in general.*

Few students (23.7% at the high scorers) felt that procrastination in *any* area was "nearly always" or "always" a problem for them. However, most students "wanted" or "definitely wanted" to reduce procrastination in *each* area, with these considered most troublesome:

> *65.0% for writing a term paper.*
> *62.2% for studying for exams.*
> *55.1% for reading their weekly assignments.*

The scale on p. A7 identifies the *factors* (categories) affecting your tendency to procrastinate. The *Fear of Failure* factor measures anxiety about meeting others' expectations and your own standards and lack of self-confidence (add up items 1, 6, 15, 21, 24 = ____). Women students scored higher on this factor than men students did (means = 10.63 vs. 8.52).

The *Aversiveness of the Task and Laziness* factor assesses lack of energy and task unpleasantness (add up items 9, 10, 16, 17, 25 = ____). There was no gender difference for this factor. A little fewer than half the students endorsed at least one reason from this factor, but it was not the only factor explaining procrastination for this group of students.

The other factors (*Dependency, Risk-Taking, Lack of Assertiveness, Rebellion Against Control*, and *Difficulty of Making Decisions*) were much less important reasons for procrastination. Items for each of these factors are easy to pick out.

Here are general findings using this scale. The *Fear of Failure* factor correlated with measures of depression, irrational thoughts, low self-esteem, delayed study behavior, anxiety, and lack of assertiveness. The *Aversiveness of the Task and Laziness* factor correlated with depression, irrational thoughts, low self-esteem, and delayed study behavior. Behaviorally, self-reported procrastination on writing a paper, studying for exams, and doing weekly readings was related to putting off taking quizzes that could be taken at any time during the semester. These findings indicated that procrastination is *not* just a case of poor study habits or time management, but is related to a wide range of thoughts, feelings, behaviors, and role conflicts (as you will see when you read about procrastination in Chapter 2).

Source for this scale:
Solomon, L. J., & Rothblum, E. D. (1984). Academic procrastination: Frequency and cognitive-behavioral correlates. *Journal of Counseling Psychology, 31,* 503-509.

This test assesses the type of academic goals that are most important to you and will help you understand and apply the information in Chapter 4.

The Goals Inventory

Use this scale to indicate your degree of agreement with each item. Write your score next to the item's number.

    1 = strongly disagree
    2 = mildly disagree
    3 = neither disagree nor agree
    4 = mildly agree
    5 = strongly agree

    1. I enjoy challenging school assignments.
    2. It is important for me to get better grades than my classmates.
    3. I persevere even when I am frustrated by a task.
    4. Academic success is largely due to effort.
    5. Sticking with a challenging task is rewarding.
    6. I try even harder after I fail at something.
    7. I adapt well to challenging circumstances.
    8. I am willing to cheat to get a good grade.
    9. I work hard even when I don't like a class.
    10. I am very determined to reach my goals.
    11. Personal mastery of a subject is important to me.
    12. I work very hard to improve myself.
    13. I like others to think I know a lot.
    14. It bothers me the whole day when I make a big mistake.
    15. I feel angry when I do not do as well as others.
    16. I am naturally motivated to learn.
    17. I prefer challenging tasks even if I don't do as well at them.
    18. Every student can learn to be a successful learner.
    19. Learning can be judged best by the grade one gets.
    20. My grades do not necessarily reflect how much I learn.
    21. Mistakes are a healthy part of learning
    22. I feel most satisfied when I work hard to achieve something.
    23. I would rather have people think that I am lazy than stupid.
    24. It is important to me to always do better than others.
    25. I give up too easily when faced with a difficult task.

Roedel, Schraw & Plake, *Educational & Psychological Measurement,* **54. Copyright 1994 by Sage Publications. Reprinted by permission of Sage Publications, Inc.**

Scoring. First, reverse your score for item 25 (i.e., change a 1 to a 5, 2 to 4, etc.). Then add up your scores for these items (with #25 still reversed) as follows:

> ➢ ***Learning orientation:*** 1, 3, 6, 7, 9, 10, 11, 12, 16, 17, 22, <u>25</u> = _____ .
> ➢ ***Performance orientation:*** 2, 13, 14, 15, 24 = _____ .
> ➢ Items 4, 5, 8, 18, 19, 20, 21, 23 are "filler" items and don't need to be added up.

Dweck and Leggett's (1988) ***social-cognitive theory of motivation*** predicts a relationship between your goal orientation and subsequent behaviors in academic settings. A ***learning orientation*** (i.e., a concern for personal improvement and mastery) leads to adaptive responses, such as strategy shifting, increased effort, low test anxiety, and persistence in the face of difficulty (e.g., Ames, 1992). A ***performance orientation*** (i.e., a concern for high performance, even if it means attempting only easy tasks) predicts more maladaptive behaviors, such as boasting and "badge collecting," lack of persistence, concern with other's performance relative to yours, and learned helplessness (i.e., feeling you have no control over whether you will succeed on a task) (e.g., Blumenfeld, 1992; Meece, Blumenfeld, & Hoyle, 1988). A high performance score is also associated with tension and worry about academic issues and general test anxiety.

Source and other references for this scale:

Ames, C. (1992). Classrooms: Goals, structures, and student motivation. *Journal of Educational Psychology, 84,* 261-271.

Blumenfeld, P. C. (1992). Classroom learning and motivation: Clarifying and expanding goal theory. *Journal of Educational Psychology, 84,* 272-281.

Dweck, C. S., & Leggett, E. S. (1988). A social-cognitive approach to motivation and personality. *Psychological Review, 95,* 256-273.

Meece, J. L., Blumenfeld, P. C., & Hoyle, R. H. (1988). Students' goal orientations and cognitive engagement in classroom activities. *Journal of Educational Psychology, 80,* 514-523.

Roedel, T. D., Schraw, G., & Plake, B. (1994). Validation of a measure of learning and performance goal orientations. *Educational & Psychological Measurement, 54,* 1013-1021.

This scale measures your tendency to rewa   yourself and will help you understand the material in Chapters 5-7 on self-manageme   and other academic skills.

Frequency of Self-Re   forcement Attitudes

Below are a number of statements concerning be.   's or attitudes people have. Indicate whether the statements are characteristic and descriptive o   ou by circling *T*, if the statement is somewhat or very ***true*** for yourself. Circle *F* if the   atement is somewhat or very ***false*** for yourself. Please be as honest as possible so you ca   et accurate feedback.

T F 1. When I fail at something, generally I ar   till able to feel good about myself.
T F 2. I can stick to a tiresome task that I need   complete for a long time without someone encouraging me.
T F 3. I don't often think positive thoughts abou   ìyself.
T F 4. When I do something right, I take time to   ìoy the feeling.
T F 5. I have such high standards for what I dema   of myself that I rarely meet those standards.
T F 6. I seem to blame myself when things go wro   and am very critical of myself.
T F 7. There are pleasurable activities which I enjo   oing alone at my leisure.
T F 8. I usually get upset when I make mistakes bec   se I rarely learn from them.
T F 9. My feelings of self-confidence and self-esteer   luctuate a great deal.
T F 10. When I succeed at small things, I become enco   aged to go on.
T F 11. Unless I do something absolutely perfectly, it g   s me little satisfaction.
T F 12. I get myself through hard things mostly by plam   g to enjoy myself afterwards.
T F 13. When I make mistakes, I take time to criticize m   ›lf.
T F 14. I encourage myself to improve by feeling good al   it myself or giving myself something special whenever I make some progres
T F 15. If I didn't criticize myself frequently, I would cont   ìe to do things poorly forever.
T F 16. I think talking about what you've done right is bein   oo boastful.
T F 17. I find I feel better and do better when I silently prais   nyself for even small achievements.
T F 18. I can keep trying at something when I stop to think o   'hat I've accomplished.
T F 19. The way I keep up my confidence is by acknowledgin   ìny success I have.
T F 20. The way I achieve my goals is by rewarding myself ev   v step along the way.
T F 21. Praising yourself is being selfish and egotistical.
T F 22. When someone criticizes me, my self-confidence is sha   ·ed.
T F 23. I criticize myself more frequently than others criticize m
T F 24. I have a lot of worthwhile qualities.
T F 25. I silently praise myself even when others do not praise me
T F 26. Any activity can provide some pleasure regardless of how   :omes out.

T F 27. If I don't do the best possible job, I think less of myself.
T F 28. I should be upset if I make a mistake.
T F 29. My happiness depends more on myself than it does on other people.
T F 30. People who talk about their own better points are just bragging.

Scoring.

> Give yourself one point if you circled "T" (true) for these items: 1, 2, 4, 7, 10, 12, 14, 17, 18, 19, 20, 24, 25, 26, 29 = ____
> Give yourself one point if you circled "F" (false) for these items: 3, 5, 6, 8, 9, 11, 13, 15, 16, 21, 22, 23, 27, 28, 30 = ____
> Add the two scores together to get your self-reinforcement score: ____

The higher your score, the more you believe in self-reinforcement rather than just criticizing your mistakes. Heiby (1983) found the average for a group of college students was 17, and that scoring 13 or less probably indicated too little self-reinforcement and 20 or more reflected a high frequency self-reinforcement. Scores of 15-19 showed an "average" level of self-reinforcement.

You might also think about what types of behaviors you will and won't reinforce yourself. Areas in which you reward yourself are those you consider important and those in which you feel more confident (feel more self-efficacy). Areas in which you withhold self-reinforcement include those you may consider unimportant or too "easy" and those in which you expect perfection (and so have little chance to receive self-reinforcement). For these latter behaviors, you might want to reread the material on perfectionism in Chapter 4 again.

Self-reinforcement is defined as the process of controlling overt (obvious, public) and covert (silent, private) positive consequences of your own behavior (e.g., making a good grade on a test or paper, standing up for yourself when someone is trying to persuade you against your wishes). Low levels of self-reinforcement may even be related to development of depression when external sources of reinforcement are low.

Those who are quick to criticize or berate themselves, but slow to congratulate or reward emselves, tend to have perfectionistic standards for their behaviors. Thus, they "expect" good havior and see no reason to congratulate themselves when it results. Because of low self- nforcement, they are also at the mercy of others to provide both reinforcement and feedback. However, others are inconsistent with praise and may only reinforce behaviors they both notice a approve of—behaviors which may be more reflective of what *they* want or expect to see ra er than what is "correct" or even good for the person performing the behavior.

Source for this scale:
Hei E. M. (1983). Assessment of frequency of self-reinforcement. *Journal of Personality and Social Psychology, 44,* 1304-1307.

This scale will show you how anxious you feel when facing or thinking about academic tasks. The knowledge you gain will help you apply the material in Chapter 7 on test taking.

Achievement Anxiety Test

For each item, circle the number that best characterizes your experience in that situation.

1. **Nervousness while taking an exam or test hinders me from doing well.**
   Always   *1 2 3 4 5* *Never*

2. **I work most effectively under pressure, such as when the task is very important.**
   Always   *1 2 3 4 5* *Never*

3. **In a course where I have been doing poorly, my fear of a bad grade cuts down my efficiency.**
   Never   *1 2 3 4 5* *Always*

4. **When I am poorly prepared for an exam or test, I get upset and do less well than even my restricted knowledge should allow.**
   This never   *1 2 3 4 5* *This practically*
   happens   *always happens*

5. **The more important the examination, the less well I seem to do.**
   Always   *1 2 3 4 5* *Never*

6. **While I may (or may not) be nervous before taking an exam, once I start, I seem to forget to be nervous.**
   I always forget   *1 2 3 4 5* *I am always nervous*
   to be nervous   *during an exam*

7. **During exams or tests, I block on questions to which I know the answers, even though I might remember them as soon as the exam is over.**
   This always   *1 2 3 4 5* *I never block on*
   happens   *questions to which*
   to me   *I know the answer*

8. **Nervousness while taking a test helps me do better.**
   Never helps   *1 2 3 4 5* *Always helps*

9. **When I start a test, nothing is able to distract me.**
   Always true   *1 2 3 4 5* *Never true*

10. **In courses in which the total grade is based mainly on *one* exam, I seem to do better than other people.**
    Never   *1 2 3 4 5* *Almost always*

11. **I find that my mind goes blank at the beginning of an exam, and it takes me a few minutes before I can function.**
    Almost always   *1 2 3 4 5* *Never blank*
    blank out at first   *out at first*

12. **I look forward to exams.**
    Never   *1 2 3 4 5* *Always*

Alpert, R., & Haber, R. N. (1960). Anxiety in academic achievement situations. *Journal of Abnormal and Social Psychology, 61,* 207-215.

13. **I am so tired from worrying about an exam that I find I almost don't care how well I do by the time I start the test.**

    Never feel   *1*   *2*   *3*   *4*   *5*   *Almost always*
    this way   *feel this way*

14. **Time pressure on an exam causes me to do worse than the rest of the group under similar conditions.**

    Always seems to   *1*   *2*   *3*   *4*   *5*   *Never seems to*
    make me do worse   *make me do worse*
    than others on exams   *than others on exams*

15. **Although "cramming" under pre-examination tension is not effective for most people, I find that if the need arises, I can learn material immediately before an exam, even under considerable pressure, and successfully retain it to use on the exam.**

    Always able to   *1*   *2*   *3*   *4*   *5*   *Never able to use*
    use "crammed"   *"crammed" material*
    material successfully   *successfully*

16. **I enjoy taking a more difficult exam than an easy one.**

    Always   *1*   *2*   *3*   *4*   *5*   *Never*

17. **I find myself reading exam questions without understanding them, and I must go back over them so that they will make sense.**

    Never   *1*   *2*   *3*   *4*   *5*   *Almost always*

18. **The more important the exam or test, the better I seem to do.**

    This is true   *1*   *2*   *3*   *4*   *5*   *This is not true*
    of me   *of me*

19. **When I don't do well on a difficult item at the beginning of an exam, it tends to upset me so that I block on even the easy exam questions later on.**

    This never   *1*   *2*   *3*   *4*   *5*   *This almost always*
    happens to me   *happens to me*

Scoring. This scale measures both positive and negative aspects of test anxiety.
  ➤ First, *reverse* your score (5 = 1, 4 = 2, 2 = 4, 1 = 5) for the following items: 1, 2, 5, 6, 7, 9, 11, 17, 18, 19.
  ➤ Use the *reversed* scores to compute the two aspects (reversed items are underlined).
  ➤ ***Facilitating anxiety:*** 2, 6, 8, 9, 10, 12, 15, 16, 18 = _____ .
  ➤ ***Debilitating anxiety:*** 1, 3, 4, 5, 7, 11, 13, 14, 17, 19 = _____ .

Alpert and Haber (1960) found that grade point average and score on a final exam correlated positively with ***facilitating anxiety*** and negatively with ***debilitating anxiety*** (i.e., the former type of anxiety helps your performance and the latter hurts it). Compare your score on each aspect of anxiety to the norms from 379 college students:
  ➤ ***Facilitating anxiety:*** Mean = 27.38; SD = 4.27.
  ➤ ***Debilitating anxiety:*** Mean = 26.33; SD = 5.33.

Source for this scale:

Alpert, R., & Haber, R. N. (1960). Anxiety in academic achievement situations. *Journal of Abnormal and Social Psychology, 61,* 207-215.

This scale measures your thoughts and tendencies that can be self-destructive. Knowing how you score on each type (factor) of self-destructiveness will help you understand and apply the information in several chapters (e.g., stress, stress management, drinking, drugs).

Multidimensional Self-Destructiveness Scale (MSS)

Please be sure to portray "How you *really are*" rather than worrying about "How your *should* or *could* be." We're interested in you feelings and tendencies. There are no "right" or "wrong" answers!

To help you portray yourself more accurately, we have divided the items into **"Frequency of Occurrence"** (*how often* this is true for you) and **"General Thoughts or Tendencies"** (*how you are*, not how often you are like that).

FREQUENCY ITEMS (USE THIS SCALE):

1	2	3	4	5	6	7
Never	Almost Never	Occasionally	About half the time	Very often	Almost always	Always

____ 1. I have a regular exercise "workout."

____ 2. Others (family, lover, or friends) have told me they wish I would exercised <u>less</u>.

____ 3. I drink to "fit in" and be accepted by those I am with.

____ 4. I drink alcohol (or use illegal drugs) because people pressure me to.

____ 5. I have driven while drunk (or high).

____ 6. I have destroyed property <u>accidentally</u> while drunk (or high).

____ 7. I have destroyed property <u>on purpose</u> while drunk (or high) due to being angry, sad, etc., or because of being with others doing the same.

____ 8. I have forced someone to do something against the person's will while drunk (or high).

____ 9. I have asked someone to help me control my drinking (hold my money, remind me not to drink, etc.)

____ 10. I have stayed away from a particular location (bar, party house), a party, or certain people because I knew I would probably lose control and drink too much there or with the person(s).

____ 11. I have ridden with a driver who was drunk (or high).

____ 12. I have done something dangerous because I was drunk (or high) that I wouldn't have done if I had been sober.

____ 13. I have engaged in sexual behaviors while I was drunk (or high) with someone with whom I would <u>not</u> have gotten sexual if I hadn't been drunk (or high).

Contact either author: C. R. Persing, Lehigh University, Department of Psychology, 17 Memorial Drive, Bethlehem, PA 18105, <u>capf@lehigh.edu</u> *or* Connie Schick, Ph.D., Bloomsburg University, Department of Psychology, 400 East 2nd Street, Bloomsburg, PA 17815, <u>cjschi@bloomu.edu</u> or <u>cjschick@uplink.net</u>

1	2	3	4	5	6	7
Never	Almost Never	Occasionally	About half the time	Very often	Almost always	Always

_____ 14. I have been with, and not tried to stop, someone who did something antisocial or dangerous because the person was drunk (or high).

_____ 15. I have played dangerous drinking games (ones involving very high consumption or risky activities).

_____ 16. Others (family, lover, or friends) have told me they wish I would diet <u>less</u>.

_____ 17. I take disappointments so seriously that I can't put them out of my mind.

_____ 18. I get so depressed that even easy tasks become difficult.

_____ 19. If someone makes me angry in a public place, I will "cause a scene."

_____ 20. When I am angry, I take it out on whoever is around.

_____ 21. I strike out at whatever infuriates me.

_____ 22. I respond to frustration with irritation and anger.

_____ 23. I have engaged in sexual activities with someone I met while out or someone I dated, even though I had a relationship with someone else at the time.

_____ 24. I have engaged in sexual activities with a friend (someone I did not consider a significant other or a date).

_____ 25. I have engaged in sexual activities with a "hook up" (someone I met at a party, bar, etc., and had sex with once or twice).

_____ 26. I have gone to a party, bar, or other casual setting with the hope of meeting someone new to have sex with that night (whether or not you actually found someone).

_____ 27. I tend to feel worthless.

_____ 28. I feel like a failure.

ITEMS ON *WHO YOU ARE* AND *WHAT YOU GENERALLY BELIEVE* (USE THIS SCALE)

1	2	3	4	5	6	7
Never true of me	Almost never true of me	Occasionally true of me	True of me about half the time	Very often true of me	Almost always true of me	Always true of me

_____ 29. I feel "guilty" that I have somehow "let myself down" if I miss my regular exercise session.

_____ 30. I do/would exercise even if I have/had an injury that might get worse from exercising.

_____ 31. I will turn down invitations to interesting social events if they interfere with my exercise schedule.

_____ 32. My regular exercise program is more important to me than my other obligations (school, people) are.

_____ 33. I have an eating disorder (frequent dieting, anorexia nervosa, bulimia).

_____ 34. I am prone to be a risk taker.

_____ 35. I crave excitement.

_____ 36. I do dangerous things just for the thrill of it.

1	2	3	4	5	6	7
Never true of me	Almost never true of me	Occasionally true of me	True of me about half the time	Very often true of me	Almost always true of me	Always true of me

____ 37. Once I am angry, I stay that way for longer than other people do.

____ 38. Something makes me angry almost every day.

____ 39. When someone hurts or uses me, I will get even with the person even though it may take a long time.

____ 40. At times, I feel angry for no specific reason.

____ 41. I find it easy to hate someone.

____ 42. I have gotten a raw deal from life.

____ 43. I believe it is safer to trust no one.

____ 44. People can bother or irritate me just by being around.

____ 45. I find that people exaggerate their misfortunes to get sympathy and help from others.

____ 46. I think most people are not very competent and don't care if they are.

____ 47. I feel that beneath the facade, human nature is basically evil.

____ 48. I make decisions on the spur of the moment.

____ 49. I defy people in authority.

____ 50. I ignore everything else (friends, duties, school) when I am in a dating relationship.

____ 51. I ignore everything else (friends, duties, school) when I am trying to get someone to be in a relationship with me.

____ 52. I am willing to do whatever my dating partner wants me to if it means keeping the relationship.

____ 53. I change my opinions (or the way I do things) in order to please someone else or win their favor.

____ 54. I wait to see what someone is going to do in a situation or if someone else is going to solve a problem so I don't have to think about how to act or what to do.

____ 55. I expect others to work as hard as I do.

____ 56. I feel that people are bound to get angry with me, no matter what I do.

____ 57. When it comes to matching my friends' accomplishments, I am pessimistic about my chances.

____ 58. I feel left out or alone more than other people do.

____ 59. Others don't care about me as much as I care about them.

____ 60. I think I have more than my share of bad luck in sports, school, relationships, and other measures of "talent" and personality.

____ 61. In order to get along and be liked, I act like people expect me to rather than being myself.

____ 62. I feel that I have often been punished without cause.

____ 63. I believe that religious commitment gives me a purpose in life that I would otherwise not have.

____ 64. I believe that everyone will be judged by God someday.

____ 65. I believe that hardship strengthens character.

Scoring: The Multidimensional Self-Destructiveness Scale (MSS) measures 17 types of maladaptive behaviors and beliefs in young adults. These types (factors) were related to college student's maladaptive drinking, drug use, and sexual behavior in studies that developed and validated the MSS (Persing & Schick, 1999; 2000). To see which types you score high on, *add your scores for the items in each factor.* To see which factors you are high on relative to other factors, you can then *divide the total score for each factor by the number of items in that factor.*

- *Despondency:* 27, 28, 42, 56, 57, 58, 59, 60, 61, 62 = ____ (divide by 10 for average = ____)
- *Hopelessness:* 17, 18, 27, 28, 59 = ____ (divide by 5 = ____)
- *Sexual Permissiveness:* 13, 23, 24, 25, 26 = ____ (divide by 5 = ____)
- *Relationship Obsession:* 50, 51, 52 = ____ (divide by 3 = ____)
- *Conformity:* 3, 4, 61 = ____ (divide by 3 = ____)
- *Social Dependency:* 53, 54, 61 = ____ (divide by 3 = ____)
- *Antisocial Drinking:* 6, 7, 8, 12, 14, 26 = ____ (divide by 6 = ____)
- *Dangerous Drinking:* 5, 11, 12, 14, 15 = ____ (divide by 5 = ____)
- *Attempts to Control Alcoholism:* 9, 10 = ____ (divide by 2 = ____)
- *Excessive Exercising:* 1, 2, 16, 29, 30, 31, 32, 33 = ____ (divide by 8 = ____)
- *Excessive Exercising (without eating items):*...1, 2, 29, 30, 31, 32 = ____ (divide by 6 = ____)
- *Disordered Eating:*...2, 16, 33 = ____ (divide by 3 = ____)
- *Brooding Anger (Anger In):*...37, 38, 39, 40, 41, 44 = ____ (divide by 6 = ____)
- *Frustrated Anger (Anger Out):* 19, 20, 21, 22 = ____ (divide by 4 = ____)
- *Hostility/Cynicism:* 43, 44, 45, 46, 47 = ____ (divide by 5 = ____)
- *Thrill Seeking/Risk Taking:* 15, 34, 35, 36, 48, 49 = ____ (divide by 6 = ____)
- *Asceticism:* 63, 64, 65 = ____ (divide by 3 = ____)
- *Demandingness:* 55 = ____

Sources for this scale:

Persing, C. R., & Schick, C. (1999, April). *Development of a Multidimensional Self-Destructiveness Questionnaire for young adults.* Poster session presented at the meeting of the Eastern Psychological Association, Providence, RI.

Persing, C. R., & Schick, C. (2000, March). *Validation of the Multidimensional Self-Destructiveness Scale (MSS) for young adults.* Poster session presented at the meeting of the Eastern Psychological Association, Baltimore.

Contact either author: C. R. Persing, Lehigh University, Department of Psychology, 17 Memorial Drive, Bethlehem, PA 18105, capf@lehigh.edu *or* Dr. Connie Schick, Bloomsburg University, Department of Psychology, 400 East Second Street, Bloomsburg, PA 17815, cjschi@bloomu.edu or cjschick@uplink.net

This scale assesses your beliefs about what will happen in the future and how everything will "turn out." It will also help you understand Chapters 9 and 10 on coping with stress.

Life Orientation Test

Use this scale to indicate your agreement with each item:

      0 = strongly disagree
      1 = disagree
      2 = neutral
      3 = agree
      4 = strongly agree

_____   1. In uncertain times, I usually expect the best.
_____   2. It's easy for me to relax.
_____   3. If something can go wrong for me, it will.
_____   4. I always look on the bright side of things.
_____   5. I'm always optimistic about my future.
_____   6. I enjoy my friends a lot.
_____   7. It's important for me to keep busy.
_____   8. I hardly ever expect things to go my way.
_____   9. Things never work out the way I want them to.
_____   10. I don't get upset too easily.
_____   11. I'm a believer in the idea that "every cloud has a silver lining."
_____   12. I rarely count on good things happening to me.

Scoring.

➤ First, reverse (0 = 4, 1 = 3, 3 = 1, 4 = 0) your score for these items: 3, 8, 9, 12.

➤ Then, add up your score (using reversed scores) for these items: 1, 3, 4, 5, 8, 9, 11, 12 = ____

➤ The average score is 21, so you can compare your score and find out if you are more optimistic (higher score) or pessimistic (lower score).

This scale assesses your *optimism*—your expectations that the future will turn out favorably, no matter how bad things may look at the moment. Here are some research findings comparing pessimists and optimists:

➤ Optimists generally had a higher level of subjective well-being (happiness).

➤ Optimism was related to less stress 3 months into freshmen students' first semester in college.

Scheier, M., & Carver, C. (1993). On the power of positive thinking: The benefits of being optimistic. *Current Directions in Psychological Science, 2,* 26-30.

- ➢ Optimists were more likely to cope by taking action when a stressful situation was within their control and were more realistic about a situation.
- ➢ Optimists are more willing to persevere in the face of difficulties.
- ➢ Optimists tended to view a stressful situation as a "growth situation" and to "make the best of it."
- ➢ Pessimists, on the other hand, tend to deny or use maladaptive coping techniques (e.g., avoidance, escape through use of drugs, alcohol, or food).
- ➢ In extensive health psychology studies, optimists consistently have better physical well-being, report less pain, recover from illness and surgery quicker, and cope with acute and chronic illnesses better than pessimists do.

Optimism and pessimism are not just learned attitudes. Research suggests that at least 25% of an individual's orientation is inherited. Of course, experience also contributes to your attitudes, as do the beliefs and teachings of your parents, your culture, and your religion.

Optimism isn't always adaptive (e.g., misjudgment may suggest a situation is controllable when it isn't). An unhealthy version is *unrealistic optimism* (e.g., refusal to recognize the reality of a situation, expecting things to turn out OK without any effort on your part). An especially dangerous belief is *illusion of invulnerability* (Weinstein, 1984; Weinstein & Klein, 1996). People under 25 are more prone to this belief, which is a tendency to think nothing bad will happen to you if you take risks that you realistically realize are dangerous for your peers (e.g., believing that drinking and driving, smoking cigarettes, or having unprotected sex won't result in negative consequences for you despite recognizing that they are hazardous for your peers).

On the other hand, all pessimism isn't bad for you. Some people who practice *defensive pessimism*, at least in controllable situations, are as realistic as optimists. They use their pessimism as a motivator to really think out a stressful situation, assess all the bad things that *could* happen, and plan how to avoid or cope with potential negative outcomes (this isn't the same as worrying about something). As long as a person doesn't use this technique as a *general* coping technique, which can result in "freezing" or excessive negative affect, a little defensive pessimism can be helpful. For instance, if you are going to give a speech, thinking about how you can keep from getting too much "stage fright" or what you'll do if you forget something can actually help you prepare *and* consequently feel less stressed about giving the speech.

Source and other references for this scale:

Scheier, M., & Carver, C. (1993). On the power of positive thinking: The benefits of being optimistic. *Current Directions in Psychological Science, 2,* 26-30.

Weinstein, N. D. (1984). Why it won't happen to me: Perceptions of risk factors and susceptibility. *Health Psychology, 3,* 431-457.

Weinstein, N. D., & Klein, W. M. (1996). Unrealistic optimism: Present and future. *Journal of Social and Clinical Psychology, 15,* 1-8.

Here is a test you can take to assess your current health behaviors and see if there are some habits you need to stop or start to keep you healthier. This knowledge will also help you when reading Chapter 9 on coping with stress, as well as several other chapters.

A Health Self-Test

	Almost Always	Sometimes	Almost Never
Cigarette Smoking			
(If you _never smoke_, enter a score of 10 for this section and go to the next section on *Alcohol and Drugs*.)			
1. I avoid smoking cigarettes.	2	1	0
2. I smoke only low-tar, low-nicotine cigarettes or a pipe.	2	1	0
Smoking Score: ____			
Alcohol and Drugs			
1. I avoid drinking alcoholic beverages *or* I drink no more than 1 (for women) or 2 (for men) drinks a day.	4	1	0
2. I avoid using alcohol or other drugs (especially illegal drugs) as a way of handling stressful situations or the problems in my life.	2	1	0
3. I am careful not to drink alcohol when taking certain medicines (for example, medicine for sleeping, pain, colds, and allergies), or when pregnant.	2	1	0
4. I read and follow the label directions when using prescribed and over-the-counter drugs.	2	1	0
Alcohol and Drugs Score: ____			
Eating Habits			
1. I eat a variety of foods each day, such as fruits and vegetables, whole grain breads and cereals, lean meats, dairy products, dry peas and beans, and nuts and seeds.	4	1	0
2. I limit the amount of fat, saturated fat, and cholesterol I eat (including fat on meats, eggs, butter, cream, shortenings, and organ meats such as liver).	2	1	0
3. I limit the amount of salt I eat by cooking with only small amounts, not adding salt at the table, and avoiding salty snacks.	2	1	0
4. I avoid eating too much sugar (especially frequent snacks of sticky candy or soft drinks).	2	1	0
Eating Habits Score: _____			

National Health Information Clearinghouse, P.O. Box 1133, Washington, D.C. 20013

	Almost Always	Sometimes	Almost Never

Exercise/Fitness

	Almost Always	Sometimes	Almost Never
1. I maintain a desired weight, avoiding overweight *and* underweight.	3	1	0
2. I do vigorous exercises for 15-30 minutes *at least* 3 times a week (examples include running, swimming, brisk walking).	3	1	0
3. I do exercises that enhance my muscle tone for15-30 minutes *at least* 3 times a week (examples include yoga and calisthenics).	2	1	0
4. I use part of my leisure time participating in individual, family, or team activities that increase my level of fitness (such as gardening, bowling, golf, and baseball).	2	1	0

Exercise/Fitness Score:_____

Stress Control

	Almost Always	Sometimes	Almost Never
1. I have a job or do other work that I enjoy.	2	1	0
2. I find it easy to relax and express my feelings freely.	2	1	0
3. I recognize early, and prepare for, events or situations likely to be stressful for me.	2	1	0
4. I have close friends, relatives, or others whom I can talk to about personal matters and call on for help when needed.	2	1	0
5. I participate in group activities (such as church and community organizations) or hobbies that I enjoy.	2	1	0

Stress Control Score:_____

Safety

	Almost Always	Sometimes	Almost Never
1. I wear a seat belt while riding in a car as a driver or passenger.	2	1	0
2. I do not drive while under the influence of alcohol and other drugs or ride with a driver who is under the influence of alcohol or other drugs.	2	1	0
3. I obey traffic rules and the speed limit when driving.	2	1	0
4. I am careful when using potentially harmful products or substances (such as household cleaners, poisons, and electrical devices).	2	1	0
5. I avoid smoking in bed.	2	1	0

Safety Score:_____

What Your Scores in *Each Section* Mean to YOU

A score of 9 and 10 in a section

Excellent! Your answers show that you are aware of the importance of this area of your health. More importantly, you are putting your knowledge to work for you by practicing good health habits. As long as you continue to do so, this area should not pose a serious health risk. It's likely that you are setting an example for your family and friends to follow. Since you received a very high test score on this part of the test, you may want to consider other areas where your scores indicate room for improvement.

A score of 6 to 8 in a section

Your health practices in this area are good, but there is room for improvement. Look again at the items you answered with a "Sometimes" or "Almost Never." What changes can you make to improve your score? Even a small change can often help you achieve better health.

A score of 3 to 5 in a section

Your health risks are showing! Would you like more information about the risks you are facing and about why it is important for you to change these behaviors? Perhaps you need help in deciding how to successfully make the changes you desire. In either case, help is available. Many campuses have programs or groups that can help, your local YMCA or local chapter of the American Heart Association may have help, and you can also contact your local health department or the National Health Information Clearinghouse.

A score of 0 to 2 in a section

Obviously, you were concerned enough about your health to take the test, but your answers show that you may be taking serious risks with your health. Perhaps you are not aware of the risks and what to do about them. You can easily get the information and help you need to improve, if you wish. The next step is up to you.

Source for this scale:
A Health Self-Test. National Health Information Clearinghouse, P.O. Box 1133, Washington, D.C. 20013

This scale identifies coping techniques you employ in stressful situations. Knowing how you choose to cope will help you understand the material in Chapter 10.

Multidimensional Coping Scale (COPE)

This scale measures how individuals respond when they confront difficult or stressful events. There are many ways to try to deal with stress. This scale asks you to indicate what *you* generally do and feel when *you* experience stressful events. Although different events bring out somewhat different responses, think about what you *usually* do when under a lot of stress.

Treat each item separately from every other item, since you may tend to use one or several techniques to the same or different extents for each one. Remember, there are no right or wrong answers. Be sure you answer for what *you* do—not what "people in general" do. Decide on your response choice for each item and place the corresponding number in front of that item:

> **I usually don't do this at all = 1**
> **I usually do this a little bit = 2**
> **I usually do this a medium amount = 3**
> **I usually do this a lot = 4**

____ 1. I take additional action to try to get rid of the problem.
____ 2. I concentrate my efforts on doing something about it.
____ 3. I do what has to be done, one step at a time.
____ 4. I take direct action to get around the problem.
____ 5. I try to come up with a strategy about what to do.
____ 6. I make a plan of action.
____ 7. I think hard about what steps to take.
____ 8. I think about how I might best handle the problem.
____ 9. I put aside other activities in order to concentrate on this.
____ 10. I focus on dealing with this problem, and if necessary, let other things slide a little.
____ 11. I keep myself from getting distracted by other thoughts or activities.
____ 12. I try hard to prevent other things from interfering with my efforts at dealing with this.
____ 13. I force myself to wait for the right time to do something.
____ 14. I hold off doing anything about it until the situation permits.
____ 15. I make sure not to make matters worse by acting too soon.
____ 16. I restrain myself from doing anything too quickly.
____ 17. I ask people who have had similar experiences what they did.
____ 18. I try to get advice from someone about what to do.
____ 19. I talk to someone to find out more about the situation.
____ 20. I talk to someone who could do something concrete about the problem.
____ 21. I talk to someone about how I feel.

I usually don't do this at all = 1
I usually do this a little bit = 2
I usually do this a medium amount = 3
I usually do this a lot = 4

____ 22. I try to get emotional support from friends or relatives.
____ 23. I discuss my feelings with someone.
____ 24. I get sympathy and understanding from someone.
____ 25. I look for something good in what is happening.
____ 26. I try to see it in a different light, to make it seem more positive.
____ 27. I learn something from the experience.
____ 28. I try to grow as a person as a result of the experience.
____ 29. I learn to live with it.
____ 30. I accept that this has happened and that it can't be changed.
____ 31. I get used to the idea that it happened.
____ 32. I accept the reality of the fact that it happened.
____ 33. I seek God's help.
____ 34. I put my trust in God.
____ 35. I try to find comfort in my religion.
____ 36. I pray more than usual.
____ 37. I get upset and let my emotions out.
____ 38. I let my feelings out.
____ 39. I feel a lot of emotional distress and I find myself expressing those feelings a lot.
____ 40. I get upset and am really aware of it.
____ 41. I refuse to believe that it has happened.
____ 42. I pretend that it hasn't happened.
____ 43. I act as though it hasn't even happened.
____ 44. I say to myself "this isn't real."
____ 45. I give up the attempt to get what I want.
____ 46. I just give up trying to reach my goal.
____ 47. I admit to myself that I can't deal with it and quit trying.
____ 48. I reduce the amount of effort I'm putting into solving the problem.
____ 49. I turn to my work or other substitute activities to take my mind off things.
____ 50. I go to the movies or watch TV to think about it less.
____ 51. I daydream about things other than this.
____ 52. I sleep more than usual.
____ 53. I drink alcohol or take drugs in order to think about it less.

Scoring. To determine how likely you are to use each type of coping, add your scores for that category and divide the sum by 4 (the number of items in a category). You can then compare your average for different types of coping to see how you usually act when stressed.

Active Coping	1. I take additional action to try to get rid of the problem. (.42)	_____
	2. I concentrate my efforts on doing something about it. (.37)	_____
	3. I do what has to be done, one step at a time. (.33)	_____
	4. I take direct action to get around the problem. (.29)	_____
	Total score (____) divided by 4 = ____	

Planning	5. I try to come up with a strategy about what to do. (.73)	_____
	6. I make a plan of action. (.68)	_____
	7. I think hard about what steps to take. (.53)	_____
	8. I think about how I might best handle the problem. (.49)	_____
	Total score (____) divided by 4 = ____	

Suppression of Competing Activities	9. I put aside other activities in order to concentrate on this. (.68)	_____
	10. I focus on dealing with this problem, and if necessary, let other things slide a little. (.55)	_____
	11. I keep myself from getting distracted by other thoughts or activities. (.51)	_____
	12. I try hard to prevent other things from interfering with my efforts at dealing with this. (.48)	_____
	Total score (____) divided by 4 = ____	

Restraint Coping	13. I force myself to wait for the right time to do something. (.71)	_____
	14. I hold off doing anything about it until the situation permits. (.67)	
	15. I make sure not to make matters worse by acting too soon. (.62)	_____
	16. I restrain myself from doing anything too quickly. (.40)	_____
	Total score (____) divided by 4 = ____	

Seeking Social Support for Instrumental Reasons	17. I ask people who have had similar experiences what they did. (.66)	_____
	18. I try to get advice from someone about what to do. (.65)	_____
	19. I talk to someone to find out more about the situation. (.60)	_____
	20. I talk to someone who could do something concrete about the problem. (.55)	_____
	Total score (____) divided by 4 = ____	

Seeking Social	21.	I talk to someone about how I feel. (.71) ____
Support for	22.	I try to get emotional support from friends or relatives. (.71) ____
Emotional	23.	I discuss my feelings with someone. (.69) ____
Reasons	24.	I get sympathy and understanding from someone. (.58) ____
		Total score (___) divided by 4 = ___

Positive	25.	I look for something good in what is happening. (.75) ____
Reinterpretation	26.	I try to see it in a different light, to make it seem more positive. (.59) ____
and Growth	27.	I learn something from the experience. (.23) ____
	28.	I try to grow as a person as a result of the experience. (.19) ____
		Total score (___) divided by 4 = ___

Acceptance	29.	I learn to live with it. (.68) ____
	30.	I accept that this has happened and that it can't be changed. (.60) ____
	31.	I get used to the idea that it happened. (.43) ____
	32.	I accept the reality of the fact that it happened. (.38) ____
		Total score (___) divided by 4 = ___

Turning to	33.	I seek God's help. (.95) ____
Religion	34.	I put my trust in God. (.88) ____
	35.	I try to find comfort in my religion. (.84) ____
	36.	I pray more than usual. (.81) ____
		Total score (___) divided by 4 = ___

Focus On and	37.	I get upset and let my emotions out. (.79) ____
Venting of	38.	I let my feelings out. (.76) ____
Emotions	39.	I feel a lot of emotional distress and I find myself expressing those feelings a lot. (.57) ____
	40.	I get upset and am really aware of it. (.45) ____
		Total score (___) divided by 4 = ___

Denial	41.	I refuse to believe that it has happened. (.75)	____
	42.	I pretend that it hasn't happened. (.72)	____
	43.	I act as though it hasn't even happened. (.52)	____
	44.	I say to myself "this isn't real." (.46)	____

Total score (____) divided by 4 = ____

Behavioral Disengagement	45.	I give up the attempt to get what I want. (.49)	____
	46.	I just give up trying to reach my goal. (.42)	____
	47.	I admit to myself that I can't deal with it and quit trying. (.37)	____
	48.	I reduce the amount of effort I'm putting into solving the problem. (.30)	____

Total score (____) divided by 4 = ____

Mental Disengagement	49.	I turn to my work or other substitute activities to take my mind off things. (.45)	____
	50.	I go to the movies or watch TV to think about it less. (.43)	____
	51.	I daydream about things other than this. (.28)	____
	52.	I sleep more than usual. (.23)	____

Total score (____) divided by 4 = ____

| **Alcohol-Drug Disengagement** | 53. | I drink alcohol or take drugs in order to think about it less. | ____ |

Carver, Scheier, and Weintraub (1989) found two clusters of coping types. These clusters were negatively correlated with each other, meaning that if you used techniques within one cluster, you were likely to avoid using those in the other cluster. The first cluster consisted of *more adaptive* strategies, including **Active Coping, Planning, Suppression of Competing Activities, Restraint Coping, Positive Reinterpretation and Growth,** and **Seeking Out Both Instrumental and Emotional Social Support**. Acceptance was also related to this cluster, but to a lesser degree. The second cluster consisted of *less adaptive* strategies, that may even damage your chances of coping with a problem and solving a solvable problem. This cluster consisted of **Behavioral and Mental Disengagement, Denial, Focusing On and Venting of Emotions,** and **Alcohol-Drug Use**. Seeking social support was related to **Focusing On and Venting of Emotions**, but to nothing else in the second cluster (i.e., social support can be a good or a bad strategy depending on why you seek it).

Carver et al. (1989) also found the different types of coping to be related to these personality characteristics.

> *Active Coping* and *Planning* were positively related to optimism, the feeling of being generally able to do something about stressful situations (stress-coping self-efficacy), self-esteem, hardiness, and Type A behavior. *Active coping* was negatively related to trait anxiety.

> *Positive Reinterpretation and Growth* was positively related to the same traits, except Type A behavior.

> *Restraint Coping, Acceptance*, and *Turning to Religion* were positively related to optimism.

> *Denial* and *Behavioral Disengagement* were positively related to trait anxiety and was negatively related to optimism, stress-coping self-efficacy, self-esteem, hardiness, and (for *Behavioral Disengagement* only) Type A behavior.

> *Mental Disengagement* was positively related to trait anxiety and was negatively related to optimism and stress-coping self-efficacy.

> *Focusing On and Venting Emotions* was positively related to trait anxiety, monitoring (dwelling on the problem), and slightly to Type A behavior and was negatively related to stress-coping self-efficacy, internal locus of control, and, to a lesser extent, to optimism.

> Monitoring was also positively related to *Instrumental Social Support* and *Turning to Religion* and was negatively related to *Behavioral Disengagement*.

Source for this scale:

Carver, C. S., Scheier, M. F., & Weintraub, J. K. (1989). Assessing coping strategies: A theoretically based approach. *Journal of Personality and Social Psychology, 56,* 267-283.

This scale assesses the degree to which you are willing to stand up for your own rights without violating the rights of others. It will help you apply the material in Chapter 11.

Assertion Inventory

Many people experience difficulty in handling interpersonal situations requiring them to assert themselves in some way (e.g., turning down a request, asking a favor). Indicate your *degree of discomfort or anxiety* in the space to the *left* of each item using the following scale:

> **1 = none**
> **2 = a little**
> **3 = a fair amount**
> **4 = much**
> **5 = very much**

Next, go through the items again, indicating to the *right* of each item the *likelihood that you will display the behavior if actually in that situation*. For example, if you rarely apologize when you are at fault, you would mark "4" after that item. (It is important to assess your *discomfort* rating independently from your *response likelihood*, so put a piece of paper over your *discomfort* ratings while responding to the items for your *response likelihood*. Use this scale:

> **1 = always do it**
> **2 = usually do it**
> **3 = do it about half the time**
> **4 = rarely do it**
> **5 = never do it**

discomfort			*response likelihood*
____	1.	Turn down a request to borrow your car	
____	2.	Compliment a friend	____
____	3.	Ask a favor of someone	____
____	4.	Resist sales pressure	____
____	5.	Apologize when you are at fault	____
____	6.	Turn down a request for a meeting or date	____
____	7.	Admit fear and request consideration	____
____	8.	Tell a person you are intimately involved with when he/she says or does something that bothers you	____
____	9.	Ask for a raise	____
____	10.	Admit ignorance in some area	____
____	11.	Turn down a request to borrow money	____
____	12.	Ask personal questions..	____
____	13.	Turn off a talkative friend	____
____	14.	Ask for constructive criticism	____
____	15.	Initiate a conversation with a stranger	____
____	16.	Compliment a person you are romantically involved with or interested in	____

Gambrill, E., & Richey, C. A. (1975). An assertion inventory for use in assessment and research. *Behavior Therapy, 6*, 547-549. (Available in Gambrill & Richey, 1985, p. 71.)

____	17.	Request a meeting or a date with a person	____
____	18.	Your initial request for a meeting is turned down and you ask the person again at a later time	____
____	19.	Admit confusion about a point under discussion and ask for clarification	____
____	20.	Apply for a job	____
____	21.	Ask whether you have offended someone	____
____	22.	Tell someone that you like them	____
____	23.	Request expected service when such is not forthcoming (e.g., in a restaurant)	____
____	24.	Discuss openly with the person his/her criticism of your behavior	____
____	25.	Return defective items, e.g., store or restaurant	____
____	26.	Express an opinion that differs from that of the person you are talking to	____
____	27.	Resist sexual overtures when you are not interested	____
____	28.	Tell the person when you feel he/she has done something that is unfair to you	____
____	29.	Accept a date	____
____	30.	Tell someone good news about yourself	____
____	31.	Resist pressure to drink	____
____	32.	Resist a significant person's unfair demand	____
____	33.	Quit a job	____
____	34.	Resist pressure to "turn on"	____
____	35.	Discuss openly with a person his/her criticism of your work	____
____	36.	Request the return of borrowed items	____
____	37.	Receive compliments	____
____	38.	Continue to converse with someone who disagrees with you	____
____	39.	Tell a friend or someone with whom you work with when he/she says or does something that bothers you	____
____	40.	Ask a person who is annoying you in a public situation to stop	____

Indicate the *situations you would like to handle more assertively* by circling the item number.

Morton, Richey, and Kellett (1981) suggested a scoring scheme to identify areas in which you feel uncomfortable. Transfer your *discomfort* scores (the ones *in front of* each item) from above.

Turning down	1	Turn down a request to borrow your car	____
a request	4	Resist sales pressure	____
	6	Turn down a request for a meeting or date	____
	11	Turn down a request to borrow money	____
	27	Resist sexual overtures when you are not interested	____
	31	Resist pressure to drink	____
	32	Resist a significant person's unfair demand	____
	34	Resist pressure to use drugs	____

Morton, J. C., Richey, C. A., & Kellett, M. (1981). *Building assertive skills A practical guide to professional development for allied dental health providers* **(pp. 259-262). Mosby. (Available in Gambrill & Richey, 1985, pp. 72-73.)**

Expressing personal limitations	3	Ask a favor of someone	_____
	5	Apologize when you are at fault	_____
	7	Admit fear and request consideration	_____
	10	Admit ignorance in some area	_____
	19	Admit confusion about a point under discussion and ask for clarification	_____
	21	Ask whether you have offended someone	_____
Expressing negative concerns	8	Tell a person with whom you are intimately involved when he or she says or does something that bothers you	_____
	13	Turn off a talkative friend	_____
	28	Tell a person when you feel that he or she has done something that is unfair to you	_____
	36	Request the return of a borrowed item	_____
	39	Tell a friend or co-worker when he or she says or does something that bothers you	_____
	40	Ask a person who is annoying you in a public situation to stop	_____
Expressing positive feelings	2	Compliment a friend	_____
	16	Compliment a person you are romantically involved with or interested in	_____
	22	Tell someone that you like him or her	_____
	30	Tell someone good news about yourself	_____
	37	Receive compliments	_____
Engaging in social contacts	12	Ask personal questions	_____
	15	Initiate a conversation with a stranger	_____
	17	Request a meeting or a date with a person	_____
	18	Your initial request for a meeting is turned down and you ask the person again at a later time	_____
	29	Accept a date	_____

Handling criticism	14	Ask for constructive criticism	____
	24	Discuss openly with a person his or her criticism of your behavior	____
	35	Discuss openly with a person his or her criticism of your work	____
Disagreeing	26	Express an opinion that differs from that of the person with whom you are talking	____
	38	Continue to converse with someone who disagrees with you	____
Handling service situations	23	Request expected service when such is not forthcoming, for example, in a restaurant	____
	25	Return defective items in a store or restaurant	____

Scoring. To find your *average* level of discomfort for each factor, add your scores for that cluster and then divide the sum by the number of items in that factor. You can then compare your average for each factor to see in which types of situations you are most comfortable being assertive and in which types you are least comfortable. You can also get insight concerning the types of situations in which you do not act *as you would like to* because of your discomfort. (Of course, you may *really not care* about acting in a situation, but just be sure you aren't using "I don't care" as a rationalization when you really would like to act!) You will find examples of other situations that require assertiveness in Chapter 11.

Sources for Assertion Inventory and the Item Cluster Worksheet:

Gambrill, E., & Richey, C. A. (1975). An assertion inventory for use in assessment and research. *Behavior Therapy, 6,* 547-549.

Gambrill, E. D., & Richey, C. A. (1976). *It's up to you: Developing assertive social skills* (pp. 158-159). Millbrae, CA: Les Femmes.

Gambrill, E., & Richey, C. A. (1985). *Taking charge of your social life* (pp. 70-73). Belmont, CA: Wadsworth.

Morton, J. C., Richey, C. A., & Kellett, M. (1981). *Building assertive skills A practical guide to professional development for allied dental health providers* (pp. 259-262). Mosby.

In his book *When I Say No, I Feel Guilty* Manuel Smith developed the following list of assertive rights (1975, as cited and adapted in Alexander, 2000). He believed these rights are necessary for healthy adult relationships. Understanding these rights can give you a better sense of the kind of thinking and treatment you can reasonably and appropriately expect from other people. If you know there are certain areas in which you would like to be more assertive, you might want to hang these rights someplace where you will see them often as a reminder to respect yourself (as well as others).

Assertive Rights

1. You have the right to judge your own behaviors, thoughts and emotions, and to take responsibility for their initiation and consequences.

2. You have the right to offer no reasons or excuses for justifying your behavior.

3. You have the right to judge whether you are responsible for finding solutions to other people's problems.

4. You have the right to change your mind.

5. You have the right to make mistakes-and to be responsible for them.

6. You have the right to say , "I don't know."

7. You have the right to be independent of the goodwill of others before coping with them.

8. You have the right to be illogical in making decisions.

9. You have the right to say, "I don't understand."

10. You have the right to say, "I don't care."

Alexander, T. (2000). *Adjustment and human relationships.* Upper Saddle River, NJ: Prentice Hall.
Smith, M. J. (1975). *When I say no, I feel guilty.* New York: Bantam.

This scale will help you understand the material on drinking and alcoholism in Chapter 14.

The TWEAK Questionnaire

1. How many drinks can you "hold" (drink before you begin to feel "high")? ____
2. Have close friends or relatives worried or complained about your drinking in the past year (or ever, if you have stopped drinking)?   No   Yes
3. Do you sometimes take a drink in the morning when you first get up?   No   Yes
4. Has a friend or family member ever told you about things you said or did while you were drinking that you could not remember?   No   Yes
5. Do you sometimes feel the need to cut down on your drinking?   No   Yes

---

TWEAK is an acronym for these items, which are accepted symptoms of being alcoholic:
➤ *T = Tolerance:* "How many drinks can you 'hold'?" (i.e., before beginning to feel high)
➤ *W = Worried:* "Have close friends or relatives worried or complained about your drinking in the past year?"
➤ *E = Eye-opener:* "Do you sometimes take a drink in the morning when you first get up?"
➤ *A = Amnesia (blackouts):* "Has a friend or family member ever told you about things you said or did while you were drinking that you could not remember?"
➤ *K(C) = Cut Down:* "Do you sometimes feel the need to cut down on your drinking?"

Scoring.

First method. Studies have used different scoring schemes depending on the population studied. This scale was originally developed for use with pregnant, inner-city residents. A total score of 2 or more indicated a higher likelihood of being a "risk" drinker (Russell et al., 1994). Russell and Skinner (1988) found three TWEAK items (*Worried, Amnesia,* and *K/Cut down*) identified 70% of obstetric patients reporting two or more indications of problem drinking, a number associated with lower birth weight, Apgar scores, and head circumference at birth (Russell & Skinner) and with cognitive deficits at age 6 (Russell et al., 1991).

Russell's scoring is based on a 7-point total possible score:
➤ For the first item (*T*olerance), you receive 2 points if your answer is 3 (or more) drinks.
➤ For the second item (*W*orry), you receive 2 points if your answer is "yes."
➤ For the last three items, you receive 1 point for each item you answered "yes."

Second method. The TWEAK has been used in several studies with traditional-aged college students, mostly 17- to 19-year-olds (e.g., Parillo & Schick, 1998; Sudol & Schick, 1999; Trauger, Schick, Astor-Stetson, & Beck, 1998). Since proportionally more college students drink—and drink heavily—than in other age groups, scoring was modified to reflect that (a) college students define bingeing as one more drink than do experts in the field and (b) parents and peers don't see drinking as a "serious problem" as easily as they do for those younger or older.

Russell, M. (1994). New assessment tools for risk drinking during pregnancy: T-ACE, TWEAK, and others. *Alcohol Health & Research World, 18,* 55-61.

We used a total possible score of 5, with each item given equal weight (1 point each). The cut-off for item 1 (*Tolerance*) was still 3 or more drinks. Here are typical findings (Parillo & Schick, 1998) for 17- to 22-year-old college students (most were 18-20 in this study).

> In a step-wise regression analysis, the predictors for those scoring 3 or more (vs. 2 or fewer) were ($r^2 = .78$): (a) drinking more on the day of the week they drank the most, (b) drinking on more days in the week, (c) having more frequent blackouts, (d) drinking more often to "loosen up" around others, (e) drinking more often to blame "what I might do (have sex, do something embarrassed) on alcohol," and (f) spending more hours per week "consuming" hard-core pornography and media portraying sexual violence against women.

> Using 2 as the cutoff (which resulted in including more females as "alcoholic" and more drinkers who were "nonfrequent" bingers, having binged fewer than three times in the last 2 weeks), the predictor items were ($r^2 = .45$): (a) drinking more on the day of the week they drank the most, (b) having more frequent blackouts, but (c) *less* likelihood of saying "I have been a problem drinker."

> Using actual score (0-5), the predictor items were ($r^2 = .66$): (a) drinking more total alcoholic drinks a week, (b) using other drugs (e.g., nicotine, marijuana) on more days a week, (c) drinking more often to blame "what I might do (have sex, do something embarrassed) on alcohol," and (d) spending more hours per week "consuming" hard-core porn and media containing sexual violence against women.

Source and other references for this scale:

Parillo, K., & Schick, C. (1998, February*). Effect of Hypermasculinity/femininity, gender, and type of video seen on beliefs about, justifications for, and political views and statistics on date rape.* Poster session presented at the meeting of the Eastern Psychological Association, Boston.

Russell, M. (1994). New assessment tools for risk drinking during pregnancy: T-ACE, TWEAK, and others. *Alcohol Health & Research World, 18,* 55-61.

Russell, M.; Czarnecki, D. M.; Cowan, R.; McPherson, E.; & Mudar, P. (1991). Measures of maternal alcohol use as predictors of development in early childhood. *Alcoholism: Clinical and Experimental Research, 15,* 991-1000.

Russell, M., Martier, S. S., Sokol, R. J., Mudar, P., Bottoms, S., Jacobson, S., & Jacobson, J. (1994). Screening for pregnancy risk-drinking. . *Alcoholism: Clinical and Experimental Research, 18,* 1156-1161.

Russell, M., & Skinner, J. B. (1988). Early measures of maternal alcohol misuse as predictors of adverse pregnancy outcomes. *Alcoholism: Clinical and Experimental Research, 12,* 824-830.

Sudol, K. Y., & Schick, C. (1999, April). *Relationship of attachment style and parental drinking to background, sexual and drinking beliefs and behaviors, reasons for drinking, and alcoholism in teenage college students.* Poster session presented at the meeting of the Eastern Psychological Association, Providence, RI.

Trauger, H., Schick, C., Astor-Stetson, E., & Beck, B. L. (1998, February). *Billy Joel was wrong: Relationship of attachment style, religion, and alcohol use to college students' sexual and intimacy-related beliefs, behaviors, and traits.* Poster session presented at the meeting of the Eastern Psychological Association, Boston.

This scale will help you understand the material on drinking and alcoholism in Chapter 14.

Alcohol: Reasons For Use Scale (ARU; Are You?)

One drink = a 12-oz beer, a 4 oz glass of wine, a wine cooler, or 1 1/2 oz of 80-proof
    whiskey, vodka, tequila, or other "hard" liquor.
If you have **stopped** drinking, answer for the **last 6 months** you were drinking.

Do you now—or have you in the past—drunk alcohol?   NO   YES

On average, in a typical week, how many TOTAL drinks of alcohol do you consume? (circle one)
    0   1   2   3   4   5   6   7   8   9   10   11   12   13   14   15   16   17
    18   19   20   21   22   23   24   25   26   27   28   29   30 or more

On how many days a week do you usually drink ANY alcohol?
    0   1   2   3   4   5   6   7

On the ONE day of the week you drink the MOST alcohol, how many drinks do you usually drink?
    0   1   2   3   4   5   6   7   8   9   10   11   12   13   14   15   16 or more

WOMEN ONLY: In the last two weeks, on how many days did you drink 4 or more alcoholic
drinks?
    0   1   2   3   4   5   6   7   8   9   10   11   12   13   14

MEN ONLY: In the last two weeks, on how many days did you drink 5 or more alcoholic
drinks?
    0   1   2   3   4   5   6   7   8   9   10   11   12   13   14

**Use this scale to answer these items concerning *how often* you drink for different reasons.
Consider *all* the reasons you may drink on each occasion when answering.**
    1 = never or almost never
    2 = Occasionally
    3 = Often
    4 = Almost always

How often do you drink "just to be social"?	1 2 3 4
How often do you drink because it makes you feel "good"?	1 2 3 4
How often do you drink "to get drunk"?	1 2 3 4
How often do you drink to stop feeling "bad"?	1 2 3 4
How often do you drink to "fit in"?	1 2 3 4

Schick, C., Astor-Stetson, E., & Beck, B. L. (1996). Alcohol: Reasons for Use Scale. Unpublished
scale, Bloomsburg University. (Dept of Psychology, 400 East 2nd St., Bloomsburg, PA 17815;
cjschi@bloomu.edu)

1 = never or almost never
2 = Occasionally
3 = Often
4 = Almost always

How often do you drink alone?	1	2	3	4
How often do you drink to forget about something?	1	2	3	4
How often do you drink because it makes a social gathering more fun?	1	2	3	4
How often do you drink to "loosen up" when with others?	1	2	3	4
How often do you drink so others won't think you are "bad" if you do something embarrassing or something they might not approve of?	1	2	3	4
How often do you drink so you can blame something you might do (have sex, do something embarrassing) on alcohol?	1	2	3	4
How often do you drink so you can blame something you might not do (study for a test, be "faithful") on alcohol?	1	2	3	4
Have you even been a "problem drinker" (driven drunk, had a serious physical fight, battered or assaulted someone, shoplifted, destroyed property, committed vandalism, forced someone to do something against the person's will, etc.)?	1	2	3	4
Have you ever had a blackout (done or said things for any period of time and not remembered it even when someone told you about it later)?	1	2	3	4
Have you ever had a drink or two before going to a social gathering just in case there wouldn't be much to drink or much chance to drink there?	1	2	3	4
Have you ever gotten drunk when you intended to stay sober or drunk more than you meant to or promised yourself you would?	1	2	3	4
Have you ever asked someone to help you control your drinking (hold your money, remind you not to drink, take you home if you drank too much)?	1	2	3	4
Have you ever stayed away from a particular location (bar, party house), a party, or one or more other persons because you knew you would probably lose control and drink too much there or with the person(s)?	1	2	3	4
Have you ever driven when you know you were drunk or otherwise impaired?	1	2	3	4
Have you ever done something antisocial or dangerous (vandalism, had unsafe or forced sex, taken chances you wouldn't have otherwise taken) because you were drunk?	1	2	3	4
Have you ever stayed drunk for more than 1 day?	1	2	3	4

Have you ever stopped drinking for any period of time because you had experienced negative social, school, professional, or health problems related to your drinking?   No   Yes

Have you ever limited your drinking for any period of time because you were experiencing negative social, school, professional, or health problems related to your drinking?
No   Yes

Can you hold your liquor better than other people can?   No   Yes

How old were you when you first because a <u>regular</u> alcohol drinker—not just experimented with it, but used alcohol on a regular basis, even if it was just a few times a month?

10 or less   11   12   13   14   15   16   17   18   19   20 or older   never drank

---

A national study of college binge drinking (Wechsler, Dowdall, Davenport, & DeJong, 1995) found 50% of men and 39% of women binged (4 or more drinks for women; 5 or more for men), and 25% did so frequently (3 or more days in the past 2 weeks). Of frequent bingers, 73% of men and 68% of women said drinking to get drunk was an important reason why they drank. While 26% of men and 17% of women reported having drinking problems, only 3% had ever sought help for a problem with alcohol. Nearly half of frequent bingers reported five or more drinking-related problems that school year, and this group was 7 to 16 times more likely than non-binge drinkers to have missed class, fallen behind in school work, had unplanned or unprotected sex, had trouble with campus police, damaged property, and been physically injured. The majority reported having hangovers and doing things they regretted, and 40% admitted having blackouts.

The Alcohol: Reasons for Use Scale (Schick, Astor-Stetson, & Beck, 1996) was developed for use with traditional-age college students, most of whom are under drinking age. It has been used in several studies with this age group (usually with 18- to 19-year-old college students), and items from it were related to maladaptive risk taking, including dangerous and antisocial sexual activities (e.g., forcing a partner or having been forced into vaginal intercourse or other serious sexual behaviors, having gone out seeking someone new with whom to have sex that night). Items asking about amounts and frequency of drinking alcohol were designed to allow researchers and those planning intervention programs with college students to examine binge drinking in their school's population. Here are some results from Sudol and Schick (1999) that are typical of those we have found in several studies in the past 5 years:

➢ Students from families in which a parent drank socially admitted drinking more total drinks a week than those from families in which a parent was a problem drinker or in which neither parent drank. Men from social-drinking families were especially heavy drinkers, and women from nondrinking families drank the least.

➢ Students from problem-drinking families drank on more days a week than those from nondrinking families.

➢ On the day they drank the most, students from social drinking families drank more than those from nondrinking families, and men drank more than women. (However, both men and women averaged enough to meet the criteria for binge drinking, which is 4 for women and 5 for men).

➢ In terms of frequent bingeing (two or more times in the last 2 weeks), men and women from social-drinking families and women from problem-drinking families outscored others.

➢ Compared to others, men from social-drinking families and women from problem-drinking families reported more frequently drinking enough to get drunk during the past 6 months.

➢ Women reported more frequently drinking to be social and to get drunk than men did.

➢ Men reported drinking alone more often than women did.

- Compared to secure men and women, men and women with an insecure attachment style reported drinking more often to forget about something and to have something to blame if they either did something bad (e.g., have sex, do something embarrassing) or didn't do something they should have (e.g., study for a test, be "faithful").
- Men from social-drinking families and women from families in which a parent was a problem drinker more frequently drank as an excuse in case they did something they shouldn't.
- Those with social-drinking families reported both taking a drink or two before going to a social gathering and blacking out more frequently than did those from nondrinking families.
- Insecure women admitted a higher frequency of drinking more than they had planned to.
- Women from problem- or social-drinking families and men from nondrinking families reported more often asking others to help them control their drinking (e.g., hold their money, remind them not to drink, take them home if they were drinking too much).
- Women from problem-drinking families and men from either problem-drinking or nondrinking families admitted that they more often had done something antisocial or dangerous because they were drunk (e.g., vandalism, had unsafe or forced sex, taken chances you wouldn't have otherwise taken).
- In terms of insecurity, anxious-ambivalent and preoccupied women and avoidant men scored higher than others on maladaptive, antisocial, and dangerous reasons for drinking.

Source and other references for this scale:

Schick, C., Astor-Stetson, E., & Beck, B. L. (1996). *Alcohol: Reasons for Use Scale.* Unpublished scale, Bloomsburg University. (Dept of Psychology, 400 East 2nd St., Bloomsburg, PA 17815; cjschi@bloomu.edu)

Sudol, K. Y., & Schick, C. (1999, April). *Relationship of attachment style and parental drinking to background, sexual and drinking beliefs and behaviors, reasons for drinking, and alcoholism in teenage college students.* Poster session presented at the meeting of the Eastern Psychological Association, Providence, RI.

Wechsler, H., Dowdall, G. W., Davenport, A., & DeJong, W. (1995). *Binge drinking on campus: Results of a national study* (Publication No. ED/OPE95-8). Newton, MA: The Higher Education Center for Alcohol and Other Drug Prevention. (On-line). Retrieved May 10, 2001. Available: http://www.edc.org/hec/pubs/binge.htm

This Exercise lets you assess your ability to identify different behaviors as abnormal rather than just a little strange. After deciding if each is abnormal or normal, you can test your ability to actually define "abnormal behavior." The knowledge you gain will help you understand the material in the Chapters 15 and 16 on depression and eating disorders.

What is Normal?

Individually or in small groups identify whether or not each case represents abnormal behavior. Provide reasons for why or why not. When you finish, give a definition of abnormal behavior.

1. A businessman is convinced that his colleagues are out to get ahead of him in the company. He has accused them of stealing his reports and believes they are following him to learn company secrets when he goes on field assignments. He locks himself in his office every day and works 10-12 hours to stay ahead. His boss reports that he is very productive.

2. A 28 year old woman requests that her partner be tied to the bed during their sexual encounters. She also requests that each dress in the other gender's clothes during sex, and indicates that this is the only way she can really get excited. Her partner is quite willing. Things often get rough during sex with cuts and bruises suffered by each individual.

3. A 47 year old male is seen in the downtown area giving all his possessions away. He is very religious and states that God told him to rid himself of his worldly possessions and to spend his time in full-time ministry for the sick and needy.

4. A college psychology major is intent on getting into graduate school in clinical psychology. To accomplish this, she goes to class then straight to the library, normally putting in 18 hours a day. She has no friends or social life and does not go home to visit family. She is maintaining a 4.0 GPA.

5. A woman becomes depressed every month before her menstrual cycle begins. She is usually ineffective at her job during these times and is difficult to get along with. She often goes on screaming fits with her husband and children with only the slightest provocation.

6. Two 27 year old lesbian women have been living together for four years. They report a very close monogamous relationship. Wanting to spread their love to future generations, they are endeavoring to adopt a child.

7. A second semester freshman is experiencing a drop in her grades. Although she is a good student, she is struggling to maintain a "C" average. She frequently is seen at local bars, stays out late, and is smoking 3 packs of cigarettes per day.

American Psychiatric Association (2000). *Diagnostic and statistical manual of mental disorders* (4th ed. text revision). Washington, DC: Author. (Scale constructed by B. L. Beck for this book.)

8. A homeless woman is sleeping on a hot air vents on the streets of New York City. When people approach her, she yells and chases them away. Being denied public facilities, she has to urinate and defecate in public. She refuses any public assistance.

9. A 22 year old woman has been married for 5 years. Her life revolves around her husband, and she has no independent friends or hobbies. He has engaged in numerous extramarital affairs and is verbally abusive to her. Her parents tell her to leave this man. She knows that she does not love him but stays with him for financial support.

10. A conservative couple has a daughter who is in need of an operation. Without it, she has a 50/50 chance of living. The parents' religion forbids medical attention; therefore, they do not allow it.

Your Definition of Abnormal Behavior:

Scoring: There is no particular scoring for the 10 clinical vignettes. The exercise is based on common diagnostic controversies still evident in clinical literature. Whether each of the cases would be considered "abnormal" has changed over time. The purpose of the exercise is to see whether you are consistent in applying your implicit rules of abnormality and to sensitize you to the difficulties of these judgments. Labeling a behavior as "abnormal" is always a societal judgment that is influenced by one's culture and values.

Models of Abnormality

When mental health professionals make judgments about abnormality, they often consult the *Diagnostic and Statistical Manual of Mental Disorder–Fourth Edition Text Revision* (DSM-IV; APA, 2000). The DSM-IV contains over 400 diagnoses of mental disorders. The diagnosis of a behavior as "abnormal" usually is a combination of the following three models: statistical, personal discomfort, and norm violation. Each model has its inherent strengths and weaknesses.

The ***statistical model*** states that one who deviates from the average on any characteristic is abnormal. It does a good job of diagnosing behaviors such as mental retardation or schizophrenia. These behaviors are diagnosed because of their deviation from the norm. However, the model has weaknesses when applied to behaviors like genius or depression. True genius is just as rare as mental retardation. According to the statistical model, it should be diagnosed as a mental disorder, but it is not. Similarly, depression is a very common behavior; in fact, it is known as the "common cold of mental disorders." According to the statistical model, it should not be diagnosed as a disorder, but it is.

In the ***personal discomfort model*** people are judged to be abnormal if their behavior causes great distress and torment to themselves. It does a good job of diagnosing behaviors such as anxiety (e.g., phobias) or clinical depression, in which the person is clearly uncomfortable. However, it does a poor job in diagnosing other behaviors, like antisocial personality disorder (i.e., a person with no conscience) or the manic phase of bipolar disorder, in which the person is engaging in very counterproductive and even criminal behaviors but is not bothered by it.

Finally, in the ***norm violation model*** abnormal behavior is whatever violates social norms and threatens or makes anxious those observing it. It does well in diagnosing the norm-violating behaviors of antisocial personality disorder and mania. It accounts for unacceptable behaviors, such as pedophilia and exhibitionism, that are clearly at odds with society's norms. However, sometimes society is just wrong and the dominant values may change over time. For example, homosexuality was removed as a diagnostic category in 1973 because same-sex relationships were no longer seen as abnormal. Recently in China, individuals were labeled with a disorder and placed in psychiatric hospital simply because their political beliefs differed from those in power. Similarly, societal attitudes can reinforce dangerous behaviors. In the US, we have multibillion dollar industries (e.g., fashion, weight loss) that promote a dangerously thin body type for women. Research suggests they have a direct connection to the high rates of eating disorders found in our society. So who is abnormal? The person evidencing the eating disorder or the society that promotes it?

When it is boiled down, abnormal behavior is that which deviates from some ideal state or interferes with day-to-day functioning. It usually is diagnosed by some combination of the three models mentioned above with consideration to current societal values.

Source for this scale, which was constructed by Brett L. Beck (2001) for this book:
American Psychiatric Association (2000). *Diagnostic and statistical manual of mental disorders* (4th ed. text revision). Washington, DC: Author.

Here are sample items from a scale that assesses your belief in three types of perfectionism in academic and personal life. These items will help you apply the material in Chapter 3.

Multidimensional Perfectionism Scale (Sample Items)

Below are several statements concerning your personal characteristics and traits. Using the scale below, indicate your degree of agreement with each item. Write your score next to the item's number.

1	2	3	4	5	6	7
Strongly disagree			Neither agree nor disagree			Strongly agree

___   4.   I seldom criticize my friends for accepting second best.
___   6.   One of my goals is to be perfect in everything I do.
___   11.   The better I do, the better I am expected to do.
___   16.   I have high expectations for the people who are important to me.
___   18.   The people around me expect me to succeed at everything I do.
___   23.   It makes me uneasy to see an error in my work.
___   29.   The people who matter to me should never let me down.
___   32.   I must work to my full potential at all times.
___   33.   Although they may not show it, other people get very upset with me when I slip up.

Scoring. The 45-item scale measures three types of perfectionism: *Self-Oriented Perfectionism*, *Other-Oriented Perfectionism*, and *Socially-Prescribed Perfectionism*. The sample of this scale contains 3 items assessing each type. Agreement with items from each subscale will alert you to your perfectionistic beliefs.

➢ *Self-Oriented Perfectionism:* 6, 23, 32
➢ *Other-Oriented Perfectionism:* 4 (reverse your score for #4: 1 = 7, etc.), 16, 29
➢ *Socially-Prescribed Perfectionism:* 11, 18, 33

      Burns (1980) described perfectionism as a compulsive striving to meet unreasonable or unattainable standards in which an individual's entire self-worth is based upon achieving these impossible goals. Developed to measure dimensions of perfectionism not assessed by Burns' self-oriented perfectionism scale, the Multidimensional Perfectionism Scale (Hewitt, Flett, Turnbull-Donovan, & Mikail, 1991) has found negative consequences related to each type. *Self-Oriented Perfectionism* (SOP), measuring one's personal expectations, was linked to excessively high standards, self-criticism, self-blame, exaggerated importance of performance and goal attainment, guilt, disappointment, anger, obsessive-compulsive disorder, depression, anxiety, interpersonal over-sensitivity, hostility, phobias, and paranoia. ***Other-Oriented Perfectionism*** (OOP), assessing one's unreasonably high expectations for significant others, was related to hostility, assessing one's unreasonably high expectations for significant others, was related to hostility, blaming others, authoritarianism, dominance, family problems, lack of trust, loneliness, and cynicism. ***Socially Prescribed Perfectionism*** (SPP)—the dimension most strongly related to negative adjustment, low self-concept, and psychological distress—measures beliefs that significant others hold unrealistic expectations for one's behavior and that one must strive to meet these standards. SPP was related to demand for approval from significant others, fear of negative evaluation, external locus of control, inflated importance of meeting other's goals and standards, procrastination, anger, anxiety, depression. self-criticism, self-blame, and overgeneralization of failure. Not surprisingly, SPP was closely related to suicide threat and intention, with SPP predicting variance in suicide scores that was not accounted for by depression or hopelessness (Hewitt, Flett, & Turnbull-Donovan, 1992).

Bognatz & Schick (1996), assessing Type A/B personality and both the 3-choice (Hazan & Shaver, 1987) and 4-choice attachment styles (Bartholomew & Horowitz, 1991), found SPP higher for insecurely attached college students than for secure students. Anxious-ambivalent students were higher than secure students on SOP, and there was also a trend for preoccupied, fearful, and dismissing students to outscore secure students. (OOP was unrelated to attachment style.) Type A's scored higher than Type B's on all three types of perfectionism. For those currently in a romantic relationship, being either Type A or male predicted higher OOP scores, showing Type A's and males expect too much from others just as they do from themselves.

Perfectionists' traits put them at risk for interpersonal unhappiness. They dwell on past or potential failure to meet standards and report loneliness and problems in personal relationships. They expect rejection from others when they are imperfect and are defensive when criticized. Defensiveness alienates others, which just reinforces their belief that perfectionism is requisite for acceptance. Additionally, they fear that divulging thoughts and feelings will make them appear foolish or inadequate, and they assume that any sign of weakness will result in rejection. Thus, the chance for intimate communication is forfeited, resulting in failure to receive the unconditional acceptance perfectionists crave but believe to be contingent upon perfect performance.

Source and other references for this scale:

Bartholomew, K., & Horowitz, L. M. (1991). Attachment styles among young adults: A test of a four-category model. *Journal of Personality and Social Psychology, 61,* 226-244.

Bognatz, G., & Schick, C. (1996, March). *Relationships among attachment style, Type A behavior pattern, and perfectionism in teenage college students.* Poster session presented at the meeting of the Eastern Psychological Association, Philadelphia.

Burns, D. D. (1980, November). The perfectionist's script for self-defeat. *Psychology Today,* pp. 34-52.

Hazan, C., & Shaver, P. (1987). Romantic love conceptualized as an attachment process. *Journal of Personality and Social Psychology, 52,* 511-524.

Hewitt, P. L., Flett, G. L. , & Turnbull-Donovan, W. (1992). Perfectionism and suicide potential. *British Journal of Clinical Psychology, 31,* 181-190.

Hewitt, P. L., Flett, G. L., Turnbull-Donovan, W., & Mikail, S. F. (1991). The Multidimensional Perfectionism Scale: Reliability, validity, and psychometric properties in psychiatric samples. *Psychological Assessment, 3,* 464-468.

Feedback from a True Survivor

The worth of a book is to be measured by what you can carry away from it. — James Bryce

In the final chapter we asked you to identify information you found especially helpful and topics you think should be included in the 3rd Edition of this book. Please include advice for new students, study techniques, constructive criticism (how we could made a section more useful), and reading material and Web sites you think we should include. Thank you! Send your response to:

Drs. Schick, Astor-Stetson, and Beck
Department of Psychology
Bloomsburg University
400 East Second Street
Bloomsburg, PA 17815

Information and sections you found especially helpful:

Information you didn't find particularly useful and think we should change or drop:

Tips, topics, readings, and Web sites you would like us to include next time:

Other comments: